All Our Yesterdays

All Our Yesterdays

A collection of 100 stories of
people, landmarks and events
from Montreal's past.

EDGAR ANDREW COLLARD

Published by

The Gazette
MONTREAL

ACKNOWLEDGMENTS

I wish to say how much I appreciate the work of the two artists, John Collins and Tex Dawson, who have illustrated this book.

John Collins is a colleague from old *Gazette* days. We went to work at the paper about the same year, and were closely associated on the editorial page when he was the cartoonist. Tex Dawson took over when John left for a stay in Florida after his retirement. They have sketched in different styles — John with his strong impressions of historic places, and Tex (an architect by profession) with his detailed sense of the features and structures of old buildings.

Both have spared no effort to get the needed sketches, though it has often meant considerable travelling, in all seasons and weather. It has been a great pleasure to work with both of them.

I also wish to say how much I have appreciated, over the years, the interest of the readers of my column. Many have sent me their own reminiscences of people, places, and events. These have enriched my files and have frequently been used in the columns. The interest of readers has been a constant encouragement and a great reward. I am grateful to every one of them.

Published by

The Gazette

245 St. Jacques St.,
Montreal, Que., Canada H2Y 1M6

Illustrations — John Collins, Tex Dawson
Cover — Reproduction of John Collins watercolor
Book design — Tom Carbray
Author photo — Pierre Home-Douglas
Co-ordination — Margaret Lester

Canadian Cataloguing in Publication Data

Collard, Edgar Andrew, 1911 — All Our Yesterdays

All of these stories were published first in *The Gazette.*
ISBN 0-9692315-1-2

1. Montréal (Quebec) — History. 2. Montréal (Quebec) — Description. I. Title.

FC2947.3.C64 1988   971.4'281   C89-090002-7   F1054.5.M84C64 1988

I am often asked one of two questions — or both. The first is: "How did you have the idea of writing your *All Our Yesterdays* column in the *The Gazette?*" The second is: "How have you been able to keep it up for 44 years without a break?"

I never thought of asking myself either of these questions. It was just natural for me to start writing the column and just as natural to keep writing it. Neither the beginning nor the continuation was a conscious decision. Both were spontaneous.

The idea of writing the column was not the outcome of long consideration. It came suddenly — in a moment. It happened on a mid-June day about five o'clock in the late afternoon. I was sitting on a bench in the old Governor's Garden in Quebec (the little park overlooking the St. Lawrence, near the Château Frontenac).

I had spent the whole day visiting Quebec's historic buildings. The thought came to me: Montreal is also an ancient city — why not write a column about its history? That same summer the first of these columns was published. "All Our Yesterdays" has appeared on the editorial page of *The Gazette* every week since then.

Obviously, however, the idea of writing this column had far deeper roots than seeing Quebec's historic buildings on a fine June day. These roots, in fact, go back far into my childhood, even to my earliest memories.

My father had the historical instinct. He was a real Victorian, born in 1875, with all the studied dignity of Victorian manners. He formed the most voluminous private library I have ever seen. Nearly all of it was historical.

Under the weight of books the upper floor of our house began to give way. This alarming development did not deter my father. He brought in a contractor. New pillars were inserted, from the cellar upwards. The floor was jacked back into position.

I spent many evenings with my father in that library. He would show me history books and read passages from them. One evening, I remember, he was reading about Montreal in the 1830s. He wanted to show me a map of the city as it was in those days but he could not find it. After I had gone to bed, and been asleep for about an hour, he came into my room and woke me up to show me the map which he had just found in another book.

On weekends my father and I went on excursions to historic places. He took me to the fort at Chambly, or to the ruins of old Fort Senneville. We went on walking tours together in Old Montreal. One autumn we explored historic stone houses from Lachine to the end of the island.

This column's ultimate origin was in my father's historical enthusiasm. I am glad he lived to see the first years of *All Our Yesterdays* in print. In a very real sense it was his column, and remains so.

Then there is the second question I am asked — the question of how I have been able to sustain the effort of producing a column every week, without a single intermission, for 44 years. It might seem a lot of work, yet I have never felt it in the least burdensome. I have always liked the saying of James Matthew Barrie that work isn't really work unless you would rather be doing something else. I have enjoyed writing these columns, and have never felt that I would rather be doing something else.

But I must admit that I had trouble at times in meeting the deadlines. This was especially difficult during the 17 years I was *The Gazette's* editor, and had many other obligations. Often on a Thursday night (my deadline), I was unable to get to work on the column until late in the evening.

I have been blessed with the perfect wife. She has at all times understood my problems. Frequently on Thursday nights we would have dinner together downtown. She would come back with me to the office. While I worked on my column, she would do research in the old files of *The Gazette* in connection with her own historical writing on the history of pottery and porcelain in Canada. We would come home together at two or three in the morning, or even later, sometimes at dawn. We look back with happy memories of those evenings.

In this book I have selected 100 of my columns. It has not been an easy choice, since there have been over 2,250 of them. I shall be more than satisfied if my readers, old and new, find as much pleasure in reading these columns as I have had in writing them.

All Our Yesterdays

Illustrations by John Collins

CONTENTS

Illustrations by Tex Dawson

CONTENTS

Montreal as "The Silver Town"

Montreal was once known as the "Silver Town" — the town with the shining roofs and spires. All lights illuminated them. They shimmered white in the noonday sun; glowed like fire in the sunset; glimmered luminously in the light of the moon.

All such splendor of roof and spire came from ordinary tin. And tin had been used for the most practical reasons. It was waterproof; it was durable; but above all, it would not burn. "The town has suffered by fire very materially at different times," wrote a visitor in the 1790s, "and the inhabitants have such a dread of it, that all who can afford it cover the roofs of their houses with tin plates instead of shingles."

This practical adoption of tin for roofing resulted in spectacular effects, having nothing to do with fire prevention. The "Silver Town" amazed and attracted visitors. J. G. Kohl, a German traveller in the 1850s, expressed his wonder at the enchantment of shining tin: "... we had... several miles to go before we saw anything of the handsome 'Silver Town.' At last something glimmered silvery through the mist, namely the tin-covered houses and churches of Montreal. This metal, *un-precious* as it is, nevertheless preserves its white brightness a long time without rusting, and when the moon or the setting sun plays on the roofs and cupolas they produce an effect that Canaletto... or any other painter of cities and houses would be enchanted with."

Radiance from so much tin did much to brighten Montreal's appearance. Narrow streets of grey limestone buildings, otherwise sombre and depressing, took on an almost aggressive brilliance.

Some visitors even thought this glare excessive. A tourist in the 1830s, T. R. Preston, could not bear to look at it. "The majority of the streets...," he wrote, "are dark and gloomy, and narrow.... The glittering tin roofs... afford some little relief to the general monotony; but the effect which they produce upon the eye when the sun is shining brightly on them is very distressing, and when thereto is added the reflexion of the solar rays from the snow, the sight has to undergo a trying ordeal."

Most tourists, however, were not complainers. They found pleasure in a town where roofs shone like "polished silver." The effect to them was "novel and agreeable." From Mount Royal the view was enhanced by the gleam of silver steeples in the vast green panorama. Summer and winter alike gave the tin gleam a memorable loveliness. In June, 1826, a lieutenant of the Royal Navy, driving by coach from Montreal to Lachine, gazed on the distant tin steeples as the town receded from his view: "The morning was beautiful.... As we receded from the city, its glittering tin steeples were seen to great advantage through the rich foliage, finely relieved in the background by the lofty and wooded mountain of Montreal."

Though the tin glitter might become a wintry glare to some eyes, it was a superb winter's feature in the eyes of others. An Englishman from Kent, Rt. Rev. Ashton Oxenden, was spending his first winter as Montreal's new Anglican bishop in 1869-70. In a little book on his first Canadian experiences, intended for English readers, he wrote: "The roofs of the houses and the Church spires are often of zinc, and their appearance is very dazzling and pretty." On his winter tours through the country parishes of the Montreal diocese he admired the gleaming spires: "Few objects are more striking than a country church with a zinc spire glittering in the noon-day sun."

Church spires were transfigured in the evening, when they caught the slanting rays of the sinking sun. J. G. Kohl thought this sunset effect was magnificent: "... the church towers under the rosy light of evening... seemed to glow with an internal fire." Another visitor said they had "the appearance of huge lamps in the sky." In the colder autumn air the roofs and spires of Montreal grew even richer in their sunset reflections. They closed the chill evenings with a blaze of splendor.

One aged Montrealer recalled those evening effects when describing the orchards on the slopes of Mount Royal in the days of his youth — about the beginning of the 19th century. Young people, supervised by their "good mammas," went on picnics in these orchards. Before and after the picnic lunch beneath the trees, they would pick apples and make them ready for the market. In their homecoming down the mountain slope they saw the evening blaze on roof and spire: "When the sun was setting, and the air was becoming sharper and even cold, we made ready to return home. As we came down we would look at the lovely effect in the sky as the golden shafts fell on the gathering clouds and the purple-red of the twilight, or on the gleaming steeples and fiery roofs of the city."

Tin roofs had still another effect: a soft glimmer on moonlit nights. This effect was best appreciated from the mountain. Montreal's poet, Charles Heavysege, wrote in the 1860s of the poetry of moonlight on tin roofs. From the mountain "the outstretched city... lying on the arm of the St. Lawrence, with tin-covered domes, spires, cupolas, minarets, and radiant roofs, showing like molten silver in the moonbeams... presented an enchanting-looking scene of glory and of gloom." The roof of the old Bonsecours

SKETCHBOOK
John Collins *Spires and Shining Rooftops*

Church was "refulgent as if cut from some rock of diamond." The convent of the Grey Nuns wore a "spangled canopy." The Collège de Montréal was "luminous as a moon-lit lake."

Snowshoers saw the same moonlit glimmer on their evening tramps over Mount Royal. At the mountain summit the leader called a halt. The snowshoers were given a "breather." During this pause the snowshoers looked down over the city: "Away below, the moon's rays flash from soaring spires... an effect that is magical in its strange beauty."

Tin roofs had one further effect. It differed from all others — almost surrealist in its spectacular weirdness. This effect was produced by neither sun nor moon. It was the sinister reflection on tin roofs of the dancing, leaping flames when neighboring buildings were on fire. To see to advantage roofs quivering with such reflected firelight a cold night

was best — the colder the better. T. R. Preston, the visitor to Montreal in the 1830s, felt the spectacle was so startling that no one should miss it, even if it meant getting out of a warm bed and going out into the winter's cold. "A very scenic effect," he wrote, "is produced by the agency of these tin roofs, if a fire (as is frequently the case) chances to take place at night in the winter season. Their glitter, in combination with the lurid glare of the flames, relieved by the surrounding snow, and a clear blue moon-lit sky, completes a tableau perfectly unique, such as it is well worth your while, how cold soever may be the temperature, to start from your bed to witness."

Tinsmiths who roofed houses and churches were not only doing a practical, useful job. Incidentally, they were giving Montreal a whole spectrum of dramatic (even theatrical) effects — from noonday glare, to sunset gleam, to moonlit glimmer, to the fantastic devil's dance reflected from flames in a neighborhood fire on a cold winter's night.

The Awful Majesty of King Cook

They called him a king. He was magnificently robed. He sat on a throne. A crown was placed upon his head. His coronation, in fact, took place every year. And this ceremony was re-enacted for years, almost for generations. This king was James Cook. He was the janitor of the Medical Building at McGill University. But every year the medical students held their grand celebration. Cook, on his throne, was the centre of it all. He was addressed, with awe and obeisance, as "His Awful Majesty Cook, absolute monarch of the realm of medical science."

The centre of such extravagant honors was an odd-looking little man, splay-footed, and walking with a waddle, double-chinned, with rosy cheeks adorned by Dundreary whiskers. In performing his duties as janitor of the Medical Building he always dressed in a brass-buttoned, black Prince Albert coat, starched shirt, cutaway collar and huge bow tie. He wore an imposing cap, suggested, perhaps, by a military example. The visor was edged with brass; the band was fastened at either end by large brass buttons.

James Cook was not king only for one night in the year. He was regal all year long. He ruled the McGill Medical Building like a monarch. And he had the special authority of a long reign. He had come to McGill in the 1860s. He was there till his death in 1911. Dr. A. D. Campbell, a McGill medical graduate of 1911, recalled Cook and his tone of despotic command: "Inside the main door was a glorified sentry-box which Cook referred to as his 'office'. During the cold weather he sat inside the cubicle, and addressed any passers-by through the window. When the days were less frigid, he sat in pontifical attitude, in a comfortably armed Captain's chair outside the door as if to guard his sanctum. He truly was the sentry, alert to duty at all times. With the approach of footsteps, he defiantly emerged from his kennel to bark in a high-pitched rasping voice: 'My boy, where are you going? What do you want?' No matter how often one heard that piercing voice, it never failed to send a shiver down the spine, as I afterward learned from experience."

One of King Cook's rules was that no student must ever enter the Medical Building by the front door. That door was reserved for the professors. Students had to enter by a lesser door, more appropriate to their lower status.

It was not surprising that the medical students should think of crowning Cook as king, when they had their yearly celebration. And though it was all a rowdy farce, Cook entered into the performance as though he were king in fact, accepting his rightful homage. As one account says,

"Old Cook sat in an exaggerated style meant to convey the idea of his greatness and his subjects' unworthiness."

King Cook was driven to his annual coronation in a state coach (a two-horse dray). He might be dressed in yellow trousers, scarlet jacket, and three-cornered hat, or in a bright orange coat of the Cromwellian period. A banner bobbed its way at the head of the procession. "Kow-Tow to Cook" was emblazoned on it. Students, cheering, ran and swarmed about his carriage.

The usual procedure at the McGill Union was to seat King Cook upon his throne. The courtiers were in costumes of the Middle Ages. They had titles: Viscount McNutt, Black Rod Clouston, the Lord High Chambermaid, the Great and Only H.H. McKenzie. A toast was read to His Majesty from a long, richly illuminated scroll. The oration was largely meaningless, with the longest words to be found in the dictionary. Vulgarity and obscenity were slipped in. The greater this devious ingenuity, the louder the outbursts of laughter. Then the pages would come forward. The nail-keg, with hundreds of coopers in plaster of Paris, would be laid at the king's feet.

When the banquet was over and Cook had been crowned he was accorded a royal departure. "It was usually arranged," wrote Dr. Campbell, "that he be escorted to his humble lodgings by his pages in a landau drawn by two grey, high-stepping horses, adorned for the occasion and resplendent with ribbons and bows. He was followed by scores of students in a glittering array of carriages and by a cheering mob of plebian pedestrians — an entourage indeed fitting to the coronation of such an Emperor, who ruled by divine authority."

King Cook had a shocking experience in the spring of 1907. The Medical Building at McGill burned down. Arson was suspected, though not proved; the Macdonald Engineering Building had burned down only a few days earlier. Cook had closed up the Medical Building about midnight and turned off all the lights. He had gone to bed in his living quarters in the basement. The fire roared through the building; still Cook slept. Outsiders had to break into the building to rouse him.

The report of the fire says: "The old man lost control of himself completely when he heard of the hold which the flames had taken, and he had to be put into a cab and taken to the Royal Victoria Hospital." He could not speak coherently until he had rested a while in one of the wards. Cook was a king whose kingdom had been destroyed in a night. But Lord Strathcona gave McGill a new Medical

Building. Cook was reinstated in his old rights and privileges.

But the king was growing very old, very infirm, very venerable. He was crowned for the last time on February 22, 1911. King Cook made his last solemn, dramatic entry. "Leaning on the arm of one of the officers of the class," says the account of the proceedings, "and arrayed in gorgeous robes, the 'king of the medical faculty' entered the room amid the cheers of the students ...."

King Cook died less than six months later. McGill's Medical Faculty went into mourning. In his lifetime he had received mock honors. In his death the true respect emerged. And it went very deep. Like any king who reigns long, King Cook had become the thread of tradition, binding generations together in a common loyalty. One of the tributes paid him declared that "as the decades passed,

and deans and professors came and went, Mr. Cook became 'King' Cook, the only abiding thing in the Faculty, the golden thread, as it were, that linked together the successive generations in continuity of policy and prestige."

The pride of all students in their faculty was symbolized by Cook's attitude towards it. To him it was never "the Medical Faculty." Always it was "my Faculty." There was really no other. When Dean Bovey invited him to visit the other faculties, King Cook perceived at once the danger of lese majesty. He explained his refusal: "The Dean doesn't understand. If I was to go visiting the other faculties, those other janitors would think I was on a level with them, and they'd probably take liberties. You know what those people are."

James Cook was a man born to be king.

SKETCHBOOK

John Collins

The KING ON HIS THRONE
From a photo of the time

When Bullets Hit the Bank

Bullet scars are visible in the sandstone of the old Molsons Bank at the southeast corner of St. James and St. Peter (rues St-Jacques and St-Pierre). They have been there since a St. James Street riot in 1867. When Molsons Bank was merged with the Bank of Montreal in 1925, the building became the Bank of Montreal's St. Pierre Street Branch. This branch was closed on the last day of October 1981, after having been the scene of banking for 115 years.

In the federal election of 1867 Thomas D'Arcy McGee, as one of the Montreal members, was seeking re-election. He had set up his committee rooms in the Mechanics' Institute, just across St. Peter Street from Molsons Bank, at the southwest corner of St. James. McGee had known turbulent campaigns; but that last campaign of his life became savage. He had denounced and exposed Montreal's Fenians. This secret society of Irish terrorists was part of the international Irish Fenian organization. Already, in

1866, they had raided Canada from the United States. It was rumored they would do it again — and they did, in 1870.

Montreal's Fenians shared a belief that Ireland's hope of freedom from British rule might be indirectly promoted by striking at British rule in the colony of Canada — or, as it was called, "twisting the Lion's tail." Fenian hatred of McGee was heightened by the fact that McGee himself had been an activist in Ireland. He had fled to America, pursued by the police, a price on his head. In America his views underwent a change. While remaining a supporter of Irish freedom, he rejected the idea that overseas quarrels should be fought on Canadian soil. All who settled in Canada (whatever their backgrounds) owed loyalty to their new country. This loyalty was called for more than ever, now that Canadians, under Confederation, had the chance to build a new country, with opportunity for all, and with friendship and goodwill amongst all its people.

In that election of 1867 McGee published in *The Gazette* his exposure of Fenian conspiracies in Montreal. He received a death threat. That, too, he published in *The Gazette*. It would be an example of the Fenians' terrorist methods. McGee soon had warnings of what was to come. He advertised a campaign meeting for August 2, at the corner of St. Catherine and St. Lawrence. "On the appearance of Mr. McGee," said an eyewitness, "the storm of hootings and groanings was so great that he did not even attempt to speak, but looked around bewildered."

In the evening of the election date, September 6, when the votes were being counted, about 1,000 of McGee's friends stood about on St. James Street, in front of his committee rooms in the Mechanics' Institute. They were watching a big wooden bulletin board. Results were being posted as they were received. The bitter contest proved close. At last the final returns arrived. McGee had won. But his majority was only 262. Before the election he had boasted to his chief, Sir John A. Macdonald, that he would beat his opponent easily by 1,000.

McGee's friends scarcely had time to cheer. An ugly roar was echoing along St. James Street. The mob was coming. Minutes later windows in the Institute's first two floors were splintering under volleys of stones. Rioters made a rush for the door. McGee's friends beat them back. Fighting spread in the street. Stones had shattered the bulletin board. Rioters armed themselves with its pieces. Some of Montreal's prominent citizens, McGee supporters, were in the thick of the battle — and doing well. Alfred Perry, always dependable in danger, was knocking men over, now here, now there. The mob turned on him. He sank to the pavement, "brutally kicked when down."

Inside the Mechanics' Institute defenders appeared at upper windows. At a window on the St. Peter Street side a McGee man had an arsenal of flowerpots. He aimed well. Rioters were going down on the street, as if struck by lightning. His success was his undoing. He became the target for a concentrated shower of three-cornered macadamizing stones. He was seen to drop a flowerpot, clasp both hands to his head, and stagger back from the window.

Fury escalated. Slashing and smashing were not enough — not even with fists, wooden boards, walking sticks, bludgeons, pieces of iron pipe with "elbows" on them. Firearms were the last resort. Both sides carried them; both sides began to use them. One man was struck in his right arm; the bullet came out above the wrist. Another man was hit in the heel. Most shots seemed to be fired to threaten or warn. Perhaps some were aimed high. This would explain why they ricocheted off Molsons Bank on the other side of St. Peter Street.

After half an hour troops arrived. They came from opposite directions. Police arrived, too, many of them, under Chief Penton. Penton pleaded with the mob. Nothing happened. He ordered his men in, batons swinging. Troops cleared a space in front of the Institute. But rioters still tried to break through. A "fellow driving a wagon made a dash against them." Other rioters attacked the lines in wedge-shaped flying columns. By this time the forces of order were too strong to be scattered. McGee's enemies, cursing and yelling, straggled off.

Some accounts say that McGee was not in his committee rooms that night — that the mob had been mistaken in thinking they would find him there. But two reporters on the scene of the riot saw and heard him. One of them wrote: "Mr. McGee evidently suffering considerable excitement then appeared outside the window, being supported on the ledge so that he could be more distinctly seen, and called for three cheers for the Queen, for the New Dominion, for the Chairman, and members of his Committee. He was then withdrawn." Another reporter saw him later come out of the Mechanics' Institute, enter a carriage, and drive off, under military escort, to his house on St. Catherine Street.

Something ominous hovered over that riot in Montreal in 1867. "Let no man be deceived," McGee warned, "a mob unpunished is a fatal precedent." Seven months later McGee was assassinated on a moonlit street in Ottawa, as he was putting the key into his lodging house door. Someone crept up behind him. A bullet passed through his neck and mouth. It sent him sprawling over the wooden sidewalk.

After the election riot of 1867 the glass fragments were swept up on St. James Street before they could harm the horses' feet. The Mechanics' Institute replaced the glass in its windows. Stones bouncing into its rooms had broken glass shades on its gaseliers and shattered interior doors. These, too, were repaired. The neighboring Molsons Bank had more difficulty. Grooves and pits made by bullets in its sandstone walls could not be repaired without making the scars more obvious still. They were left as they were. Time-darkened, they remain — relics of D'Arcy McGee and the St. James Street Riot of 1867.

The Magic That Was Drury's

Long after Drury's had gone, tourists were still asking how they could find it. They had been there on a previous visit, or had been recommended to go there by friends. It was little wonder they could not find Drury's. Not only had this restaurant been demolished. Even the street on which it stood was gone. Much of Drury's charm had been its location. It stood facing the southern end of Dominion Square. But here everything had changed. That lower half of Dominion Square had its name altered to Place du Canada. And the street where Drury's stood, Osborne Street, was shuffled out of existence.

Actually Drury's was not built to be a restaurant. It was a big stone Victorian house. It dated back to the middle years of the 19th century. At that time the streets round about Dominion Square were being developed as Montreal's new residential area. They then marked almost the limits of Montreal's westward movement. Before long Dominion Square was becoming the tourists' centre in Montreal. Montreal's biggest and grandest hotel, the Windsor ("the Palace of Canada") was opened on the west side of the square in 1878. Eleven years later the first section (the upper section) of Windsor Station was completed. A square with an hotel and a railway station would be an obvious spot for a first-class restaurant. Drury's moved to the south side of the square in 1887.

It did not come as a parvenu. It had been close to the square since it was founded by John Drury in 1868. It had stood around the corner, on the west side of Windsor Street, about midway between Osborne and St. Antoine. The restaurant passed from John Drury to his son Jimmy. In 1938 it was bought from Jimmy by Léo Dandurand. Dandurand brought to Drury's his own fame as sportsman and sports promoter, prominent in football, hockey and horse racing. When he acquired Drury's he was about 49 years of age. For more than 20 years he presided over Drury's. He could command the ease of manner of someone educated by the Jesuits at St. Mary's College. But his long years in sport had also adjusted him to all sorts and conditions of men. He had developed the open friendliness and ready conversation that often characterize sports characters. He could be hail fellow and well met.

The Victorian house south of the square had its entire facade rebuilt. It was made to look like an old London chophouse. Architecturally the style might be hard to define exactly. Perhaps "Tudor" was closest. Six tall windows, in stone frames, filled most of the front wall. The windows had panes of opaque colored glass. The restaurant was entered from the western side under an iron canopy and old-fashioned lamps. A massive wooden door increased the sensation of entering into a bygone world. In its interior, Drury's had kept much of the atmosphere of an old house. No attempt had been made to create one large room. The dining area was divided into a number of rooms, with much the same dimensions they must have had when the building was a Victorian residence.

Mellowness was the word for Drury's. Modernity was in the behind-the-scenes organization. It did not obtrude. The dark panelling of the walls, the large chairs with their high backs and leather upholstery, tacked with brass, contributed to the mood of chophouse solidity. Occasionally muted sounds echoed from the street, for Drury's was close to the roadway. The crushing of tires through the ice, or the flash of an auto's headlights on the colored glass windows were reminders of the preoccupied, chilling world outside. Such reminders only deepened the sense of comfort, warmth and seclusion within.

Nothing at Drury's was hurried. It was no place for those who had to eat and drink quickly and be off. It was the place for the long lunch and, better still, for the leisurely evening dinner. It was a place for savoring good food, for relishing good wine, all in reassuring surroundings. The mood of Drury's was in the old-world tradition of mature dining. Someone out of the 18th-century could have strayed into Drury's and found himself at home. Dr. Samuel Johnson, that great figure of 18th-century London, might have said of Drury's, as he said of the London inns of his own day: "As soon as I enter the door... I experience an oblivion of care, and a freedom from solicitude; when I am seated, I find the master courteous, and the servants obsequious to my call; anxious to know and ready to supply my wants. Wine there exhilarates my spirits, and prompts me to free conversation and exchange of discourse...."

At Drury's the food was substantial and good and the wines excellent. The cellar had been so exceedingly well supplied that even during the war years Drury's was able to sell a brandy nobody else had — at $3 a glass or $40 a bottle. Drury's mood and manner, and its strategic position on Dominion Square, brought to it famous diners from other countries. A Montrealer at Drury's, looking across one of its crowded rooms, might recognize celebrities he had never expected to see in the flesh. He might identify Sir Anthony Eden, Charles Boyer, Fiorello LaGuardia, Mrs. Franklin D. Roosevelt or Maurice Chevalier. Drury's met the test of international standards.

This restaurant became so much part of Dominion Square that one could scarcely be thought of as existing without

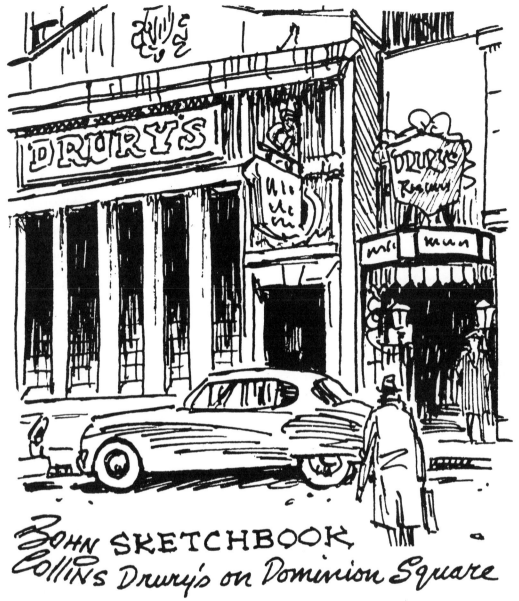

John Collins SKETCHBOOK
Drury's on Dominion Square

the other. But crisis came in the 1950s. Plans were drawn up to reshape the entire area south of the square. La Gauchetière Street would be realigned in a northwesterly direction to join Osborne west of Peel. The portion of Osborne going eastward from Peel to Cathedral would be obliterated. Dominion Square would be extended southward as far as La Gauchetière's new line.

Mayor Drapeau had realized the value and meaning of Drury's in the life of the city. He had intended that the famous restaurant should not be a victim of the plans. He would divert the new line of La Gauchetière around Drury's. The old restaurant would survive, as a heritage landmark. Drapeau, however, was defeated in the next civic election. The succeeding administration in City Hall ruled that Drury's would have to give way. Léo Dandurand was given notice with startling abruptness. On October 22, 1959 he was informed he would have to be out of his restaurant by November 30. "That left us no time at all to

try to move the building or set up elsewhere," he complained.

Montrealers, appalled by the threat to Drury's, rallied to Dandurand's support. A petition of protest was sent to Premier Paul Sauvé. It was too late. Léo Dandurand could do nothing but clear out his restaurant as best he could. Many Montrealers went to Drury's for a last dinner. They asked for souvenirs, or they took them — sugar bowls, salt and pepper shakers, silverware. One American tourist sent in $2 to cover two hand towels he had taken as his souvenirs. Most of the equipment went to the auction block.

The sad end of Drury's Restaurant on Dominion Square had at least one happier side. Drury's had never known decline. Its reputation, like its silverware, was untarnished. The memory of Drury's is of something that vanished at its best. No wonder visitors to Montreal might be encountered still searching for Drury's.

Those Old Simple Holidays

Some wag sent a joke to *The Gazette* in March, 1929. Sir Henry Seagrave had just set a world record for speed on land, in his racing car Golden Arrow. This humorist in *The Gazette* asked a question: In this age of speed, what always goes faster than anything else? The answer was: The two-week holiday. Holidays went fast in those days because they were so short. Two weeks a year was the standard. Those at the top could command more. But the vast working middle class had two weeks, and that was that. Nor was there much chance of long weekends. The regular working week included Saturday till noon. Today, Place d'Armes is almost deserted on Saturday. But then, when it was the heart of the office district, it was covered with surging crowds on a Saturday at noon. For most Montrealers holidays had to be simple. There just was not time enough to go far away and get back again.

Simplicity was imposed by another restriction. Incomes were small. Office workers were mostly engaged in ill-paid routines. The age of technology, with its business machines, was only dawning. Computers were still so far away they were beneath the horizon. Office work was mostly manual — methodical, repetitious keeping of office records. It used to be said that if you went to work in an office, you learned the job in a week and you did it for the rest of your life. Most office workers had to settle down to the realization that they would never earn much and would have to live as best they could on very limited means.

With little time and little money, many Montrealers stayed at home for their two weeks' holidays. They could take little holiday excursions. In summertime, steamship lines offered "boat trips for the day." Steamboats, old paddle-wheelers, left early in the morning for trips through the Lachine Canal and up the Ottawa River to Oka. There the boats docked for an hour to give passengers a chance "to stretch their legs" on shore. Then they returned downstream. In the early evening, in the softening light, came the concluding excitement — shooting the Lachine Rapids. Other day trips were available. The little steamboat *Beauharnois,* built in the 1850s and still operating in the 1920s, crossed Lake St. Louis to Châteauguay, Beauharnois and other places along the south shore of the St. Lawrence. Other excursions went downstream to Sorel or Trois Rivières. These "days on the water" were quietly satisfying. Passengers sat on deck on little wooden chairs and watched the river shores going slowly by. Families brought picnic lunches, supplemented with packages of biscuits and soft drinks bought aboard. When the holidaying family was brought back to the Montreal wharf, it made its way in the evening light over the cobblestones of the waterfront and took a streetcar home — rested, pleased, content and not restless or hankering after grander recreations.

Steamboat trips were only one of many simple holiday excursions. There was always Stony Point in Lachine. A streetcar went there over the nine miles from Montreal, swaying rather quickly on a route among the fields. Verchères boats could be rented by the hour at a little wharf opposite the Post Office. Seen from out on the water, the shoreline was made picturesque by distance, with its old elms along the roadside and the huge gleaming dome of the convent chapel. Back on land, the picnic hampers were opened on the stony shore. Supper took place under the evening sky, with the view of the broad river and the sun going down in tranquillity.

Streetcars were not only a means of transportation on excursions, they became excursions in themselves. The Park & Island Railway, at the turn of the century, offered trips to the Rivière des Prairies (the Back River). Passengers would be taken on a holiday far north of the city through the farmlands, passing the rural villages of St. Laurent and Cartierville, even on to Ahuntsic or Sault-au-Récollet.

Vivid advertising pictured the pleasures of these brief holidays in the country. "Rushing onward," said the railway's promotional literature, "the returning flush of health already in the cheek, drinking in with long respirations the pure refreshing air ... we view with rekindled eye the wave of spreading orchard branches, quaint and picturesque hedges and farm buildings, the distant shimmer of silver water and glint of rural spire...." Such a holiday in the country, on the excursions of the Park & Island Railway, would blow "the cobwebs from the brain," and invigorate "those ... hot and tired, or worried and annoyed by the cares and labors of daily life."

Montreal also had holiday excursions in town on its "Golden Chariots." These were the special holiday excursion streetcars — open cars, painted in gleaming gold and with seats rising in tiers towards the rear. Built for recreation only, they took passengers on summer trips around the mountain. They ran in the evenings, as well as by day. In earlier years, when the area behind the mountain was still countrified, it was (as one account says) "indeed a pleasant ride on a warm summer evening, accompanied by a certain glamor and exhilaration as the car rushed along the dark roads behind the Mountain, with the white beam of its arc headlight leading the way." The Golden Chariots were the longest-lasting of the simple holiday pleasures. They began running in 1905. They continued (except for 1943-44) until 1958. The number of other holiday amusements, requiring little time and little money, were almost endless. Among them were the trips by ferry to Ile Ste. Hélène, and the amusement parks, with the exhilarating mood of the outdoor fair.

Though the simple holidays were brightened by the little excursions, they were spent mostly at home, on the big front verandahs. Those big verandahs, often roofed over and sometimes screened against flies and mosquitoes, were a feature of many family homes. They linger, though now not much used. They are relics of the simple life. Big verandahs were family verandahs. There father read his paper, mother crocheted, and children played (generally on the steps). They were also communal gathering places.

There on summer evenings friends came over for talk and for soft drinks and home-baked cookies. Conversation on a warm evening might go on till late. In the darkness, talkers became voices only, indicated by a glowing bowl of a pipe or the burning tip of a cigarette.

Today it all seems amazingly simple — those 1-1/2-day weekends and the annual two-week holiday, and the excursions here and there for a few hours, and the big balconies where the out-of-doors in summertime could be enjoyed at home. But such simplicity was believed to be wholesome, with the satisfactions of a steady and dependable life. ''Home-keeping hearts are happiest'' was a motto of the time. And in the simplicity of those home holidays many felt it was true.

JOHN COLLINS SKETCHBOOK — The Front Porch

Introducing Montreal to the Bicycle

When did Montrealers first have the bicycle and its advantages demonstrated for them? The year was 1869. The day was February 23. The place was the Crystal Palace on St. Catherine Street. Excitement is preserved in the accounts of the time. "That great sensation the velocipede may now be considered fairly upon us," wrote one commentator. "At length," wrote another, "Montrealers have been gratified with the advent of 'velocipedes' to the city on the St. Lawrence."

Velocipedes were sensationally new. This early form of the bicycle had been on display at the Paris Exhibition of 1867. It was a tremendous advance on the previous type of bicycle — the hobbyhorse. Those first bicycles had only been a sort of adult kiddy car. Drivers propelled themselves by pressing one foot, then the other, along the ground. The velocipede was a far more advanced invention. The driver turned a huge front wheel by a system of cranks and pedals. "Velocipede" was a name taken from the French "vélocipède." And the French had made up the name by combining the Latin words for "swift" and "foot." The velocipede was a means of becoming swift of foot. The rider ceased to be the plodding pedestrian. He flew onward like a skater, and, commentators believed, with an equal "ease and beauty" of motion.

By February 23 a "Mr. A. Millet" and his troupe arrived. Montrealers made their way to the Crystal Palace. The floor of this exhibition hall proved suitable for demonstrating an outdoor vehicle indoors. The palace had been built in 1860. It was a reproduction, more or less, of one of the transepts of London's Crystal Palace, built for the Great Exhibition of 1851 (first of the world fairs). The central floor was so extensive it had been recently used for the manoeuvres (in a military show) by the Montreal Field Battery, guns and all. Millet and his professional riders gave a dazzling display. Speeding at nearly ten miles an hour, they threaded the posts and pillars on which the galleries rested. At this "break-neck speed" one of them demonstrated "the capabilities of the machine by kneeling on the saddle with one leg in the air."

Velocipedes seemed formidable machines for such antics. They had two wheels, one behind the other. The front wheel was enormous, the back wheel tiny. Bicycles were so new in Montreal that they were described in terms of horses. Commentators that day in the Crystal Palace called them "mechanical horses," or "skeleton steeds." Pedals were likened to stirrups, seats to saddles. In the eyes of such observers, everything about the velocipedes appeared as novelties. They recorded what they saw with naive literalness: "By an alternate upward and downward movement the apparatus is started. The great difficulty consists of balancing oneself...."

The purpose of Millet in coming to Montreal was not only to demonstrate the velocipede. He would conduct a school, where the art of riding would be taught. That day at the Crystal Palace members of the audience were invited to come out on the floor. They could try a velocipede for themselves. Most hesitated. Velocipedes, in their height, were intimidating. Since the front wheel was so big, and the pedals had to be worked from the middle of it, the rider's seat had to be raised high above the ground. Old drawings show that when an adult rider was standing beside his velocipede, the handle bars were about the level of his eyes.

Mounting a velocipede was even more formidable than mounting a horse. The horse, at least, might be expected to stand still on four legs while the rider slung himself into the saddle. Wheels on a velocipede were only about an inch thick. The rider had to swing himself into the saddle and start the velocipede moving before it flopped over. If it flopped, the rider, being a long way from the ground, could, like Humpty Dumpty, have "a great fall." Even if the driver mounted successfully and propelled himself forward, he faced the problem of eventually getting off. The art of descent demanded as much skill as the art of mounting.

Most of the gentlemen at the Crystal Palace had made the mistake of bringing ladies with them. Velocipedes challenged their manhood. The ladies, as a writer observed, seemed to expect the gentlemen to rise to the occasion: "Several gentlemen, perhaps prompted by the ladies, of whom there were a fair number, essayed to ride the skeleton steed...." First to respond to the challenge was "a venerable legal dignitary." Once he had come forward, younger men could hardly hang back. He was followed "by a number of military and sporting gentlemen, and corporation officials."

At the beginning, the ordeal was not as terrifying as it might otherwise have been. Each volunteer "was held on to and supported by his best friends, the erratic course of the cavalcade giving one the idea that it was not conducted on temperance principles." The moment of truth came when such friendly support was withdrawn: "The gentlemen riders were at last abandoned by their friends, and left to struggle for themselves, which resulted in the most absurd efforts to get to shore, and considerable amusement on the part of the spectators."

Most of the beginners came to some sort of grief. Some got the machine to go, and even to go fast. But not knowing how to stop it, they crashed into a wall. They found the forewheel of a velocipede "very like a donkey's neck, in its grand capability of being pulled in any direction, without influencing the movement of the animal." Sometimes the front wheel seemed to turn round on a rider, catch his foot in its spokes and tumble him down.

Nevertheless, the first demonstration of February 23 had made a deep impression on the Montrealers who saw it. "Great interest was taken in the exercises of the afternoon," wrote a reporter, "and a number of persons expressed their intention of undergoing a course of instruction in the art of velocipedestrianism." So it proved.

Velocipedes began to appear on the streets of Montreal. They were not inexpensive, costing up to $300.

Montreal was far ahead in velocipedestrianism. Nine years after Millet's demonstration, the Montreal Bicycle Club was formed. It was the first bicycle club on the continent, except for the one in Boston. And it was one of the athletic clubs that joined in forming the MAAA in 1881. By 1889 the Montreal Bicycle Club had nearly 200 uniformed riders. They were seen in procession, touring the countryside. They even cycled to Toronto. Bicycles have undergone many changes, many improvements since the velocipedes were demonstrated in Montreal on that snowy February day in 1869. But basically the principle of self-propulsion remains the same. It is accomplished today, as it was in the Crystal Palace, "by an alternate forward and downward movement" of the rider's swift feet.

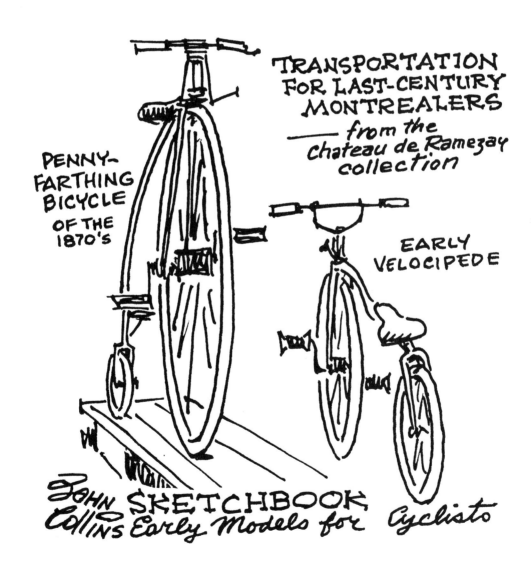

TRANSPORTATION FOR LAST-CENTURY MONTREALERS — from the Chateau de Ramezay collection

PENNY-FARTHING BICYCLE OF THE 1870's

EARLY VELOCIPEDE

John Collins SKETCHBOOK Early Models for Cyclists

Songs of the Voyageurs

In the summer of 1826 an officer of the Royal Navy — Lieutenant the Honorable F. Fitzgerald de Roos — was crossing from Montreal to St. Helen's Island (Ile Ste Hélène). On his way he heard for the first time in his life a song of the French Canadian voyageurs. Such songs, he said, were "so celebrated in Europe." Word from travellers had spread. These French Canadian voyageur songs, they said, were like no other songs in the world. Those rough voices, heard on the Canadian lakes and rivers, had a rugged plaintiveness more moving by far than the arias in any opera, even when rendered by the best of professional singers.

Much of the fame of the voyageurs' songs had been spread abroad by the Irish poet, Thomas Moore. He had heard them in 1804, on a three-day journey by bateau down the St. Lawrence from Kingston to Montreal. "Our voyageurs," Moore had said, "had good voices, and sang perfectly together. The original words of the air ... appeared to be a long incoherent story, of which I could understand little... but I remember when we have entered, at sunset, upon one of those beautiful lakes, into which the St. Lawrence so grandly and unexpectedly opens, I have heard this simple air with a pleasure which the finest compositions of the first masters have never given me; and now there is not a note of it that does not recall to my memory the dip of our oars in the St. Lawrence, the flight of our boat down the Rapids...."

The fame of the French Canadian river songs, reaching as far away as Europe, came not because they were distinctively Canadian. Actually they were not really Canadian songs at all. References in them to anything Canadian could scarcely be found. They were songs of old France — ancient and fanciful, full of allusions almost medieval. They might be about a meeting on the road with two well-mounted cavaliers; or the three daughters of a prince; or the grand gold musket used by the king's son when he went to shoot ducks; or about the rich brocades — gowns that stood up by themselves. Even the most popular song of all — "A la claire fontaine" — was hardly Canadian, with its references to nightingales. To the voyageurs, in a canoe or in a bateau, the words seldom seemed to matter. The songs had been brought to Canada from old France long ago. Time and association had made them part of French Canadian life.

When the voyageurs set out from Lachine on their canoe journeys to the Northwest, their parting song was often "La Belle Rose." In this song a travelling troubadour describes a virtuous young woman. She is declining naughty offers made to her, though these offers are backed by a settlement of 100 francs a year. "La Belle Rose" declares she will sleep with no man until she has first of all married him:

"Je ne couche point avec un homme.
"Hors qu'il m'épouse auparavant."

The voyageurs would sing with all the more relish about La Belle Rose's virtue because they obviously doubted it. Neither the words of these voyageur songs, with their garbled antiquity, nor even the engaging tunes explain their appeal. Rather, it was the time and the place — the voices over the water. Here was "water music" at its most attractive.

Lieutenant de Roos, first hearing a voyageur's song on his way from Montreal to St. Helen's Island, heard other songs in his journey on the St. Lawrence. Of these other songs he wrote: "On re-embarking the weather cleared up and revived the spirits of our rowers, who now commenced their boat-songs to our great delight. The conductor had previously made many apologies for not having any of his best singers on board, but the songs produced gave us a good idea of their general style. The boat-songs are joyous French airs, sung to the quick movement of the oars; the stanza is given by the steersman, and the rowers join in chorus at the end. On a summer's evening, to hear the echo of these wild melodies, softened by the distance, is indescribably pleasing."

"Indescribably pleasing" — these seem to be the key words. Somehow the voyageurs' songs transformed reality for the listeners. They enveloped every river scene with glamor, rough yet wistful. This enchanting river mood was perhaps best expressed by the Scottish traveller, John M. Duncan, journeying down the St. Lawrence to Montreal in 1819: "Towards evening it began to rain.... I could have endured the rain for an hour or two, to listen to the boat songs of the Canadian voyageurs, which in the stillness of the night had a peculiarly pleasing effect. They kept time to these songs as they rowed; and the splashing of the oars in the water, combined with the wildness of their cadences, gave a romantic character to our darksome voyage."

Voyageurs' songs also gave a special liveliness and drama to departures and arrivals. Sir George Simpson, governor of the Hudson's Bay Company at its Canadian headquarters in Lachine, was well aware of their stirring effect. He made the most of it. When setting out on his regular visits to the company's posts in the Northwest he gave instructions that the voyageurs were to break out into a song the moment their canoes left the Lachine waterfront. And as he approached each of the remote trading posts in

A Great Lakes Canoe

A Portage —

John Collins SKETCHBOOK Canada's Singing Voyageurs

the wilderness, he again commanded them to burst into song. Being by nature imperious, with a high sense of the dignity of his position, he felt these bursts of song lent impressiveness to his official comings and goings.

The same thought was in Sir George Simpson's mind in 1860, when he made arrangements for entertaining the Prince of Wales at a luncheon on Dorval Island in Lac St. Louis. The prince was to be rowed in a barge to the island from the lakeshore road. Sir George planned to have the barge escorted by 100 Iroquois voyageurs from Caughnawaga, "costumed en sauvage... with feathers, scarlet cloth, and paint." *The Gazette* reported: "As soon as the barge carrying the Prince pushed off... the fleet of canoes darted out from the island to meet him, in a line abreast, and to the inspiriting cadences of a voyageur song."

The appeal of the voyageurs' songs came not only from their picturesque plaintiveness. For the managers of the fur trade such songs had economic value. They were good for employee morale, as sea chanties were to sailors.

This advantage was seen by an observant British businessman, John Gray, who was staying in Canada from 1806 to 1808. Gray saw the voyageurs setting out from Lachine on their long journeys of unremitting labor into the Northwest. "They strike off," he wrote, "singing a song peculiar to themselves, called the *Voyageur Song*.... It is extremely pleasing to see people who are toiling hard, display such marks of good humour and contentment...."

In addition to helping employee morale, the voyageur songs stimulated the employees' productivity. As Gray noted: "The song is of great use: they keep time with their paddles to its measured cadence, and, by uniting their force, increase its effect considerably." It can be understood why an exceptionally good singer in the crew of a canoe or bateau was worth more and paid extra. He was an economic asset.

Comforting Heat of the Old Wood Stoves

No country on earth, in proportion to its population, made greater use of the stove than Canada. Hard experience had proved that the stove was the simplest, most effective means of fighting off the formidable cold of Canadian winters.

The complaint against the stove was not that it did not produce heat enough, but that it worked only too well. Some found the heat of stove-warmed rooms to be stifling. But these complainers were generally people from overseas. They had grown accustomed to fireplaces and chilly houses.

Even the complainers from overseas, if they stayed in Canada long enough, overcame prejudices. Fireplaces had lost the battle with Canada's winter cold. They tended to burn the face while freezing the back. It was not long before those from overseas had installed stoves and were grateful for the change.

One of them was Hugh Gray, an English businessman who came to Canada in 1806.

"I, like all other Englishmen, came to this country strongly prejudiced against stoves and warm rooms," he admitted, "but I have found that warm rooms are very comfortable in cold weather, and they are more likely to be comfortable, if heated by a stove, than by an open fireplace."

Some Englishmen coming out to Canada even failed to recognize a stove when they saw one. A box stove (so named for being in the shape of an iron box) particularly puzzled them.

Captain Basil Hall of the Royal Navy was visiting a French Canadian farmhouse in 1827. He gazed at the box stove; he walked around it; but his inspection made him no wiser. To him it looked like the money chest of some wealthy merchant, but a merchant's money chest in a farmhouse seemed improbable.

"Ah, Monsieur," said the French Canadian housewife, "you have not wintered in Canada, or you would not ask what this is for." She patted the stove.

If it looked like a money chest it was because the stovepipes had been removed for the summer. "Were it not for this fellow," she continued, patting the stove again, "we should all die of cold here."

Not only country houses but city houses were often heated by stoves, even the big limestone Victorian houses lingering here and there today. These city houses also had

fireplaces. But these fireplaces were mostly for show. Seldom were they used.

Many were never used at all. When such houses were being demolished in recent years, the white marble of their fireplaces was found unstained by any smoke, even though they may have been 100 years old, or more.

These big city houses had their hall stoves. They were recalled by Mrs. Florence May Ramsden, in her memoirs of her Victorian childhood in Montreal. She wrote: "There were few furnaces in those days in private houses, but we had a large friendly hall stove with mica windows that gave out a rosy glow. It had a protecting guard on which we hung our wet mitts."

Her account of the old stoves, like many others, speaks of the windows. These windows had been in the doors. They were filled with transparent mica, often called isinglass.

Mica could be had in a number of colors. The light of the fire behind it gave the agreeable glow to which Mrs. Ramsden refers. Sometimes the mica was white and clear. It could then be decorated with scenes.

Among the advantages of stoves was that their pipes could be used as a form of central heating. The stovepipes could be extended into other rooms, to spread the warmth in the house. They served as radiators.

Stoves had yet another usefulness — as humidifiers. Evaporators were part of some stoves' equipment. A simpler, if cruder, method was to place a pan of water on the stove.

The stove, though a simple and efficient heater, had a tedious drawback. The pipes had to be taken down every spring, put up every fall. J. W. Hughes, a 19th-century Montreal plumber, commented: "Imagine what a domestic disturbance it was every spring taking down the stoves and pipes, cleaning them and storing them away in the attic or woodshed. Then in the fall they had to be taken out and refitted. This was the tinsmith's harvest time — the plumber was a point above that sort of work."

Not only houses were heated by stoves but also churches, schools, courts, public halls, hotels. Some hotels featured very elaborate stoves in their lobbies. One of them was in a hotel on St. James Street (rue St-Jacques), near the old Bonaventure Station.

This stove stood about six feet high. It was of cast iron, with nickel-plated trimmings. Its four feet resembled lion's paws. The sides were moulded into scenes from Canadian history.

The mica windows in the two stove doors were decorated with pictures. One was of a French Canadian woman making bread in an old-fashioned outdoor oven. The other depicted a hunter returning through the forest, with the trophies of the hunt slung over his shoulders. These pictures on the transparent mica were illuminated from behind, when the fire had been lighted.

Crowning the whole stove was a handsome, classical urn, nickel-plated on copper. It was decorated with the Canadian coat of arms and by representations of sailing vessels and steam locomotives. All around the base of the stove was a nickel-plated footrest.

This gigantic stove, a metal tour de force, was Canadian not only in its decorations but in its origin. It was the creation of the Bélanger Stove Manufacturing Company, then situated on Craig Street (now St. Antoine), near St. Denis.

Travellers staying at the hotel sat around this stove, their feet on the circular fender. Conversation among strangers could always begin with remarks on the wonderful stove. Few travellers, even men who had stayed at many hotels, had ever seen anything quite like it.

Serious efforts to provide coal burning stoves began to be made in the 1830s. At the end of 1833 "Dr. Nott's Patent Stoves for Burning Coal" were being advertised. Coal-burning stoves had many advantages over those burning wood. They needed to be attended to only twice during the day; and coal would burn far into the night. But wood-burning stoves continued to be favored. Nothing could quite take the place of the dancing flames, or the whiff of wood smoke. With stoves, long-lasting fires were not everything. One Old Montrealer writes: "There was a much different heat from these old stoves that modern heating appliances can never attain. It was a sort of soothing (not harsh) comforting heat. Sort of mellow, the flames no doubt contributing to the pleasing sensation."

JOHN COLLINS

SKETCHBOOK

BOX STOVE

CAST FROM SAINT-MAURICE FORGE

1 APR 72

sketched at McCord Museum

The False Armistice

Montrealers did not celebrate their first Armistice on November 11, 1918. They celebrated it on November 7. And it was a false Armistice.

From about the beginning of November rumors were flying about that an Armistice was drawing near. They were enough to keep Montreal in a high pitch of excitement.

About noon on Thursday, November 7, a cabled message came. An Armistice had been signed, it said. Hostilities had ended. That message came from a source that could hardly be questioned. It was from Brest in France, from the headquarters of Admiral Wilson, commander of American forces in French waters.

The admiral had passed it on to United Press, and United Press had sent it to all newspapers suscribing to its services. These newspapers ran it up on bulletin boards in front of their offices.

Nor was it a newspaper report only. The same dispatch was arriving in every stockbroker's office that had a private wire service. Sir Charles Gordon, a director of the Bank of Montreal, happened to be in Washington. He heard the news there and sent it on to the Canadian government.

John Collins SKETCHBOOK Armistice Memories

In Montreal the burst of joy was spontaneous. Thousands streamed from offices into St. James Street (rue St-Jacques). Those who had not heard the news at once guessed what it was. They saw fire wagons parading through the streets, decorated with flags and streamers, sounding sirens. Church bells swung and clanged with extraordinary vigor and persistence.

Montreal's mayor and city council received the dispatch. At once they declared a half-holiday for City Hall's staff. Munitions and railway factories no longer felt the urgencies of war. Their workers were running outdoors. From noon on no one seemed to work, except harried girls at the telephone exchanges.

But Admiral Wilson had made a mistake. Misinformed himself, he had passed the misinformation on to United Press. Efforts were made as soon as possible to qualify the first cable. New dispatches were sent over the wires. They warned that reports of an Armistice were still unofficial and unconfirmed.

A whole hour passed. At last the official statement arrived. No Armistice had been signed. Actual negotiations for an Armistice had not even begun. The Western Front was far from quiet. Fighting continued. Casualties were still being reported.

It was too late to stop the celebration. St. James Street was crowded from wall to wall. Those still indoors joined the celebration by sending streams of paper flying from upper office windows.

Slowly word spread that no Armistice had been signed. It was all a mistake.

No longer did it matter. Celebration had begun. Nobody could stop it. Revellers, told the truth, only shrugged. "What's the difference?" they asked. The end of the war was coming soon anyway. Why not start celebrating it? A perfectly good party was under way. Why be a kill-joy?

Along the waterfront ships discharged rockets or fired cannon. Crowds surged into hardware stores. They came out with saucepans or frying pans — anything that could be beaten to make a noise. Singsongs were going on everywhere.

Bars were jammed. Private clubs were arranging big dinner parties. Hotels had processions of demonstrators marching through their lobbies, in by one door, out by another.

The celebration, beginning on St. James Street, moved up the hill to St. Catherine. Montreal's entire police force was out, doing its best to keep traffic moving. It had to tolerate interruptions. A sailor might start dancing a hornpipe at an intersection. A crowd soon surged round, to cheer him on. Even street cars had to wait till he finished.

All the crowding, shouting, singing, eating and drinking went on, quite without regard to the risks of Spanish Influenza. Only weeks earlier the epidemic had been killing Montrealers by hundreds. It was by no means over.

Underlying fierceness in the crowds hailed the premature appearance of a float — one made ready for the victory bond parade of the coming Monday. On it was the stuffed figure of the Kaiser. He was kneeling, begging for mercy. Above him stood a Canadian soldier. He held a rifle with the bayonet at the Kaiser's throat.

Cheers were sent up as the float lumbered by. They rose to screams of approval when the Kaiser's head was cut off and held up at the end of a pole.

A military parade was improvised. Fifty men of the French Foreign Legion were in Montreal. They marched through the town.

As the parade neared the corner of St. Catherine and Peel, fireworks flared from the office windows of the Drummond Building. At the corner, the Salvation Army's band, with flags flying, pounded out patriotic airs.

Long after midnight the false Armistice celebration went on, outdoors and indoors. Only the still light of dawn awakened Montrealers to the realization that war was still being waged.

Yet few seemed to regret the celebration of the false Armistice. All felt they had a right to celebrate. They had waited long enough.

The weekend came and went. Late on Monday morning the true message reached Montreal. War had really ended.

The true Armistice of November 11 was celebrated with happy gratitude and relief. But Montrealers on that Monday could not recapture the wild foretaste of peace and victory they had celebrated in the false Armistice of the preceding Thursday.

On November 12 an onlooker remarked: "The peace celebrations in Montreal yesterday were not so noisy or unrestrained as those which took place on the receipt of the premature peace news last Thursday.

"With the Armistice actually signed, the feeling among the majority of citizens was one of quiet thankfulness that the great struggle was over, and although there was much noisy jubilation among the younger generation, the majority of citizens celebrated in a quiet way and by 11 o'clock at night there was little to indicate anything out of the ordinary...."

Anticipation had brought an exhilaration that realization could never equal.

Montreal Once Had a Pillory

pillory used to stand in Montreal — just south of Nelson's Monument in Jacques Cartier Square. There was good reason why this particular spot was chosen. The criminal in the pillory faced the market below; and it was the custom in all cities and countries that the pillory should stand where it would be most seen — in a market-place.

The pillory was a pole or post, with a horizontal crosspiece at the top. This crosspiece was formed of two large pieces of wood, separate, but so made that they could be locked together. In each piece of wood three half-holes (like half-moons) had been cut out — one large and two small. When the two separate pieces were locked, the half-moons came together, to form three round holes. The criminal was made to take his place behind the pole. His head and hands were thrust forward, into the half-moon hollows of the bottom half of the crosspiece. Then the upper half descended into position. There he stood, his hands and neck tightly secured, in an awkward, clownish position. And he stood in the pillory as long as the judge had specified in passing sentence.

The discomfort was mental as well as physical. The criminal in the pillory was exhibited for public view and ridicule. He suffered more than the muscular strain of his unnatural position, or the stares and jeers of the market crowd. His head, thrust forward from its wooden hole, was an inviting target. And the market provided ample, ready ammunition. The refuse that lay scattered over the ground, about and under the market-carts and near the stalls, was rotten and stinking.

It was considered good sport to see who could hit the head in the pillory, as good sport as could be found at a country fair. In Montreal (as elsewhere) the pelting of the criminal in the market-place was regarded as part of his deserved punishment. He was compelled to submit to it.

To add to his distress, and heighten the sport of the market crowd, the crosspiece at the top of the pillory was placed on a pivot. Though the criminal had his head and hands fixed in the holes of the crosspiece, he could face in any direction around the pole. This freedom of movement was not intended as an easement; it was a planned torment. The common hangman was stationed behind the pillory. He held a whip in his hand. The criminal would try to turn away from the shower of market-place refuse fired at his face. He would wheel round the pole to face northwards. But every time he tried to turn, the hangman slashed at him with his whip until he faced the market again. The wretched criminal was left with a choice of miseries. He could endure the pelting of the crowd if he faced south, or

feel the whip of the hangman if he faced north. No one in the pillory could stand the hangman's whip for long; he would reluctantly wheel back to face the market.

The length of time spent in the pillory was generally one hour. The hour was always set in the forenoon, when the market crowd would be greatest: it was 10 to 11, or 11 to noon. But that one hour, twisting and turning between the barrage from the market and the cut of the whip, was considered long enough to leave a lasting impression upon the criminal, and to teach the crowd that the way of the transgressor is hard.

A pillory had stood in Montreal since the days of New France. At first it stood in the Old Market, in what was to become Custom House Square, and is now Place Royale. In 1808 the New Market was opened in what today is Jacques Cartier Square. For a time both markets were used. Then the Old Market was closed.

The pillory in the New Market was in an ideal spot. Its position, just behind Nelson's Monument, was at the height of the upward slope. The culprit could easily be seen by all, as if on a stage. Moreover, the spot was convenient: it was close to the jail. The old jail stood on the north side of Notre Dame Street, more or less opposite Nelson's Monument. The prisoner could easily be taken from the jail to the pillory, a distance of only a few feet. The common hangman, who attended the pillory, led an easy life. He was assigned free living quarters in the jail, and had only to cross the street with his whip to deal with a pilloried criminal.

In Montreal the pillory was used for only certain crimes, mostly for petty larceny. Criminals in Montreal were also pilloried for "uttering" bad money (putting bad money into circulation); receiving stolen goods; cheating; enticing a soldier of the garrison to desert. Sentences were worded much the same in all cases: "That he be carried to the Market Place of this city and be there put in and upon the Pillory and exposed to the view of the public...."

Sometimes a culprit was discharged as soon as his hour in the pillory was over; that one hour was his entire punishment. In other cases, being pilloried was only part of sentences that included periods in jail — from three months to a year. In still other cases, the culprit, after being fixed in the pillory, was whipped by the common hangman. This was not merely the random whipping, applied only if the culprit tried to turn away from the pelting of the crowd. It was the specified number of stripes imposed by the sentencing judge. The number was invariable — 39 stripes (the "forty stripes save one" of the scriptural

Place Jacques Cartier

SKETCHBOOK

John Collins

The Bonsecours Market of the last Century

Mosaic law). This number "39" had become so firmly embodied in the traditions of the law that it remained the same, even though one crime might be far more serious than another.

Such a sentence was passed on Andrew Symington in January, 1790. His crime was only petty larceny. Yet he was condemned "to be conducted to the Pillory on the public market place of the Town of Montreal, between 10 and 11 o'clock in the forenoon, then and there to be whipped by the hand of the Common Hangman upon the naked back, thirty-nine lashes and afterwards to be discharged." Women rarely appeared in the pillory in Montreal. One of the few was Mary Campbell. She was

pilloried in 1792 for petty larceny. But, as a woman, she received special consideration. She had to stand only half-an-hour in the Old Market, and was then discharged.

The pillory was a relic from a far past. It was generally abolished before the second half of the 19th century. In the United Kingdom it became a restricted punishment in 1816; it was limited to perjurors and suborners of perjury. By an Act of the British Parliament, dated June 30, 1837, it was abolished altogether.

In Canada the pillory lingered on a few years longer as a permissible punishment, for a number of crimes. It was not abolished until 1841.

The Cross by the Side of the Road

The custom of erecting wayside crosses, centuries old in Quebec, continued into the 1920s. A survey made in 1920 of the wayside crosses in and about Montreal listed about 200 of them. New crosses were still being added. Though the city was spreading out, many of the old farmlands lingered, as in the area around St. Laurent (then still a country village), along Côte St. Luc Road, out to the Back River, and westward to Ste. Anne de Bellevue. Even closer to town a few remained. One stood in a cabbage patch on the south side of the Upper Lachine Road, a short distance east of Montreal West. In Lachine itself one overlooked the highway, near St. Joseph's Hospital.

These tall crosses, about 15 to 20 feet high, were ornamented with wooden carvings of the instruments used in the Crucifixion: the hammer, the spear, the sponge of vinegar at the end of a rod, a pincers, a ladder. Often the cross was surmounted by a carved wooden cock, a reminder of the cock that crowed thrice at the time of Peter's denial. Nearly every cross, on the side facing the road, had, on its main shaft, a wooden (sometimes a wax) crucifix, or a statue of the Holy Virgin with the Infant Jesus in her arms. These images were sheltered from the elements by a little box, with a glass front.

Erecting a wayside cross was most often an act of piety on the part of a farmer. It was done at his expense; it stood on his land. At times a cross might be erected by the united action of neighbors, or by a family with many members in the parish. The cross would be dedicated on a Sunday after mass. The parish curé would officiate at the ceremony of consecration. The farmer's friends and relations would gather. It would be an important parochial event.

The custom of setting up wayside crosses in Quebec goes back far into the French Regime. The great number of these crosses was noted by the Swedish traveller, Peter Kalm, who visited the St. Lawrence Valley in 1749. He found them standing along-side the road between Montreal and Quebec, separated by only short distances. They were in the same style: ornamented with symbols of the Crucifixion, and with the little statue behind a glass pane. Kalm refers, in particular, to two crosses near Montreal: one at Laprairie and one at Sault au Récollet.

For nearly two centuries after Kalm's visit, travellers continued to describe the wayside crosses as one of the most conspicuous features of the Quebec scene. Visitors who had been recently in France felt they were back again, once they entered Quebec. The British geologist, Sir Charles Lyell, wrote of his visit in 1842: "On approaching Montreal we seemed to be entering a French province. The language and costumes... the large crosses on the public roads, with the symbols of the Crucifixion, the architecture of towers, carried our thoughts back to Normandy and Brittany, where we had spent the corresponding season of last year."

Most visitors not of the Roman Catholic faith considered these wayside crosses to be picturesque. But occasionally travellers might be irritated by the frequent pauses of their French Canadian drivers to say a prayer at each cross along the road. A British Army officer, Lieutenant Thomas Anburey, serving in this area in 1776, was among the impatient. He said: "These crosses, however good the intention of erecting them may be, are continually the causes of great delays in travelling which ... are exceedingly unpleasant in cold weather; for whenever the drivers ... come to one of them, they alight, either from their horses or carriage, fall on their knees, and repeat a long prayer, let the weather be ever so severe...."

One day Lieutenant Anburey was being driven in a open calèche. "The weather was so excessively severe," he said, "that with the assistance of fur coverings we could scarcely keep ourselves warm." They had not driven more than a mile before they came to a wayside cross. The driver stopped and got out. He said he was only going to "say a little prayer." The little prayer lasted five minutes. When he came back the passengers protested. They "complained of being almost perished with cold." The driver said it would be all right. He would just drive a little faster.

Not all travellers were so impatiently unsympathetic toward wayside prayers at wayside crosses. A Protestant clergyman from the United States, Rev. John Cozens Ogden, who was travelling in Quebec about 1799, approved of these pauses for prayer and was impressed by them. He wrote: "As the driver passes the churches and crosses, he checks the speed of the horse and stops for a minute, and taking off his hat repeats a small prayer, and replaces it on his head and drives on. Some have profanely resisted and ridiculed this practice; but to be conducted as a stranger by attendants, who constantly pay homage to the Creator and Preserver of men, must console every considerate mind."

Wayside crosses were erected not only to recall the wayfarer to prayer; they were shrines for other devotions. Those who did not live in the villages might not be able to go to church except on Sundays or on religious holidays. During the week they could go to a nearby wayside cross to say their prayers. Sometimes neighbors would gather for special, organized devotions. Some of these devotions were known as "the Month of Mary." Mothers and daughters decorated little wooden shelters, or "chapels," at the foot of wayside crosses. In these little chapels were placed statues of the Virgin Mary. Old folk and children knelt down together on the earth. They recited their rosaries in unison, and sang hymns in the open air. All knew these hymns by heart; they sang like a choir.

Times, however, were changing. When farms were broken up for buildings, some of the neglected crosses, left in vacant lots, grew weatherworn and leaning. In a gust of wind they might snap near the base and crash down. Even in the countryside itself customs changed. Motoring

brought churches nearer; shrines for local devotions were less needed. Religious customs themselves were not what they had been. Traditional ways were being abandoned.

The few wayside crosses still to be found linger to testify to the quality of the old custom. Wayside crosses had a strength, naturalness and realism that crosses in churches or on steeples can never have. Like the original cross of Good Friday, the wayside cross was under the sky, planted in the soil. It could leave an unforgettable impression of stark and simple grandeur, as it lifted up its arms, above all against a dark sky of rolling cloud and in the first drops of driving rain.

JOHN COLLINS SKETCHBOOK

ROADSIDE
CROSS
—ILE BIZARD

Houde the Humorist

It was December, 1953. Mayor Camillien Houde of Montreal was guest speaker at the Ottawa Knockers' Club. Speakers, he said, would learn more about their audiences if they just answered questions. That suited the Knockers. They fired question after question. Some of them had mean curves. He fielded them all. What did he think of the mayor of Montreal? "I may want to run again. I can't tell you that." What did he think of Ottawa's mayor — Charlotte Whitton? "I think the same as you do!" How come Toronto got ahead of Montreal with a subway? "We want to stay on the level in Montreal." And what about the song "Alouette"? "It's Canada's national anthem — after midnight." What makes Montreal attractive? "We keep a nice balance between the praying and the sinning."

It was only appropriate that Houde held a card in an entertainers' union. He was an entertainer — one of the best of them. At any gathering he brought an instantaneous mood of jollity, liveliness, sparkle. His quick wit was only one of his resources. He looked like an entertainer. He was the image of the genial fat man. How much he really weighed was a matter of speculation. No ordinary chair could have held him when he was elected member of Parliament for Montreal-Papineau in 1949. One had to be made specially for him. No glue or mortise held it together; it had to be bolted. Its seat measured 28 inches, inside massive arms. No chances were taken. They tested the chair with sandbags.

Camillien Houde would dress in black formality, whenever the occasion required it. But when free to do as he pleased, he could be as swaggering as any entertainer in choosing his clothes. In 1957 he was described as carrying a black cane, wearing a dark-blue homburg, a navy burberry coat, topped with a navy cape with a reversible green tartan lining.

His success as a public entertainer came not only from his rapid wit, his grotesque bulk, his love of displaying clothes. It came, perhaps most of all, from the mobility of his face. He had all the actor's tricks. His humor lay not merely in what he said: it was in his way of saying it. "The Houde brand of humor," remarked one commentator, "is almost untranslatable — it depends on the expression of his mobile face or the perfectly timed gesture rather than on the words." He was at an annual luncheon meeting of the Royal Automobile Club. For guest speaker, an expert in traffic control had been invited from the United States. Solemnly, in the manner of experts, he described the huge measures carried out in American cities to solve their traffic problems. In the question period,

someone asked how much similar measures would cost, if applied to a city like Montreal. The expert quoted a staggering figure. Mayor Houde was sitting at the head table. All eyes turned toward him. He said nothing. His mobile face mimicked an expression of total shock; his mammoth body shuddered. No longer was he on the spot. Everybody was laughing.

Mayor Houde never had to say anything that might embarrass him. Wit was always a means of escape. At a meeting in 1953 someone in the audience asked him a probing question. He pretended not to hear. "Pardon me?" he said. The questioner hesitated. "Perhaps," he said, "that's not a fair question." And the mayor said at once: "I'm afraid I heard you." No longer did he need to reply. Again everyone was laughing.

Houde had complete confidence in his powers as a humorist; he could be audacious in using them. No instance has been recorded of any joke of his falling flat on its face, or dying out in pained silence. He could take his chances, even in the presence of royalty. Mayor Houde presided at the banquet given at the Windsor Hotel in honor of George VI and Queen Elizabeth during the royal tour of 1939. In preparation for his role, he had himself carefully instructed in the etiquette he must observe. He had been told on no account to address His Majesty, or introduce any topic, until His Majesty had spoken first. Part way through the dinner a burst of laughter came from the King. An animated conversation ensued, punctuated by more laughter. Everyone was fascinated. All wanted to know what had happened.

The King had turned to Houde. "Did you speak to me?" he asked. "No, Your Majesty, I was talking to myself." "Why were you doing that?" "I was told before I came in here that I was not to speak to you until you had spoken to me, and as you had not spoken to me, I was talking to myself." "What were you saying?" "I was saying, 'I wish I had someone to talk to.' " At this point the King roared with laughter. Their laughing conversation continued till the banquet ended.

Camillien Houde's quick wit was not an isolated facet of his mind. He sized up any situation at once. He was as quick in action as he was in word or expression. On the night of December 7, 1950 he was addressing a political meeting in a hall on the fourth floor of the St. Henri College at 4125 St. Jacques Street. Someone in the rear of the hall screamed "Fire!" Smoke billowed into the hall. There was an odor of burning. The audience panicked. Mayor Houde grabbed the loudspeaker. "Be calm and proceed slowly,'' he urged. ''There is no real danger and no cause for anyone to get hurt.''

Panic died down. People filed out without pressure. Houde stayed on the stage; he was the last to leave. Firemen confined the outbreak to one classroom on the floor below. It was soon put out. Most of the audience came back into the hall. The mayor went on with his speech. ''Just before the interruption,'' he said, ''I was about to speak on the administration's policy for smoke control.''

Camillien Houde presided over Montreal for seven terms — a total of 17 years. As the years passed, he became the great reconciler. The fact that he had spent several of the war years in an internment camp, for advocating resistance to national registration, was lived down. He abandoned the bitterness and division of his earlier career. He had become ''Mr. Montreal,'' the symbol of a tolerant, cosmopolitan city. ''Any race in the world can feel at home in our city,'' he would say, ''whether they speak French or English or not.''

Nothing mawkish spoiled his appeals for understanding. He lightened them with humorous touches. In 1952 he was speaking about all the races that made up the city's population. When he came to the end of the list, he paused, then said: ''I hope I haven't left any out. There is an election coming.''

The same good humor appeared in his references to the Montreal English. He set the figure at 250,000. ''Sometimes,'' he added, ''I feel there are more than that, because they seem to pretty well run the city — but they pay for it.''

When Camillien Houde died in 1958 some 75,000 Montrealers attended his funeral, though he hadn't been mayor for several years. Another 100,000 lined the streets. ''A part of the city is gone,'' said Mayor Fournier. And it was a good-humored part.

CAMILLIEN HOUDE TELLING ANOTHER FUNNY STORY

"MR. MONTREAL" WITH HIS CHAIN OF OFFICE

John Collins SKETCH BOOK

Charles Dickens in Montreal

"Yesterday Mr. Charles Dickens, the well-known author, and Mrs. Dickens, arrived in town from Kingston. They proceeded to Rasco's Hotel, where it is their intention to remain for some days." This was the announcement in the Montreal *Gazette* on May 12, 1842. Rasco's Hotel still stands — the tall stone building on St. Paul Street, opposite the western end of Bonsecours Market. Somewhere in its massive interior, quite beyond identifying now, is the room that Dickens and his wife occupied for a stay of some 19 days.

Dickens's host was Francis Rasco, a fat, lively, little Italian. When he first came to Montreal, Rasco was a partner in a looking-glass business. But he soon had a hotel of his own. He went on with grander projects, until he established the new Rasco's Hotel — the massive stone building on the north side of St. Paul Street. When Dickens came to Rasco's it was just six years old. Rasco himself described it as "the largest and most splendid hotel ever erected in British North America." Rasco must have been particularly attentive to a guest so distinguished as Dickens. He was described by a Montrealer as "a model for desire

John Collins SKETCHBOOK

RASCO'S — HOTEL

to please his guests and boarders,'' a perfect blend of pride and servility, a man of ''imperturbable good humor.''

Those days Dickens spent in Montreal were among the most buoyantly happy in all his life. Everything seemed to have come together to rouse his high spirits. He was young, only a few months past his 30th birthday. He was immensely successful, intensely popular. Already he had written *Pickwick Papers, Nicholas Nickleby, The Old Curiosity Shop, Oliver Twist* and *Barnaby Rudge.* He relished the fame of what he had done; he could look forward with excitement to what he might yet accomplish. The rather sombre portraits of the later Dickens, with the grizzled beard, give little impression of the clean-shaven, laughing youth of the American tour of 1842. ''Ah, how happy and buoyant he was then!'' wrote his Boston publisher. ''Young, handsome, almost worshipped for his genius.... He seemed all on fire with curiosity, and alive as I have never seen mortal before.... What vigor, what keenness, what freshness of spirit, possessed him!''

Other reasons, more immediately relevant, enlivened him. After a long tour of North America he was nearing home. No other traveller could have been more homesick. He began to miss his London home almost before he set out. He longed for it every step of the way. One of his last North American letters ended: ''Oh home — home — home — home — home — HOME !!!!!!!!!!!!'' Just because he was heading home, Dickens was prepared to enjoy the last of his North American tour with greater freedom of mind. He was more ready to be interested and pleased. And being in Montreal was such a relief after his depressing experiences in the United States. He had come up toward Canada by the Mississippi route. Of the Americans he wrote: ''Their demeanor in these country parts is invariably morose, sullen, clownish, and repulsive....''

Montreal was a delightful contrast. It was a substantial town, with civilized people. On May 12, 1842, Dickens was writing from Rasco's Hotel: ''We have experienced impossible-to-be-described attentions in Canada. Everybody's carriage and horses are at our disposal, and everybody's servants; and all the government boats and boats' crews.'' Montreal appeared splendid in his eyes. He found it ''full of life and bustle.'' The environs abounded in ''charming rides and drives.'' He saw something agreeably substantial about everything — the ''many excellent private dwellings''; the ''great variety of very good shops''; the Government House, ''very superior to that at Kingston''; the granite quays, ''remarkable for their beauty, solidity, and extent.''

Dicken's sense of well-being was increased by coming to Montreal at the right time of the year — in spring. ''All the rides in the vicinity,'' he found, ''were made doubly interesting by the bursting out of spring, which is here so rapid, that it is but a day's leap from barren winter, to the blooming youth of summer.''

Even his entry into Montreal had a certain dash about it.

This cheerful young Dickens came down to Montreal from Kingston. The last part of the journey down the St. Lawrence to Montreal was by steamboat. Dickens arrived at Lachine. There he found that arrangements to have him met had been made by Sir Richard Jackson, commander of the forces in Canada and an old veteran of the Peninsular War. Sir Richard had sent out his four-in-hand carriage, with two young aides. Dickens says he came into Montreal ''in grand style.'' In Montreal he dined with Sir Richard and saw the best of society.

Everything seemed to go well for Dickens in Montreal. Even though he fell victim to a fraud, he never knew it was a fraud but was pleased by it. Inevitably, Dickens received many letters. In his mail at Rasco's one day was a letter that particularly appealed to his sentimentality. It was from an English laboring man who had settled in Montreal. He was writing for himself and his wife. They had heard a great deal about the ''beautiful books'' Dickens had written about ''us poor folks.'' Then came a request: would he permit them to name their baby boy after him? They promised to give the child a better education than they had had, so he would be able to appreciate more fully the works of the great novelist. If Dickens wished to reply, he could simply address his letter to ''Post Office until called for.''

Dickens, busy as he was, could not turn aside such an appeal. He wrote in reply that he would be proud to have their little son bear his name. And if, in later years, their son, influenced by the novels, developed sympathy for his fellow-creatures, he, the author, would feel his own life had been worthwhile. The letter was called for at the Montreal post office, but not by any laboring man. It was picked up by the son of an officer in the British garrison then stationed in Montreal. The letter he had sent to Dickens was a fraud. The only aim was to get the novelist's autograph.

The perpetrator of the fraud lived to be ashamed of what he had done. Later he went to India and settled in Bengal. There he came to be the proprietor of extensive plantations. Whether influenced by Dickens's letter or not, he developed into the sort of man Dickens would have commended. He had a reputation for being ''very popular among the natives for his humanity and the uprightness of his dealings.''

Charles Dickens Acts on the Montreal Stage

Dickens had never expected to act in North America when he set out on his tour in 1842. He had gone as a tourist. Like other literary tourists, he planned to write a book about his experiences. The chance to act had come about by accident. On board ship was Lord Mulgrave, an army officer returning to duty in Canada. Mulgrave told him the officers in Montreal, the Garrison Amateurs, were intending to put on plays in the spring, at the time Dickens would be there. Would he take part? And would he be the stage manager as well? Dickens seized the invitation. The prospect exhilarated him. He approached Montreal enlivened by anticipation.

When Charles Dickens had established himself at Rasco's Hotel on St. Paul Street, he did not have far to go to preside over the rehearsals at Montreal's Theatre Royal. The theatre was on the other side of the street, a little way to the east, at the southwest corner of St. Paul and Bonsecours. The eastern end of Bonsecours Market now covers the ground where it stood. The Theatre Royal was only 17 years old at the time of Dickens's visit. It is described as a neat building, with a Doric porch. It was "commodious" for the period, being two stories high, with a pit, a balcony and two tiers of boxes.

Montrealers had a special regard for the Garrison Amateurs. Their productions at the Theatre Royal had an intimacy and good humor no other performances could offer. The officers were well known in the social life of the town. The audiences that gathered for their amateur plays were seeing their friends on the stage. These plays also had local meaning, as the proceeds went to Montreal's charities. The Montreal General Hospital often benefited.

Though Charles Dickens appeared at Montreal's Theatre Royal as an amateur, he was an amateur thoroughly experienced as player and director. He was not only experienced but devoted. The stage drew him and drew him powerfully. Near the end of his days, Mrs. James T. Fields, the wife of his American publisher, wrote: "His love of the theatre is something that never pales, he says..." When he agreed to become stage manager for the Garrison Amateurs, Dickens assumed all kinds of trouble. But he relished every bit of it. To his friend, Professor Felton of Harvard, he wrote: "... if you could only stumble into that very dark and dusty theatre... and see me with my coat off, the stage manager and universal director, urging impracticable ladies and impossible gentlemen on to the very confines of insanity... and struggling in such a vortex of noise, dirt, bustle, confusion, and inextricable

entanglement of speech and action as you would grow giddy in contemplating...."

As stage manager for the Garrison Amateurs, he was faced with a difficulty: the associations of the stage were not for ladies. According to the customs of the time, as they prevailed in Montreal, the stage was appropriate for professional actresses but ladies should not expose themselves to such public display, or to those temptations that the stage was reputed to encourage.

The Garrison officers, out of respect for these social standards, used themselves to play the female roles in their stage plays. Possibly Dickens, when he began the rehearsals for the Garrison Amateurs' plays in 1842, had to try to make some of the young officers simulate the female voice and the female way of walking. Twenty-one years later, in speaking at a theatrical banquet, Dickens proposed the toast to "The Ladies." He recalled that once in his life he had missed them particularly. He had been in Canada, acting with the officers. At that time "no ladies were to be found and it was absolutely necessary that young and newly caught officers should supply their places; upon which occasion, in order that they might acquire something of the feminine walk, it was found absolutely necessary to tie their legs!"

Dickens, obviously an impatient and exacting stage manager, might have found this arrangement so unsatisfactory that female actresses were provided after all. Convention, however, had still to be respected. To spare the ladies the disgrace of appearing before the public in a public theatre, the first performance would be held in private. The theatre would still be the Theatre Royal. But no one would be admitted except by invitation. And to banish all associations of the professional stage, the very name of the playhouse would be changed for that one night. It would cease to be the Theatre Royal; it would become the Queen's Theatre.

This arrangement, ingenious as it seemed, still left one serious problem. Montreal would be hot with resentments among those who regularly attended the performances of the Garrison Amateurs, and paid for their seats, but who might find that they had not been invited to the private performance. To soothe their feelings a second performance would be held. This second performance would be open to the paying public. The playhouse would revert to being the Theatre Royal. The ladies would not appear on the stage. They would be replaced for that night by the female cast of a touring stock company that happened to be in Montreal.

JOHN COLLINS SKETCHBOOK East End of Bonsecours Market

The evening for the first performance came — the evening of May 25, 1842. The dazzling scene in the theatre was described in one of the accounts of the time: "About four hundred cards of invitation were issued to ladies and gentlemen in the city and vicinity. Soon after the doors were opened, the boxes and pit were well filled with the beauty and fashion of the city, and the gay uniforms of the officers of the different regiments in the garrison interspersed with the costly dresses and jeweled brows of the ladies fayre, presented a beautiful scene." The governor general, Sir Charles Bagot, and the commander of the forces, Sir Richard Jackson, and their suites, were present. The band of the 23rd Fusiliers formed the orchestra. It played with spirit, though rather too loud.

The plays came off splendidly — "no wait or hitch for an instant." None of the amateurs had much in the way of acting ability. But Dickens had nerved and menaced them into making the best of themselves. The props were superb. Furniture had been lent from private houses to make a good show. Dickens had even contrived a real fireplace. It went "blazing away like mad."

If efficient as a manager, Dickens was triumphant as an actor. One critic commented on his role as "Mr. Snobbington": "This was THE performance of the evening, and was most admirably acted. Mr. Dickens so disguised his person and voice that some time had elapsed after the play began before he was recognised." The

governor general did not recognize him at all until the play was over, though he had been sitting close to the actors in a stage-box.

It was not the excellence of his disguise, or the waves of laughter he brought from the audience that made Dickens's performance "the magnet" of the evening. In his acting that night was a foreshadowing of the power he was to show in later years, when he largely abandoned writing to give dramatic readings from his novels. This was the power to pass from the comic to the tragic. It was the same power he was later to use in dramatizing the murder of Nancy Hanks — a tragic presentation so intense that women in the audience often fainted, and were carried out, stiff as pokers. The next Saturday evening the Garrison Amateurs presented two of the three short plays for the paying public. Then Dickens set out for home.

Dickens had been interested in seeing Montreal. His comments on the city and its people had been favorable. But it was his performance in the theatre on St. Paul Street that had made his visit memorable. All his old love of the stage had been reawakened. Perhaps, he wondered, he had really missed his true calling. From Rasco's Hotel he wrote to Professor Felton at Harvard: "The FUROR has come strong upon me again, and I begin to be once more of opinion that nature intended me to be the lessee of a national theatre, and that pen, ink, and paper have spoiled a manager."

A Great Victory for Great Ned Hanlan

A fieldstone house faces Lac Saint Louis on Elliott Place in Dixie. It is a very old house, long the home of the Meloche family. It also was a place in the history of sport. Here Ned Hanlan, the Canadian oarsman, had his headquarters in October, 1878. In that month Hanlan defeated Charles E. Courtney in a race on the lake. Already the champion of Canada, Hanlan made himself, by his Lachine victory, the champion of America. Two years later, in a race on the Thames, he won the championship of the world.

October 2, 1878 was the day first set for the race on the lake to decide the championship of America. It seemed likely to be an ideal day for the Courtney-Hanlan race on Lac St. Louis. Morning broke fair and fresh. Not ''a breath of wind'' blew ''from any quarter of the compass.'' The Grand Trunk Railway's special excursion trains from Montreal were arriving every half-hour at the Lachine station. They were pouring forth their ''living freight… in almost a solid mass.'' Lachine had never seen such crowds. At the same time that trains were unloading hundreds of passengers every half-hour, steamboats were arriving, some of them from Ontario. They anchored on the lake near the route of the race. Passengers on deck had all the advantages of floating grandstands.

Spectators on shore had grandstands also. Owners of properties along the waterfront had built them. They were reaping profits of their own. Hucksters of every type had put up stalls. Some were offering ''eatables and drinkables.'' Gamblers were there with wheels of fortune, card tables and dice boxes. The Corporation of Lachine had licensed them all at $4 a head.

But it was a day of disappointment. Storm clouds scurried up. Rain pelted decks and grandstands. Spectators ran for cover. From the judges' barge, the referee flew a blue flag — signal of ''suspense.'' Then came the signal that the race had been called off. That night Hanlan went back to the stone house at Dixie. He rested in bed till noon the next day. His friends guarded the house. Next day — October 3 — the crowds in Montreal held back. They would not set out for Lachine again unless they heard the race would definitely take place. The word came. A telegram signed by all the judges was issued at one o'clock. The news soon spread. The GTR's special half-hour trains were again jammed — so jammed that rules were broken and men went out to Lachine clinging to the steps of cars.

They arrived under clearing skies; they saw a quiet lake. But hope soon dwindled. Storm clouds returned. Forked lightning stabbed the water. Rain turned to hail. A battering wind tore the judges' barge from its moorings. It went drifting downstream towards the rapids, until rescued and towed back. No one, it seemed, could row in wind, rain and lightning. But in very little time the sun shone through a rift in the clouds. A promising rainbow reflected its colors in quietening water. Thunder still muttered in the distance. But the lake was becoming smooth enough for a race, remaining rough only near Dorval Island, at the west end of the course.

The referee hoisted the red flag — signal for the oarsmen to prepare to race. At 4:40 Ned Hanlan appeared from his stone house at Dixie. He glided downstream to take up his position. Ned was ''the Boy in Blue'' — easily recognized by his blue shirt. Hats went off, ladies waved their ''delicate handkerchiefs.'' Courtney, looking anxious, took up his position also. Officials instructed both rowers in the rules. Then the race was on. The American Courtney took an early lead over Hanlan. At Stoney Point, he was a quarter of a length ahead. Gradually Hanlan pulled even.

At one-and-a-half miles Hanlan led by a length. Both began a tussle with the current east of Courcelle's Island. As they passed the island they moved neck and neck. Courtney won a slight lead at Dixie Island. He was pulling 32 strokes to Hanlan's 29. Hanlan was a small man, but he commanded an extraordinarily easy and powerful stroke. An English newspaper, the *Newcastle Chronicle,* described it as ''a grand sweeping stroke which, when he exerts his strength, seems almost to lift the boat out of the water, even though it always travels gracefully on an even keel.'' At the two-mile stake, Hanlan pulled even. The pace was getting faster. Both men were pushing hard to be the first to go round the turning buoys.

Hanlan was in front. At two-and-a-half miles the ''real hard struggle'' began. Courtney had been creeping up. They came to the press boat, off the east end of Dorval Island. By this time they were nearly even; perhaps Courtney had a slight advantage. Hanlan's wife was watching the race from a steamboat deck. She ''was very excited as she saw how gallantly her young husband was rowing for victory, and how his manly and plucky opponent was hanging on to him like a bull dog…. Mrs. Hanlan, although rain was coming down heavily at this moment, remained on deck waving her handkerchief to her husband, and it seemed as if he caught sight of the encouraging sympathy….'' His shell was seen at once to fly past Courtney's. But Courtney was not to be left easily behind. Off Latour's Point, both men were again almost even.

The race home ''was a most glorious struggle.'' At the

four-mile stake Courtney had increased his stroke. Hanlan was at 31. It seemed enough to pull him ahead. American supporters of Courtney had congregated at Quesnel's Point. They raised a cheer. This cheer seemed to make both men aware they had come to the final spurt. Courtney raised his stroke to 35. He was "working like a steam engine," yet working smoothly, without splashing. Hanlan kept steady at 32. They came within 200 yards of the finish line. Neither seemed to have any advantage. Cheers were going up on all sides for a struggle so close. It was either man's race. Both seemed collected and cool, "notwithstanding the excitement all round."

In the last 100 yards they entered "the death struggle for victory." Hanlan moved ahead by half a length. His unique ability almost to lift his boat out of the water now told. He was widening the difference, though Courtney was working furiously to hold him. The judges' barge was now only two or three lengths away. In a flash, Hanlan shot by. The referees pronounced him champion "by a good length."

"The Boy in Blue," now champion oarsman of America, was close to the championship of the world, which came to him in 1880. His old headquarters overlooking the lake still stands as a reminder of the man whose tribute, on his monument in his hometown of Toronto, reads: "Most renowned oarsman of any age.... His achievements are all the more worthy of commemoration by his display of the spirit of true sportsmanship, which is held in honor in all fields of sport."

SKETCHBOOK
John Collins House on Elliott Place

Noisy Nights for a Bridegroom

A mob would assemble in Montreal before the house of the bride and bridegroom. It came in the evening. As many as 200 men, even more, might be there. They were ''masqueraders in every grotesque attire.'' Clothes were on backwards; hats flashed with cocks' feathers, jangled with bells; faces might be blackened. Some arrived on horseback, with the horses gaudily decked out — ''gaily caparisoned.'' The mob serenaded the bride and the bridegroom. The noise was ear-splitting. It came from horns, cowbells, penny trumpets, whistles, kettles, tin pans. The mob also roared, shouted, hooted, screamed. Sometimes it brought shotguns loaded with peas.

These mobs were not made up of friends and well-wishers, making a normal wedding clamor. They were generally strangers, out to bully and torment. Young brides and bridegrooms were not bothered. The mob came when it was a second marriage, especially when the difference in age between bride and groom was wide and ludicrous. In Montreal, as in many other towns in Canada, these organized torments became a custom, a social institution. They were called charivaris (pronounced "shivarees"). They were a form of sport, of "raising Hell," of harassing and intimidating. For the married couple they were an annoyance or a terror; for the onlookers, they were an entertainment; for the authorities they were a problem in law enforcement. Not only the young rowdies of the town got up the charivaris. Many taking part would be middle-aged, even older. They might be respectable, prominent citizens. A writer of 1823 remarked: "The first characters of the country are often the instigators of the mob."

The mobs beat on doors with clubs and sticks. They demanded to be paid to go away. Nor would any payment do. They bargained, with pressure. Sometimes as much as £100 was extorted. A wise bride or bridegroom came to terms with a charivari. It was not good form to give in at once. The mob must be accorded a few nights to amuse itself. About the third or fourth night bargaining should begin. The rules were: joke with the mob; pretend to be easygoing; make the best deal the circumstances might allow. The price of getting rid of a charivari might come high. But better pay it with as much good nature as could be simulated. And, above all, never complain to the police, or try to bring any member of a charivari before the courts.

Not everyone could bring himself to give in. The charivari was blackmail, a "protection maney" racket, a blatant public insult. Some bridegrooms could not stand the humiliation. Pride and courage got the better of prudence and appeasement. They were determined to fight it out. Such bold stands against the charivaris were doomed from the start. It was one man against a mob, and the mob knew it. No charivari could be worn out by resistance. It might beset a house night after night, for weeks, even for months.

The charivari's mood grew increasingly vicious. Anything might happen. Crowds, unconnected with the charivari, gathered to look on, almost hoping that the mob might break the door down and drag the bridegroom out. Charivaris were illegal. From time to time the magistrates (and Montreal was long ruled by the magistrates) issued warnings that no more charivaris would be tolerated. But suppressing a charivari was not simple. A mob of 100 men or more, out for mischief, was not easily dispersed. The police by day, and the watchmen by night, were few and poorly trained. Making arrests in a mob might be almost impossible. Anyone seized was at once wrenched free by his friends.

Attempts were made to have the charivari seem like an "innocent and amusing Canadian custom." Some charity would be given the money extorted from bride or bridegroom. But abuses from the charivaris were too frequent, their illegality too evident to make such donations really acceptable. The annual report of the Montreal General Hospital for 1835 included a resolution that "no money extorted under the pretext of a charivari in future be received by this institution."

Disasters resulted when a charivari was resisted. One of Montreal's principal citizens, Colonel John Dyde, commandant of all the city's militia, used to describe what happened to his brother-in-law, a man named Holt. A charivari descended on Holt's house, because he had married a woman much younger than himself. Holt was a man of spirit. He rejected the charivari. It resorted to his house night after night. Still he refused to give in.

Colonel Dyde said he had seen "as many as two hundred persons before the house of an evening and fifty of them on horseback." One evening the mob arrived with a "transparency" — a picture on cloth or paper, with a light behind it, to make it visible in the dark. Holt peered from a window. He recognized the picture — a portrait of his wife's deceased husband. This calculated indelicacy was more than Holt could stand. He shouted to the mob; he would shoot anyone who would touch his house again. The mob was back the next night. It began to rip off one of his shutters. Holt fired. A man staggered and fell dead.

Frenzy ran through the charivari. It surged about the house. But it was unarmed; Holt had his gun. The charivari moved out of range, to plot revenge. Holt realized his mistake. He knew another night would come. The charivari would be back. This time it would be after him, armed. He did the only thing he could: he took his bride and left town. That night the charivari came at his house "like a wolf on the fold." It smashed its way in. It could not find Holt; but it destroyed "almost every article" the house contained.

The heyday of the charivari in Montreal was in the 1820s and 1830s. But it lingered far into the century. In 1887 a tremendous charivari was organized against a Pointe St. Charles man. But prosecutions in the courts were becoming more effective. In July, 1886 "seven persons" were charged in Police Court "with being concerned in the recent charivari of Mr. Bourassa at Laprairie." They were found guilty and fined $10 each, or one month's imprisonment. Once the charivari became weaker than the law, its days were numbered.

Students and their Boarding Houses

Boarding house life used to be the experience of nearly all male students from out of town who came to attend McGill University. Not until 1937, when the Douglas Residence was opened, did McGill itself provide male students with accommodation. Even then, comparatively few students could be admitted.

Boarding houses, however, abounded in the network of streets near the campus, formerly one of Montreal's principal residential areas. Victorian Montrealers, with their big families, had needed big houses, often three storeys high.

When the movement away from the city's core began, these old buildings were just what were needed for boarding houses. They had a mutiplicity of rooms, big and small.

The transition from residences to boarding houses was certainly a decline. The change was evident in the prevailing shabbiness, the scuffing and chipping from the come and go of transients. Many houses had a fustiness in the atmosphere — "the still, sad odor of humanity."

Yet the old houses retained some charming features of Victorian ancestry: high ceilings, fireplaces in some rooms, graceful curving staircases with massive bannisters and newel posts (sometimes in solid mahogany).

Even the view from the windows at the back might have a certain wistful appeal — remnants of neglected flower beds with an occasional lingering bloom, and great trees, planted long ago, and grown so high as to overreach the rooftops.

Most of these Victorian boarding house are now gone. After the Second World War, the inner core of Montreal was reconstructed. McGill University, once surrounded by street after street of boarding houses, became an enclave among the office towers.

What life was like in the old downtown boarding houses has been described by Dr. A.D. Campbell. He graduated in medicine in 1911 and went on to become a notable teacher at McGill and surgeon at the Montreal General Hospital. Conditions in these houses varied, he found. Some were infested with vermin. They smelled of insecticide (Keating's powder) — a preparation used in an inconclusive battle with cockroaches and bedbugs.

Other houses were better managed. "There was," wrote Dr. Campbell, "the clean, tidy widow, reared and steeped in Victorian manners and customs, as evidenced in her rigid bearing and the décor of her parlor." In that parlor the Victorian world had been preserved intact — a little

area of chairs covered with horsehair, draped with antimacassars. Deep picture frames enclosed artificial flowers made of colored feathers. There the widow interviewed those asking for rooms. Medical students, it soon appeared, had inherited a stigma. They were a landlady's fixed aversion. Of all students, they had the worst reputation for wildness and freakish episodes. This particular landlady slowly resigned herself to the revelation that A.D. Campbell was in fact one such student. With a show of reluctance, she invited him to inspect the room she had to let.

In this room was an iron bedstead. Though pushed into a corner, it still occupied about one-quarter of the floor space. It had a crocheted coverlet. Pillows were enclosed in embroidered covers, known as "shams." One had the embroidered precept:
"I slept and dreamed that life was beauty,
"I woke and found that life was duty."

In the room stood a commode — a washstand. On top was a huge water jug, rather handsomely decorated. It stood in a water basin of matching design.

The prospective boarder was shown the bathroom. It was divided into two parts. In one was the skylighted bathtub, "a sort of coffin designed for a giant." It was lined with tin, and enclosed in a mahogany cabinet. The other half of the bathroom lacked a skylight. Anyone using the facility here soon discovered "an umbrella was almost essential." The elevated cistern spat a "shower." After the conducted tour the landlady cleared her throat. Much as she had an aversion to medical students, she would consent to rent the room for $8 a month. She would like two months paid in advance.

Finding a room in McGill's neighboring boarding houses was the incoming student's adventure. As with most adventures, the student could never be sure what to expect. A.K. Hugessen, later an eminent lawyer and a senator, wrote of the experiences he had in 1908. He considered himself lucky. He had found a room close to the campus, on McGill College Avenue. The house was owned by an old German bandmaster, Robert Gruenwald. The bandmaster's wife kept a few boarders. "The room was comfortable and convenient, and reasonably clean," recalled Senator Hugessen. "Once, though, being attacked in the early morning, I arose and slew a bedbug! This I duly reported to my landlady, who expressed herself as being extremely shocked that such a thing could happen in her house. She asked me particularly to tell her whether the bedbug looked very tired, as if it had come a long way, but I was unable to satisfy her on that point."

John Collins SKETCHBOOK Old Houses on Lorne Avenue

Only fortunate students stayed the whole college year in the same boarding house. Most sought a new room, hoping for better conditions — a hope not infrequently disappointed. Some of the curious adventures of students were described by A. Sydney Bruneau, a McGill student in arts, then in law, and later to be the mayor of Westmount. He went looking for better quarters. So did another student, Percy Corbett, later dean of McGill's law faculty.

They came late to the search. The better rooms had already been taken. At last they found a front and back parlor, divided into two rooms by a folding door. They could rent these rooms for $10 apiece. Sydney Bruneau remembered his landlady: "The landlady was a gloomy, forbidding person, with a face rather the worse for warts, but we were not in search of beauty, and the room was decently, if plainly, furnished, and not five minutes' walk from the campus."

Bathing facilities, however, were not attractive: "We had the use of a tin bath in the basement for which the plug never seemed to be available, so that sometimes a bath had to be taken by making a paper stopper, or one hand did duty while the other washed. Evidently frequent ablutions were not encouraged."

Women students, meanwhile, were living in the considerable comforts of the new Royal Victoria College on Sherbrooke Street, Lord Strathcona's gift to McGill. There, however, they lived among regulations and restrictions, sternly enforced. The Royal Victoria College was known as "the Gilded Cage." Men students had a more rugged time in their boarding houses. Yet these students, looking back in later years, recalled their experiences with lively good humor. They had been young, roughing it a bit, but relishing the mingled hardship and freedom.

When Montreal Burned

"The fire is still raging at the hour we write. God only knows where it will stop. Our city seems to be doomed." So a Montrealer was writing in the early morning of July 9, 1852. A fire, urged on by strong winds from the west, was rushing "from street to street and from house to house like water pouring down a rapid." It was crossing roadways in "one broad sheet of red flame" yards wide.

Many Montrealers stood staring and inactive: "...all those whose dwellings were not in immediate danger seemed to sink into a state of apathy, as if despairing that any stop could be put to the march of the destroyer."

Fire had broken out between nine and ten o'clock in the morning of July 8. The Montreal banker, William Weir, never forgot that morning. "I remember the morning very well," he was writing as long afterwards as 1903. "I was walking down town with the late M. H. Gault, who then represented several fire insurance companies, and when the fire-bells rang he left me at the corner of St. James and Bleury Streets, running down the latter to discover where the fire was located. All the insurance companies suffered heavily...."

The fire started in a house on the east side of St. Lawrence Main, above Dorchester. When it reached a woodyard on St. Dominique Street, it spread beyond control. Sparks from burning wood sailed on the wind. Wherever they settled, new fires soon burst out. Everything conspired to give the fire its chance. For many dry days the city had been under a scorching July sun. Temperatures were in the 90s. Wooden buildings, wooden tiles, wooden gutters, were parched. Meanwhile the Corporation of Montreal had drained the reservoir at Côte à Baron (later the sunken playground in St. Louis Square). Old water pipes were being replaced by bigger ones. Work was still in progress when the fire came. Montreal found itself fighting fire without water. Flames danced and ran. They spread upwards and downwards, carried by the west wind behind them. They reached northward at times above St. Catherine Street, southward at times to the waterfront.

Fire fighting was then done mostly by volunteer "fire companies." They were defeated by the dry reservoir, though some were able to draw water from wells. In the heat many firemen dropped from exhaustion or the sun. Help came from the British garrison in Montreal — from the Royal Artillery and the 22nd Regiment. Military fire fighting was carried out by blowing up buildings with gunpowder. The aim was to clear open spaces in the fire's path. To prevent the gunpowder from exploding from sparks while it was being delivered, it was brought along the waterfront in canoes.

Setting charges of gunpowder in buildings near the fire was dangerous. Major George Ranken of the 22nd Regiment gave an example: "I was assisted by the artillery in placing the charge, which, on account of the proximity to the flames, and a quantity of straw which was lying about, was a service of some danger. The bugles sounded the alarm, and the majority of spectators withdrew; however, notwithstanding all the bugles, and the loud shouts of the bystanders, one man (whom, I conjecture, must have been half-drunk) persevered in maintaining his position on a log of wood close to the doomed house. Nothing would induce him to move; and I was compelled, at my own risk, to run forward, and carry him off in my arms, amidst the cheers of the mob."

Major Ranken was in the midst of the fire fighting from start to finish, in the combined heat of sun and flames. "I rode four different horses during the day," he wrote, "and was galloping about for several hours, with my clothes torn...." Almost blind with dust, exhausted by heat and exertion, he left the fire for a few minutes for a brandy and soda. He came back to find things worse than ever. Horses without bridles were thundering in frenzy through the streets. He knew in a moment the stables of the 22nd Regiment must be on fire. Many of the garrison officers lived in houses on Dalhousie Square. Major Ranken had been some distance away, helping Mrs. Dixon, wife of the colonel, to load her household goods into a cart. No sooner was the cart loaded than he saw "a dense column of smoke issuing up behind Dalhousie Square" — the square that occupied ground later covered by railway tracks behind the old Place Viger Hotel.

By the time Major Ranken reached Dalhousie Square the fire was "to the highest degree grand and terrific." An enormous building, owned by the eminent Jewish businessman, Moses Hays, was on fire. It incorporated a hotel (Hays' House), a theatre (Hays' Theatre), shops and offices. In two hours nothing was left of the building. Most of the buildings around the square went down, one after the other. Worn out, at two o'clock in the morning, Major Ranken went to his own house nearby. To his surprise, it was still there. After "a fevered sleep of an hour and a half," he got up and went to the wharf. There he saw "all around, furniture and baggage of every description, and groups of poor men and women."

About 10,000 homeless people had to be sheltered. Some were taken into convents, into City Hall, or into the Emigrant Sheds at Pointe St. Charles. Most gathered in the open on the Champ de Mars or in a big field below Sherbrooke Street, a little east of St. Lawrence Main. The garrison came to their aid with army tents. "On Sunday I visited the tents...," said William Weir. "Such a motley crowd; it looked as if all the gypsies in the world had been brought together in that field. Still, being mostly French, they bore their misfortunes with that cheerfulness which is characteristic of their race."

When the fire had burnt itself out about four o'clock in the morning of July 9, a huge portion of Montreal had been reduced to "a smoking wilderness, covered with chimneys, like a burned pine forest with its scathed and charred trees." Many of Montreal's important landmarks were among the ruins. The Roman Catholic Cathedral, on St. Denis Street above St. Catherine, and the nearby Bishop's Palace, were lost. St. Thomas Anglican Church, built by

Thomas Molson, burned. The Montreal General Hospital came close to being lost also.

The City of Montreal at once set about raising a relief fund for those who had lost dwellings and household goods. Donations came from other cities in Canada, from the United States, from England. Amidst all the far-flung generosity, the Relief Committee appreciated one gift most of all. As the report reads: "A most memorable instance of generosity was mentioned by B. Holmes, Esq., to the Relief Committee, at its meeting.... A poor discharged soldier from the 22nd Regiment, named McDouall, had scraped together, and laid up against a 'rainy day', the sum of $20. He handed $10 of this store to Mr. Holmes and insisted on giving it to the Committee to be applied to the relief of the sufferers."

John Collins SKETCHBOOK St. Louis Square — Site of the old Reservoir

The First Airplane Over Montreal

Count de Lesseps had planned his Montreal flight as a surprise. Only his brother and sister, and a few associates, knew the secret. The crowd at Lakeside, where the international aviation meet was taking place, had seen, during those eight days, aviators manoeuvring their planes above the airfield. On the evening of July 2, they had expected the Count to follow this pattern (as he had earlier in the meet). But on that Saturday evening of July 2, 1910, after circling twice above the airfield, he headed off for the lake. His plane became a diminishing speck, until vanishing altogether in the far distance.

BROOKINS' WRIGHT BIPLANE

The WRIGHT BROS. who started it all... ..back in 1903

DE LESSEPS' BLERIOT MONOPLANE

JOHN COLLINS SKETCHBOOK. Early aviation days in Montreal

Count de Lesseps was well aware of the danger of attempting so long a flight. He had taken special precautions. He felt it would be safer for him to fly, as far as possible, over the water; a crash landing would be less likely to end in disaster. A cigar-shaped bladder or float had been installed in the fuselage of his plane, from the tail to the seat. He hoped it might keep him and his plane from sinking until help could arrive. Even that help had been arranged. Two gasoline-powered yachts were in readiness to effect a rescue. One was at Valois, the other at Lachine.

Plans were also made to have his brother Bertrand and a few others follow his plane by driving along the old Lakeshore Road in a powerful 60-horsepower automobile. They left the airfield 10 minutes before the flight started. Another automobile followed them. It was driven by A.E. Rea of Montreal. With him went a *Gazette* reporter. That reporter was young John Bassett. Twenty-seven years later he was to become *The Gazette's* president. Rea's car, with the reporter, lost sight of the airplane at Dorval. The car ahead, with the aviator's brother, did a little better, but lost sight at Lachine.

About half-past six that evening Montrealers heard the steady throb of a motor. Such a sound was not unfamiliar, for Montreal had been in the new automobile age more than a decade. Yet the sound of this motor was not coming from the streets. It was coming down from the sky. People stared upwards. The evening sky was rather misty. But there could be no doubt about what they saw. An airplane was flying overhead.

Most Montrealers had never seen an airplane in their lives. No airplane had ever before appeared over the city. They were living a moment of history. The impact was sensational. From the shops streamed customers and clerks. Streetcars stopped to let impatient passengers hurry out. In street after street, people could be seen coming out of their houses, their faces turned skywards, even as they came down their front steps.

The airplane had reached Montreal by way of the river. It flew northward over McGill Street. It circled in the sky above City Hall, then passed over Mount Royal. Back it came to centretown. It passed above the Windsor Hotel, headed across the southwestern corner of Westmount, crossed St. Henri, then, at Lachine, turned out over Lac St. Louis.

The apparition came and went within a few minutes. The aviator had no time to linger. He was making an anxious long-distance flight. He had flown in all the way from Lakeside, on the Lakeshore. By the time he arrived back in Lakeside, he had travelled 30 miles. He had been in the air 49 minutes, three and three-fifth seconds. And he had maintained an average speed of 40 miles an hour. Altogether it had been an astonishing achievement for 1910.

The crowd at Lakeside was now standing on the grandstand benches. It scrutinized the sky. The returning plane came in sight, at first only a cross-like speck on the horizon. Rapidly it grew bigger. It was approaching the airfield at 50 miles an hour. The Count made an easy landing "in front of the awe-struck crowd." One account reads: "It took a few minutes for the spectators to recover from their shock. The thought ran through their minds that the thing was not possible." Then "they clapped, they threw up hats, they shrieked."

Meanwhile, an automobile was thudding up the uneven field. It came near to bouncing out its passenger — Madame de la Bégassière, the Count's sister. She was coming with roses, ordered confidently in advance. When she came near her brother, she leapt from the car, made her way through the crowd, and presented him with the bouquet. "Jacques," she said, "your face is too oily for me to kiss you, but you're a wonderful boy."

His face was certainly oily. His monoplane had an open cockpit. The fine wire screen in front of his face only partially shielded him from spurting oil. Aviators at that time seemed to fly without goggles. His eyes were bloodshot; they watered profusely. Sweat matted his hair. The fastidious Count was aware of his unpresentable appearance. He hurried away to clean up. He reappeared stylishly dressed "in his street clothes."

In all this confusion, Walter Brookins, the pilot sent to Lakeside by the Wright Brothers, descended from a flight over the field. It had been an important flight; he had established a new Canadian altitude record. The crowd was too excited by Count's return to pay much attention to Brookins. De Lesseps sought him out at once. He insisted on giving Brookins half his bouquet. They were photographed side by side. Then they got into an automobile. Together they drove in front of the grandstand, sharing the honors of the day. Honors came to de Lesseps not only on the airfield. They came from across the river, at Caughnawaga. Two days later he was made an Indian chief. They gave him the name: "The man with the great wings."

Count Jacques de Lesseps, like all pioneers of aviation, was risking his life on every flight. In the end, aviation claimed him. In 1927 he undertook an autumn flight over the St. Lawrence from Gaspé to Val Brillant. His plane ran into a wild storm. Its shattered fragments drifted ashore, before his body was found. He was buried at Gaspé. In Montreal, the year before, Count de Lesseps had drawn up a holograph will. "I wish to be buried," he wrote, "where they will find me.... I want all who have comforted me with their affection to know I was remembering them, with all my heart, till the very end."

Count de Lesseps — the Stylish Aviator

The first airplane over Montreal was flown by Count Jacques de Lesseps during the evening of July 2, 1910. And there has never been an aviator so stylish. When the count strode to his plane on the airfield at Lakeside, past the grandstand (the biggest that had ever been built in Canada), he did not wear an aviator's costume. He was dressed like a modish Parisian, out for a stroll on a boulevard. Behind walked his valet. The valet carried the "aerial costume." When de Lesseps reached his plane, he took off his fashionable black coat and handed it to the valet. Only then did he get into his aviator's overalls. The next moment "he was off in his machine and gliding easily into the air… with the utmost grace and steadiness."

For eight days an international aviation meet, one of the earliest in North America, had been taking place at Lakeside, on an improvised airfield in the farmlands above the railway station. This enterprising venture had been initiated by Montrealers who were members of the automobile club. In their enthusiasm they even went so far as to change the club's name for a couple of years to "the Automobile & Aero Club." They were joined in the venture by Ed Wilcox of the Toronto Automobile Club. A syndicate was formed and chartered as the Canadian International Aviation Association. It would promote two aviation meets — the first on the Island of Montreal, the second in Toronto.

Wilcox was influential in winning participation by the celebrated Wright brothers. These pioneers of heavier-than-air flight in the United States were too much absorbed in their research to come themselves, but they agreed to send some of their best planes and their best aviators. J.A.D. McCurdy, who had recently made a flight at Baddeck in Nova Scotia, would be present with his plane. Other aviators joined.

The meet had grown to such proportions that the club was claiming the total equipment on the field would be "larger than it was in any other meets held in America." It would make aviation history. An eminent aviator was sought in France. Count de Lesseps was approached. At first he was reluctant, but finally agreed to come for $10,000, with $5,000 for expenses. He would give exhibition flights on the Island of Montreal and in Toronto.

Count Jacques de Lesseps was a French aristocrat. His father was Vicomte Ferdinand de Lesseps, who built the Suez Canal and began the building of the Panama Canal. The Vicomte, at the age of 64, married a girl of 21 and fathered 12 children. Count Jacques de Lesseps was one of six sons. He had distinguished himself in French aviation

in his Blériot airplane, *Le Scarabée*. In this plane he had flown over the English Channel early in 1910. It was only a few months later that he gave Montrealers their first sight of an airplane over their city.

Count de Lesseps arrived in Montreal with his brother Bertrand, and his sister, Madame de la Bégassière. The secretary of the Automobile & Aero Club, George A. NcNamee, used to recall that "the gentlemen were dressed in morning coats, gloves and silk hats." Madame de la Bégassière was "delightfully attired in the latest from Paris." An airfield for the meet was being hastily improvised. The club had leased fields from several farmers at Lakeside — fields just above the Lakeside railway station. They were rough farming land. The Count de Lesseps went out to examine the site. He was "polite but nevertheless businesslike." Such a field, he said, would never do. He "simply waved his hand." That night an army of men went to work on it. They removed a snake fence. That fence had been left standing the length of the field. Later the runway was enlarged and smoothed. Ditches were filled.

"Aviation Park" was the name given this makeshift field. It was a picturesque spot. Trees bordered it on two sides. The grass was a "mass of clover and marguerites." Soon the field took on a holiday air. Tents arose along its margin. Some were for the aviators, others for the Royal Canadian Dragoons from St. Johns (now known as Saint Jean-sur-Richelieu). They were there to maintain order. The band of the 65th Regiment would entertain the crowd between the scheduled flights. Other amusements were provided by a midway. It had fancy booths, even a restaurant.

"Count Jacques de Lesseps was the hero of the meet," said George A. McNamee. He captured the favor of the crowds by being so easy in his manner, so obliging. When the scheduled flights were delayed, and the crowd was growing restless, the managers would appeal to him. Even when he had already been up several times, he would smile and agree to go up again, to give the people something to look at while they waited. The Count was then a young man, not yet 30. He was well set up, though small — suave, moustached, with soulful eyes. His manner had extraordinary ease. Today it would be called "laid back." When he flew low over the grandstand he appeared as calm "as if he were on a comfortable divan."

His flying was never a mechanical process. He made it an art. As an art it seemed his personal expression. His grace in handling his flying machine inspired onlookers to poetic

Blériot
Monoplane

Comte Jacques
de Lesseps
in his flying
togs

Wright Bros.
Biplane

John Collins SKETCHBOOK
Early days of aviation in Montreal

phrases. One observer wrote: "The symmetry, sweet motion and graceful start and finish of de Lesseps appealed to the crowd. No straining after effect, but the ease and live perfection of a stately swan in the bosom of a lake." Yet, while demonstrating his nonchalant skill, he was never an odious showoff. He was modest about it all. When congratulated on all sides, he simply said: "Merci, merci." And would add: "Ce n'est rien."

His principal competitor for the adulation of the crowd was Walter Brookins, the aviator sent by the Wright brothers. Brookins was a contrast to the count. He had the American's "hawk-like profile." Without any pretension to fashion, he rolled up his sleeves; he wore oil-stained trousers. The count won all the greater favor from the crowd by softening any rivalry with Brookins. When Brookins suggested that de Lesseps fly in his plane as a

passenger, the Count at once climbed in. He could be seen waving as they took off. When they landed, he declared at once that the Wright biplane was much firmer and safer than his own Blériot monoplane. The Count had proved himself not only a good aviator, but a good sport.

Though outwardly calm, de Lesseps was fuming inwardly. His favorite plane, *Le Scarabée* (the one he had used in his flight over the English Channel), had not arrived. It seemed to have been lost somewhere along the transportation route. He had been using at Lakeside a weaker plane. At last, on the eighth day of the meet, the delayed *Scarabée* arrived. The count's mechanics worked over it till late in the afternoon. By the early evening it was ready for flight. It was to be a flight no one had expected.

Msgr. Bruchési — Power to be Reckoned With

Msgr. Louis-Joseph-Paul-Napoléon Bruchési, Montreal's archbishop since 1897, was one of the last of the "prelate princes" — wielding immense authority, not only in matters of faith, but in the secular life of the community. When Archbishop Bruchési spoke, the city paid heed. He was a power to be reckoned with.

The archbishop granted interviews in the long red reception room of the palace, the big bare red brick building, dating mostly from the 1850s, and still standing on La Gauchetière Street, immediately behind the Cathedral-Basilica of Mary Queen of the World. Those who had seen him in procession and ritual expected, in that room, an awesome presence, heralded and attended. But the archbishop's manner was nearly informal. Almost suddenly he would enter the red room alone, with a swish of his purple-embroidered robe. He was a rather thin man, with pince-nez glasses, keen, affable. Msgr. Bruchési is described as talking "with headlong cordiality." But a visitor soon felt the sinewy power of his mind, his subtlety in finding his way among the complexities and contradictions of a difficult city. He would feel, too, that the archbishop was very much in control, with a vibrant sort of authority — a man conservative, even perhaps reactionary in his views, but well able to realize who were the opponents of the faith in a changing world.

An issue that stirred Msgr. Bruchési to action arose in 1906. Montreal had a new theatre with a new policy — the Théâtre des Nouveautés. Its manager was importing plays from Paris. They were very modern plays of the "Boulevard" school. One of these plays, *La Rafle ("The Police Raid"),* was to be performed at Easter. The archbishop felt compelled to warn his people. "As everyone knows," he said, "there exists in this city a certain theatre, where some of the most obscene representations have been offered and where dramas of a depraved taste are frequently played without scruple."

The archbishop protested. The manager was going ahead with the performance. The archbishop ordered a pastoral letter read by the parish priests. It forbade all Catholics to see the play. *La Rafle* was performed nevertheless. It was a failure. The management of the theatre agreed that all plays in future would be submitted in advance to a citizens' committee, under the archbishop's direction.

In 1907, when Sarah Bernhardt was coming to Montreal, the plays she would perform were announced. Two of them the archbishop condemned as immoral. They were withdrawn. Others, more acceptable, were substituted.

When he disapproved of the pornography that was flooding newspapers, magazines and posters, he sent a public letter to City Hall: "...You, Mr. Mayor, have in your hands the authority of municipal law. Is it possible that nothing will be done to stop such moral contamination — the worst of all epidemics?" The mayor and aldermen knew they had been put on the spot. Immediate action was taken. To those who suggested he should stay out of such matters, he replied: "We keep silence too often. In this, as in hundreds of other things, we submit, and the evildoers become hardened from day to day in their audacity and ignominy."

Archbishop Bruchési was aware that a ceaseless vigilance was needed to fight off all bad influences. These influences were penetrating his archdiocese from every quarter. His particular enemy was the American Federation of Labor. Here, in his view, was an American union, knowing nothing about the distinctive values of French Canada, but trying to inflame the workers of Montreal with radical, restless ideas.

On April 26, 1903 Msgr. Bruchési issued a pastoral letter on labor relations. It was read in every church. He warned his people to beware of those who would turn labor relations into a battleline, with violence as a weapon. Workers had every liberty to organize themselves into unions for the defence of their rights. But they had no right to ignore the rights of others. "Still this liberty," he stressed, "does not give you the right to contend for ends which are in flagrant opposition with public weal, justice and charity. This freedom of association does not invest you, for instance, with any right to use violent measures...." He entered directly and personally into strikes when violence had broken out. His influence ended the longshoremen's strike in 1907, and the policemen's and firemen's strike in 1918.

Archbishop Bruchési's administration was crowded with events. But the greatest of them all — his crowning achievement — was the Eucharistic Congress of 1910. For the first time a city on the American continent was chosen by the Catholic world. One of the celebrations of mass took place on Fletcher's Field. A hundred bishops gathered, with 2,000 priests and 200,000 lay members. A choir of 1,000 voices responded to the chants of the celebrant, Msgr. Farley, archbishop of New York. This demonstration of faith in the Roman Catholic Church, by people of many races and countries, this experience of having the Catholic world so powerfully represented in his own archdiocese, gave Archbishop Bruchési a new international prestige. Reports said that he was being "spoken of in connection with a further elevation in the church."

But the future for Archbishop Bruchési was to be tragic. Before the end of 1919 he felt his mind giving way. His firm, subtle, resolute grip was fumbling and confused. Though he remained the archbishop of Montreal, it was in name only. No longer was he fit to perform an archbishop's role. The administration of the archdiocese was carried on by Msgr. Georges Gauthier, the Archbishop Coadjutor.

In 1928, with special prayers, the 50th anniversary of his ordination as a priest was celebrated. At that time the Roman Catholic hierarchy of Montreal issued a letter, signed by Rev. Canon Harbour: "Since October, 1919, our beloved and venerable chief has worn the crown of thorns. He saw the trial before it arrived. It was Msgr. de la Dutantaye, I believe, to whom he confided. He accepted the trial with heroical submission. It was the end of a great work. After 23 years as the glory of the diocese he has now been almost 10 years the victim of sufferings. We have insisted on keeping him with us. He occupies his old quarters. It is pleasant for us to feel that we can give him tokens of our care, affection and kindness. To us he is still Monseigneur Bruchési. That means everything."

For another 11 years Msgr. Bruchési remained in seclusion. He died, at the age of 84, on September 20, 1939. He lies buried in the mortuary chapel of the bishops of Montreal, at the east side of the Cathedral-Basilica. His marble tomb is only a few feet to the northeast of the Archbishop's Palace where, before his affliction, he had presided as "the real power."

John Collins SKETCHBOOK — The Archbishop's Palace

The Great Herald Fire

On the Montrealers of 1910 the great *Herald* fire left an indelible impression. Other events were often dated from it. People would say: "That happened about the time of the great *Herald* fire."

In 1910 the *Herald* building stood on the south side of St. James Street (rue Saint Jacques) a little to the west of Victoria Square — the third building from the corner, just beyond the Imperial Bank Building.

It was a tall building for those days — five storeys. Extraordinary precautions against fire had been taken by the proprietors. Understandably, they were nervous, as fires had destroyed other buildings the *Herald* had occupied. Automatic fire alarms were installed, fire extinguishers, a fire escape at the back, together with access to the roof of the Imperial Bank Building next door.

Still the proprietors were not satisfied. They planned a crowning precaution. On the roof, toward the rear, they

erected a gigantic water tank. Thirty thousand gallons of water, weighing 300,000 pounds, were held in the tank. In case of fire, water in abundance would be instantly available. Pressure would be superb. This measure had not been undertaken without thorough preparation. Architects examined the building carefully; they reported that it would be perfectly safe. The tank was erected by experts. It was upheld by supports from a strong central wall to the eastern wall, adjoining the bank. Regularly, the tank was inspected. The last inspection had been carried out only two weeks before the calamity.

In the morning of June 13, 1910 this water tank crashed upon the roof. Its weight carried it down, storey after storey, until it sank into the basement. It came down without warning. Many workers in the building were crushed; others were dragged down with it. Water spilled out of the tank. The basement was flooded to a depth of four feet. Some, pinned beneath wreckage, drowned. Fire broke out almost at once. It was caused, apparently, by a pot of molten metal in the stereotyping plant on the third floor. Many, unable to struggle free of the debris (which piled up two storeys high at the rear of the building), lay screaming, as flames crept upon them.

Back of the *Herald* building, separated only by a lane, was a restaurant — Miss Miller's dining rooms. "It was the most terrible thing I ever saw in my life," said Miss Miller. "We heard the terrific crash when the building fell, and then there came the cries and groans of men and a terrible shrieking of women and girls. We heard them shrieking for someone to come and help them…. We saw one little girl wearing a short skirt standing near the end of the building after the first crash, and could hear her crying, 'Oh, for mother's sake do come and save me.' A moment later the floor crashed down, and she went with it."

The water tank, being near the rear of the building, carried away most of the back part of every floor. Under the impact the back wall buckled and fell into the lane. Some were rescued from the front part of the floors, before fire reached them, though all but the front wall was tottering. Gerald Bishop, photographer for the *Herald*, was working in his darkroom. He heard a crackling noise. Pieces of plaster dropped from the ceiling. He took no notice. From time to time heavy machinery was moved on the floor above. The vibration always knocked down a little plaster. A moment later he "heard a crash like thunder, and felt the whole building shake." Bishop rushed to the nearby office of Miss Heubach, the society editor. Together they found their way to a staircase. They groped through dust and darkness. Beams broke through the ceiling. Miss Heubach was cut on the head. But they scurried downstairs in time.

On the third floor down from the roof were the linotype operators. One man was sitting at his machine when he heard the first crash. He jumped back. Dust stifled the air.

He saw his machine drop down through the ripped floor. The piece of floor, where he stood, held up. He was rescued. On the top floor the girls in the bindery worked right under the tank. One of them, Maggie Starke, saw the ceiling move. She called to a friend, Olive Hart: "I am sure something is going to happen." Down came the roof. Olive was swept away with it, screaming, "Help! Help!" Maggie saw the forewoman carried down too. She herself struggled to a window, ready to jump. Firemen shouted to her from the ground, then brought her down, shaken and bruised. She was 14 years old.

Little could be done to save anyone, after the eastern and western walls gave way and tumbled. Wreckage lay deep — a weird mixture of beams, bricks, machinery, big lumps of plaster. Fire leaped up. Wilfrid Vidal was one of the few *Herald* workers rescued from the heap of wreckage. He lay above the water, his leg broken, his head cut. The flames had not yet reached him. Vidal was discovered by fireman E. C. Lamonte. Iron bars pinned him down; they would have to be sawn through. More firemen waded through to cut him loose. Father Martin, chaplain of the Fire Department, put on the regulation long boots and rubber coat and came to his side, to give him the last rites and console him. Three hours of work freed Vidal — badly injured but not drowned, crushed or burnt.

A few stayed with the trapped, until they were trapped themselves. One man was seen by the crowd as he saved two girls. "There's another in there, and I'm going after her!" he shouted. He ran back into the ruins. The rest of the building was seen coming down on him. The first body identified was that of Laura Amesse, forewoman in the bindery. The body was identified by two girls working for her on that top floor. "She could easily have saved herself," said one of the workers, "but she stood by and helped all of us to get on the ladders and reach safety. She did everything in her power to see that all of us got out of the dangerous building…. She would not listen to those of us who wished her to come down with us, and she turned back to see if she could not save those who were behind. That was the last we saw of her …."

It was a lurid night scene. Under arc lamps and searchlights 75 firemen and 40 police, as many as the space would hold, worked with shovels, picks, pitchforks. Big machines had to be pulled away before searchers could see what lay under them. Ropes were strung to nearby buildings, and fitted with pulleys. Masses of twisted steel were hauled out of the way.

Gradually the death toll rose over 30. Crowds were at the morgue, trying to make identifications. Reports that nothing was left of the *Herald* building but a heap of burning debris soon discouraged all hope. The mother of one of the girls was saying: "No, she won't come now. I know she won't. She was a good obedient girl, and well thought of."

Governess for a King's 64 Children

Those who came to afternoon tea with Mrs. Anna Leonowens on McTavish Street in Montreal would try to turn the conversation to her seven years as governess to the 64 children of the king of Siam. She was the original Anna, whose experiences at the court of King Mongkut in the 1860s were later to be seen in the movies. She had written of them in her book, *An English Governess at the Court of Siam*. In 1946, long after her death, these experiences were to be the basis of *Anna and the King of Siam*, when Irene Dunn played the part of Anna and Rex Harrison played the king. In 1956 Deborah King played Anna in *The King and I*, with Yul Brynner as king.

Anna Leonowens had applied for the position as governess in King Mongkut's court because she had been left a young widow with two children but little money. She had married Captain L.S. Leonowens, an officer in the British army in India. He died of sunstroke, on returning from a tiger-shooting safari. She opened a school for English children in Singapore. It did not pay. It was then she heard of the post of governess in Siam.

In Siam the king was an absolute monarch. He was reverenced almost as a deity. He could do what he wished, as he wished, when he wished. In his kingdom no one could feel secure. He tolerated no interference. Anna interceded on behalf of a young woman under sentence of death. He had the young woman burnt in front of the windows of Anna's house.

Anna had to be the king's secretary, as well as his children's governess. She handled his foreign correspondence. At last her strength gave way. It was not the work that exhausted her, but the tense uncertainties of her life in Bangkok. The problem was how to get out. The king refused to allow her to go. At length he granted her six months' leave of absence. She left — and never went back.

About the turn of the century Anna Leonowens came to live in Montreal. Her daughter had married Thomas Fyshe, who left the Bank of Nova Scotia to become joint general manager of the Merchants Bank of Canada. He moved to Montreal. Mrs. Leonowens came to Montreal with the family. They all lived in Thomas Fyshe's house near the top of McTavish Street on the west side (a house now gone).

Anna was to be remembered in Montreal as a handsome woman, undoubtedly, in the austere, rather formidable English way. In Montreal, as in Siam, she seemed to have a natural attraction for the worried and anguished. They came to her not for advice only, but for strengthening. Montrealers felt instinctively she had acquired something of the timeless wisdom of ancient Oriental religions. Her knowledge of other faiths was remarkable, even profound. She was a linguist, especially learned in Sanskrit. One distressed woman who went to Anna in Montreal with her troubles was told to wait a minute. They should not begin considering her problems until they had calmed their minds. She then recited a poem in Sanskrit. The woman who had come to Anna knew no Sanskrit. But the quiet, solemn incantation of the poem brought stillness to her mind. They then proceeded to consider her problems with no tensions distorting their thoughts.

As a woman of extraordinary knowledge she had a natural place in academic society and was often seen at gatherings in the homes of McGill's professors. She had, among other types of scholarship, an unusual understanding of the world's religions. As she would sometimes remark: "I am too good a Christian not to be something of a Buddhist, and too good a Buddhist not to be something of a Christian."

At once she became active in the community. As *The Gazette* said: "Here she formed many close friendships and was ceaseless in good work through lectures and writings for various societies and charities. She had a special interest in the Baby Foundling Hospital...." Her interest in infants prompted an attempt to modify the Roman Catholic custom of hurrying newborn infants to the church for baptism. She called upon the Catholic clergy, pointing out that the premature exposure of newborn infants to the cold air gave rise to pneumonia and other ailments, often fatal to them. She is said to have met with some success in modifying the old practice.

But the latter years of Anna Leonowens in Montreal were not to be a time of ease and peace. She was called upon to show all the strength and resolution of her early years. In the spring of 1902 her daughter Avis died of ptomaine poisoning and Anna became mother to her granchildren in the house of McTavish Street. In 1906 Thomas Fyshe resigned as general manager of the Merchants Bank. He could not agree with the views of the board of directors and refused to act in accordance with them. Though he left the bank, he went with a good pension.

Relations between Mrs. Leonowens and Thomas Fyshe were very different from those often existing between mothers-in-law and the men their daughters see fit to marry. They were both strong, self-assured, rather unyielding characters. But far from clashing, they admired each other's firmness of character. Thomas Fyshe was a

JOHN SKETCHBOOK
COLLINS Anna's Grave — Mount Royal Cemetery

man after her own spirit. In his many struggles with adversaries and critics, he could always count upon his mother-in-law for understanding, counsel and support. He was called out of his retirement by the prime minister, Sir Wilfrid Laurier, who appointed him to a royal commission to investigate the conditions in the civil service. Fyshe evidently influenced the final report: it was one of the most scathing reports any royal commission had ever made. And it had results. Among other things it led to the establishment of a Civil Service Commission.

Perhaps these last turbulent exertions proved too much for Thomas Fyshe. A stroke paralysed him. Anna became his nurse. She was believed to "have kept him alive, by a perfect miracle of will and watchfulness, years after the doctors had completely given him up." Anna kept her son-in-law alive until 1911. When he was gone, her own strength gave way after the long, last strains. She, too,

suffered a stroke, but seemed to make herself live by force of will. The end for her came on a January day in 1915. Christ Church Cathedral on St.Catherine Street was the scene of her funeral. She lies buried in Mount Royal Cemetery, near her daughter and her son-in-law.

The qualities of Anna Leonowens were well known and well valued in Montreal. When she died in Montreal in 1915, in her 81st year, *The Gazette* commented: "She was a woman whom it was a privilege to know; possessed of the finest qualities of heart and head, with great force of character when advocating a good cause and at the same time of gentle and kindly characteristics; beloved by rich and poor, young and old." Professor John Macnaughton of McGill, in paying her tribute, said that Anna Leonowens, of all the women he had met, was "the best, bravest and wisest."

Montrealers on the Titanic

In the evening of April 14, 1912 a prominent Montrealer, Charles Melville Hays, president of the Grand Trunk Railway, was talking with Colonel Archibald Gracie of the U.S. Army. They were aboard the *Titanic*. The ship was speeding through the darkness on her maiden voyage, about 400 miles from Newfoundland. Hays was uneasy and critical. The captain, he said, was very wrong to be sailing so fast when there was danger of encountering icebergs. The shipping companies seemed in a frenzy to break one another's records for Atlantic crossings. "The time will come," Hays prophesied, "when this will be checked by some appalling disaster."

About 11:40 p.m., as Hays and the colonel were talking, passengers felt a slight shudder. Some, looking through the windows, saw a huge iceberg passing close by. Fragments of ice lay scattered across the decks. The engines were stopped. Colonel Gracie remarked to Hays that the ship appeared to be listing. Hays, though he had just been prophesying disaster, still put some faith in the claims of the ship's owners that the *Titanic* was unsinkable. "No matter what we've struck," he said to Colonel Gracie, "she's good for eight to ten hours."

Hays went on deck with his wife, his daughter, and his 23-year-old private secretary, Vivian Payne. Men were told to stand to one side. Women and children would be lowered to the sea in the lifeboats. "We were told," said Mrs. Hays, "there was no danger, and that the boat... would float for days and that other ships were rushing to our rescue. The women were told to get into the lifeboats and that the men would be safe. There was no panic or confusion. The sea was calm as a mill pond and the sky was clear." Charles Hays and the young Vivian Payne could be seen standing by the deck's railing. Hays's wife and daughter were confident they all would soon be reunited. "We did not even think of kissing them goodbye," his daughter said.

Among other Montrealers aboard the *Titanic* was Mrs. James Baxter, returning from overseas with her daughter, wife of Dr. Fred C. Douglas, and with her son Quigley, a McGill athlete who had been studying in Europe. "My brother was not at all disturbed," said Mrs. Douglas, "and while he did not relish being parted from mother and me, he bade us farewell bravely. He was on the deck.... After that we pulled away and lost sight of the *Titanic*." Though nearly all the women left in the lifeboats, one Montreal woman went down with her husband. She was Mrs. Hudson J. Allison, married to a 30-year-old

financier, a partner with J. W. McConnell in the investment firm of Johnston, McConnell and Allison.

The Allisons had taken a trip abroad with their two children — a daughter three years old, and a son, still a baby. In the late evening of April 14, they had retired for the night to their stateroom with their little daughter. In another stateroom was the baby with a nurse, Alice Clever, an English girl. When the ship shuddered in its collision with the iceberg, Allison, partly dressed, went on deck. He soon came back. There was no danger, he reported, no cause for worry. The nurse, however, was nervous. She kept dressing. Noises and movement were heard in the corridor. She wrapped the little boy in a fur carriage rug and went on deck to see for herself what was going on. When she arrived, the lifeboats were being readied. She wanted to go back to tell the Allisons that she had the baby with her. Ships' officers would not let her go back, but forced her into a boat about to be lowered.

Meanwhile the Allisons, no longer confident that nothing serious had happened, went to the stateroom where they had left their baby and the nurse. They found it empty. They became frantic, not knowing what had become of them. Allison grabbed his little daughter in his arms. His wife insisted on staying with him. Together they dashed about the saloon and the decks, looking everywhere. While they searched, one lifeboat after another was being lowered away. The designers of the *Titanic*, it was said, confident that they were planning an unsinkable ship, had not considered it necessary to provide enough lifeboats for all passengers. While the Allisons were searching the ship, the last of the lifeboats had gone. All hope of getting off the ship had gone with it.

On the sea, some two hours later, the nurse, with the baby in her arms, saw the *Titanic* plunge downward, bow first. Lights in the cabins had never gone out. Now they flickered, came on again in one or two flashes, then went out altogether. With a quiet slanting dive, the greatest passenger ship in the world slid out of sight. The survivors, rescued from the lifeboats by the *Carpathia*, were brought to New York in the evening of April 18. Mrs. Hays arrived with her daughter, but not her husband. Mrs. Baxter arrived with her daughter, but not her son.

Other Montrealers who did not come ashore were Vivian Payne, Hays's young private secretary; Harry Markland Molson, who only a few months earlier had been described by the American publication, *Moody's Magazine*, as one of the most influential businessmen in Canada; Thornton Davidson, head of the Montreal stockbrokers, Thornton

Davidson & Company; R. J. Levy, a Montreal chemist; and Hudson Allison, his wife and daughter. Mrs. Hays had been asked: "Did you know that Mr. Hays was not among the survivors?" Her reply was grimly realistic: "I knew he was not on the *Carpathia* and that the *Titanic* had gone down."

The same could be said, with equal finality, of the other missing Montrealers. There was now no hope for any of them. Among those who came ashore, however, was the nurse with the Allison baby. "The Allison baby," said a report, "was the object of much pathetic interest.... Despite a slight attack of bronchitis, he was bright and playful, but all who took the baby into their arms had tears in their eyes." The baby was taken to Montreal. There he was turned over to the lawful guardian, his Allison grandmother.

The young friends of Hays's private secretary in the Grand Railway — more than 125 of them — erected a tablet to his memory in Christ Church Cathedral on St. Catherine Street. This memorial to Vivian Payne states that it is "an emblem of their high esteem and... a kindly expression of sympathy with his family." The inscription ends with the words, "Nearer My God to Thee." These words are from the hymn some said was played by the Titanic's orchestra as the ship went down.

The body of Harry Markland Molson was never recovered from the sea. He is commemorated nevertheless by a tablet in Mount Royal Cemetery. The epitaph is from Psalm 77, verse 19:
"Thy way is in the sea and Thy path in the great waters,
"And Thy footsteps are not known."

JOHN COLLINS SKETCHBOOK

PAYNE MEMORIAL —
CHRIST CHURCH
CATHEDRAL

The Gazette was World's First with Titanic News

It was about midnight on Sunday, April 14, 1912. *The Gazette*, being a morning newspaper, was open and busy at that hour. The telephone rang in the City Room. It was answered by John Bassett, then a reporter, later the paper's president. The call was for Stranger, *The Gazette's* marine reporter. Stranger went to the phone. He had no idea that in a matter of minutes he was to be the first newspaperman in the world to hear one of the biggest news stories of all time.

All the other end of the line was George Hannah, the Montreal passenger traffic manager of the Allan Steamship Line. Hannah was quick with excitement. He had a scoop for Stranger. A Marconi wireless message had just come in from the captain of the Allan liner, *Virginian*. And in those days wireless messages were still something of a novelty. Hannah read the message over the phone: "Titanic has struck an iceberg and sends Marconigram asking for assistance. *Virginian* going to her rescrue."

John Collins SKETCHBOOK Old Gazette Building — PICTURE OF 1907

Distress signals from the *Titanic* had been picked up by the *Virginian*. The *Virginian's* captain had then sent a Marconigram to the Allan Steamship office in Halifax, to explain why he was changing course. The message had been relayed overland to the Allan office in Montreal. George Hannah had come to know Stranger, as the marine reporter. He decided to pass the news on to *The Gazette*. In this way *The Gazette* became the first paper in the world to learn what had happened. John Bassett remembered that the office was at once alive with action. At that time *The Gazette* had an agreement with *The New York Times* for the exchange of news stories. Ted Slack, *The Gazette's* managing editor, immediately sent the message on to New York.

The message took New York completely by surprise. The very idea that the *Titanic* was in distress seemed incredible. Even the New York office of the White Star Line (the line that owned the *Titanic*) had heard nothing. The last word the White Star Line had from its magnificent ship had come hours before — at 11 o'clock that Sunday morning. It had merely given the ship's position, southeast of Cape Race. Nothing was said of any trouble. It seemed odd, anyway, that the *Titanic* should be sending out desperate SOS signals, calling other ships to steam to her rescue. She was supposed to be unsinkable. She was divided into 16 water-tight compartments. Even a collision with an iceberg should give no wild cause for alarm. Something of panic was sensed in the signals. The *Virginian* picked up more of them. They sounded blurred. At 12.27 on Monday morning came the final signal. It was hard to hear. It ended abruptly.

The front page of *The Gazette* was cleared for the latest news. Newspaper headings were not then one or two lines, as they are today. They were set in what were called "decks." Down a column one heading was set on top of another. All the main features of the following story were proclaimed.

The Gazette was flooded with calls as the morning passed. They were coming mostly from New York. Since *The Gazette* had received the first news of the disaster, New Yorkers were hoping that it was still getting news and could tell them what was developing. In London the morning newspapers had done badly. They had gone to press reporting all was well with the *Titanic* on her maiden voyage. The London papers even ran editorials congratulating everyone concerned that man's inventive genius had banished forever the perils of the sea. Only a few of the very late editions caught the news that the *Titanic* was sinking.

John Bassett recalled that all next day *The Gazette's* office was besieged by people trying to get more information. Everyone was anxious, but confidence still prevailed. Even if the *Titanic* was in trouble, it could easily remain afloat until help arrived. *The Gazette* had consulted "shipping men" on the night the first news had arrived. It reported their opinions.

"Shipping men who were communicated with late last night were inclined to the opinion that the mammoth liner was simply unable to make her way along to any extent and had been heading for Halifax when she got in communication with the *Virginian*. With her water-tight compartments, danger had been reduced to a minimum, as far as marine and engineering science could make a ship."

After all, the Allan ship, *Virginian*, was not far from the *Titanic* when she received the signal for help — only about 150 miles. And the *Virginian* was a fast ship. She would reach the *Titanic* soon.

In fact, confidence in saving all passengers was so strong that George Hannah, of the Allan Line, was being asked whether the *Virginian* was big enough to take all the *Titanic's* passengers aboard when she reached the scene.

Hannah was confident no problem would arise. The *Virginian's* passenger list on the eastbound trip was not heavy. She could "certainly take all on board if there should be need." There was also a large crew to be thought of, but the *Virginian* would "be able to bring them all ashore."

Through most of that Monday confidence was sustained. The sinking of the *Titanic* might turn out to be an exciting, dramatic adventure for the passengers. By night *The Gazette* had further news. John Bassett remembered standing, with others, around Ted Slack's desk. The managing editor was getting the latest report over the telephone. When he put the phone down, he said to those about him: "There must be loss of lives. This message mentions survivors." Montreal's interest in getting the news was more than an excited curiosity. Many Montrealers had booked passage on the *Titanic's* maiden voyage. Obviously, the unsinkable ship had gone down. Who were saved?

The Cunard liner *Carpathia* was the first to reach the scene. She arrived at dawn. The *Titanic* had vanished. The *Carpathia* found only wreckage and a few lifeboats. It rescued what survivors there were. On the morning of Tuesday, April 16, George Hannah received a message from the captain of the *Virginian*: "Arrived at scene of disaster too late. Have proceeded on voyage to Liverpool." The last message from the *Virginian* read: "Please allay any rumors that the *Virginian* has any of the *Titanic's* passengers."

The Gazette's office in 1912 (red brick faced with stone) was on the south side of St. Antoine Street. Long ago it was demolished. Its site would today be identified by drawing a line southwards from Place Ville Marie. That old building has its place in history as the first newspaper office in the world to receive word of the world's greatest disaster at sea.

When Automobiles Came to Montreal

The idea of a Victorian driving an automobile may seem a bit odd. But as far back as 1898, Alderman Ucal H. Dandurand appeared in an automobile on the streets of Montreal. Dandurand's automobile was powered by steam, not gasoline. He had bought it in Boston, from Waltham, a manufacturer of steam cars. To all appearances it was a buggy, though a buggy without shafts or a horse. It seated two persons. The second person had a rather tight fit, for Dandurand was a big man, as expansive in weight as he was in personality. These steam-driven automobiles (called "flying kettles") were slow to start. The tank had to be filled with gallons of water. Kerosene provided heat; burning kerosene made the car stink. The rising force of steam in the tank had to be watched on gauges and controlled by handles. At least half an hour was needed, if a sufficient head of steam was to be generated to make the car run.

Some of these old steam-powered automobiles, made around the turn of the century, proved amazingly durable. One type was known as the Stanley Steamer. Among those who bought a Stanley Steamer was Stephen Osgood of Cookshire, in the Eastern Townships. Mrs. Eric Brown of Greenfield Park (who spent her childhood in Cookshire) remembers a drive in Osgood's Stanley Steamer in 1924. They went to Sawyerville. On the route the car refused to mount a hill. In the end Osgood made it, by driving up backwards. This same Stanley Steamer was still running at least as late as 1930. When it was driven no motor was heard — only a faint swishing sound, a magnified sigh. It hissed to a stop.

Dandurand kept his steam-powered car for about three years. He bought a new car in 1901 — a Dion-Bouton. It may still be seen, preserved in the cellar of the Château Ramezay on Notre Dame Street. This new car had a one-cylinder internal combustion engine. Its gas consumption was moderate. Once it ran out of gas while Dandurand was driving it. The city then had no gas stations. Dandurand found a drug store. He bought a bottle of gasoline, sold by druggists for cleaning gloves. He poured it into the tank and drove away. A Dion-Bouton was not cheap. Dandurand paid $1,535 for his — a substantial sum, considering the value of money at the time.

Some reminiscences concerning Alderman Dandurand (apparently after he had bought a subsequent car) were written by George A. McNamee. In 1905, McNamee began his lifetime career as secretary of the Automobile Club of Canada (later the Royal Automobile Club). "At the turn of the century," he wrote, "I well remember seeing Mr. U.

H. Dandurand driving up Windsor St... in his gasoline buggy." Wheels were large, like buggy wheels. Springs protruded. Steering wheels, gear and brake levers were located on the right-hand side. A goose-necked horn had a rubber bulb attached. It was sounded by squeezing the bulb. Lamps were actually carriage lamps, with oil and wicks. This car, he believed, may have been equipped with a collapsible umbrella. "Mr. Dandurand," McNamee recalled, "was dressed in the garb of the day — leather cap, pea jacket, gauntlets, goggles and a cotton duster." Goggles were necessary, because these cars had no windshields. Dusters (big, loose cotton overcoats) were necessary, because swirling clouds of dust were raised wherever an automobile went.

Any claim to be "first" is certain to arouse contention. Dandurand's claim to be Montreal's first motorist was no exception. McNamee remembered these disputes: "From time to time there was much discussion and argument during Club meetings, in the press and elsewhere, as to who really owned and operated the first automobile in this part of the country. Mr. Dandurand's claim was usually upheld." The Montreal historian, Dr. E. Z. Massicotte, archivist of the Montreal Court House, researched the various claims in 1931. He reached his conclusion: "It was in November, 1898, that Mr. U. H. Dandurand bought... the first automobile that ran in Montreal."

Dandurand's enthusiasm for automobiles was buoyant. He tried an electrically-powered car, as well as those powered by steam or gasoline. He even owned a trailer, or "Pullman Automobile." His son Henri, 19 years old, designed it. In this car the whole Dandurand family could have outings together — father, mother, the 11 children, and a few friends. It could hold 26 seated, or 12 sleeping. At the back was a boarding vestibule, such as those still seen on railway cars. In fact, this trailer, more than 29 feet long, was like a miniature railway car. Inside it had curtains, electric lights, panelled woodwork, stained glass windows.

When Dandurand first began driving an automobile in Montreal, the municipal bylaws had no provision for such a vehicle. Dandurand needed a licence. City Hall's staff were at a loss to decide what sort of licence to issue. At last they considered that an automobile, with its tires, was a species of bicycle. Dandurand was charged for a bicycle licence — $1. In 1901 the provincial government took over the granting of licences. It fixed the price at $5. But no licence plates for automobiles were issued. Dandurand was required to paint the number of his licence on his car.

Those were the happy, early days. Automobiles, not yet

U.H.Dandurand parked in front of the house on Dorchester

—an early automobile on the streets of Montreal

John Collins SKETCHBOOK U.H.Dandurand and his cars

taken seriously, could be adventurous fun. They were so regarded, even by the law. When the Automobile Club was granted its charter by the Province of Quebec, it was incorporated under the Amusement Act. This sporting mood prevailed at a Gymkhana, held on an October afternoon in 1906. It was sponsored by the Automobile Club in the Montreal Amateur Athletic Association (MAAA) field in Westmount.

All sorts of contests were held to test the drivers' skills. Ucal Dandurand was there, to take part in the relay race. At a signal, each driver had to jump from his car, remove his overcoat, start the engine with a crank, put on his overcoat, light a cigarette, then drive round the cinder track. When back at the starting line, each driver had to get out, assist a passenger to the front seat, help him to a cigarette, light a match for him, get back in the car and make another circuit of the track. On the third round, each driver had to take up two more passengers and assist them

to rear seats. For the fourth and last round he had to help all passengers alight, then make the circuit alone.

It was all great fun. Dandurand was just the man to make the most of it. *The Gazette* reported: ''Mr. Duncan McDonald and Mr. U. H. Dandurand deserved special prizes because of their gallantry in having ladies as passengers, but these gentlemen spent so much time laughing at each other that they fell outside the time limit.''

Those early days were the automobile's age of innocence. Traffic jams, air pollution, the death toll on the highways, soaring gasoline prices — they were only foreseen dimly, if at all. In that age, automobiles were a lively novelty, a diversion, and still rather laughable. At such a time an automotive club, quite appropriately, could be incorporated under the Amusement Act.

"Get Yourself a Horse!"

For generations, even for centuries, the streets and roads had belonged to the horse — the horse and wagon, the horse and carriage. Then came the automobile, and it came as an intruder. Horse and automobile faced each other. The confrontation was often spectacular.

Such a confrontation was described by Murray E. Williams: "I was driving along the Senneville Road with some people one Sunday afternoon, when we heard, away in the distance, a tremendous clattering and pumping. It sounded as if a mowing machine, with every bolt loose, was being operated by a street roller. Suddenly around the corner there came, bumping and crashing, the first automobile I had ever seen. It was also the first automobile the horse had ever seen. If I remember rightly the man running the car was J.K.L. Ross. Our horse celebrated the event by standing on his hind legs, while pawing the air with his fore legs. After that he gracefully jumped the ditch and smashed into the fence. The occupants of the carriage flew out in all directions, and I awoke standing on my ear, in a field of oats."

These sensational meetings between horse and automobile have also been described by George A. McNamee, who became secretary of the Royal Automobile Club in Montreal in 1905: "In some cases in order to pass a horse-driven vehicle, the driver had to place a blanket over the horse's head and nostrils, since the exhaust fumes were sufficient to scare the animal, apart from

JOHN COLLINS SKETCHBOOK

RAINY DAY
ON
MOUNT ROYAL

the noise of the engine. On occasion these experiences brought blasphemy from the drivers of horse-drawn vehicles.''

For many years the drivers of horses felt the roads belonged to them by the rights of ancient usage. They did not see why they should accommodate themselves to the intruders. They stubbornly resisted attempts to make the roads suitable for motorists. The member of the Quebec legislature for the county of Chambly, Dr. E. M. Desaulniers, was trying to interest his constitutents in better roads. At one meeting a city councillor shook his fist in the member's face. ''If you want these fancy roads built for the automobilists,'' he shouted, ''let them buy our land and build their own roads, instead of killing our cows and chickens as they are now doing, and imposing taxes on us for these new roads.''

The most astonishing instance of this resistance was seen in the controversy over lights on wagons. The motorists soon realized the necessity of having horse-drawn vehicles carry taillights at night. A motorist, coming along a dark road, could smash into the back of a wagon before he could see it. The horse-drivers, however, refused to give in. They would not carry lights, even after it had become necessary for their own protection. They argued that lights would be expensive. If the law once required them, and their tail-light (often lit by a candle or oil) went out, they could be sued in case of a collision. They also argued that carrying flame-lighted tail lamps would be a fire hazard. The lamps might set fire to a farm load, such as hay. A light, swinging at the back of a wagon, or buggy, might set a stable on fire.

Even in Montreal itself the battle was going on. In 1930 a new bylaw was proposed. It would require horse-drawn vehicles within the city limits to carry lights at night. Alderman Bray argued that the streets of Montreal were well lighted; lights on wagons were unnecessary. To compel the carrying of lights would be to declare that Montreal was an ill-lighted city, which it wasn't. Other aldermen contended that accidents were caused by speeding motorists; the wagon-drivers were not a fault. If motorist looked where they were going there would be no accidents. The motion for the new bylaw was put to the vote. It was defeated — 16 to 6.

The horse drivers took extreme satisfaction in seeing automobiles stuck in the mud. ''Get yourself a horse!'' they shouted, as they drove by. Many farmers had a double satisfaction. They could be amused by the motorist's embarrassment and they could make money by using their horses to pull him out. The story went around about the motorist asking the farmer if his horse was afraid of automobiles. ''No,'' replied the farmer, ''he's hauled too many of them out of the mud for that.''

Farmers with their horses did particularly well on the old roads to the Laurentians. Before the Sixteen Island Road was built, clay belts, about 100 yards long, might be encountered on the flats just past Crystal Falls on the St. Jovite Road, or between Weir and Macdonald Lake. C.L. Reeve, one of the pioneer Montrealers to go to the Laurentians, remembers the horses at work, rescuing motorists in distress. ''Generally there was a farmer standing by with a horse,'' he recalled. ''And those horses knew their business. They were quiet and peaceful until the chain was hooked to the car. Then, on their master's voice, the tail would go up, mud flying everywhere and they got you to solid ground. The farmer charged $2.00 and by the end of the day he had a good harvest.''

The fears aroused by the coming of the automobile were eased by a feeling that the automobile was too unreliable to last. The motorist might be a fool, wasting his money on a toy. The horse was here to stay; the automobile might disappear. A horse-cab proprietor was interviewed in 1913. He was confident he could hold his own. He pointed out that cabs were more and more numerous in Montreal; the demand for them was greater than ever. In Montreal, the carters and the cartage companies were also confident horses would continue in service. They had great advantages over motor trucks. They could move on runners on the snow-clogged streets when motor vehicles might have to be put up for the winter.

Even in summer horse wagons were better than motors for deliveries in town. House-to-house deliveries — as by the breadman, the milkman, the iceman, the laundryman — did not need a speedy vehicle. A horse could plod along beside the driver, trained to follow the accustomed route. A driver of a motor truck would waste his time getting in and out to move his truck only a few feet. The wear and tear on the truck would be disastrous.

It seemed that live horsepower would go on forever. But technology was closing in. At the beginning of 1938 delivery by horses was discontinued by Canadian Pacific Express in Montreal. Other changes had been earlier recorded. Montreal's 660 horse cabs of 1917 were down to 140 by 1924. They dwindled still more. Today only the restriction on automobiles on Mount Royal keeps the few cabs that are left. But the horse age had put up a good long fight against the motor age. It had not gone out with a whimper.

Florence Nightingale Danced with the Devil

It was not every day that Montrealers could expect to see the Devil dancing with Florence Nightingale; or an Indian chief dancing with Cleopatra; or King Henry VIII waltzing Madame de Pompadour. Yet some 100 years ago such a spectacle might be seen two or three times every winter. And to make the bizarre combinations even more unusual, these dancers out of history or legend appeared on skates. So far from skates making them clumsy, they went moving about with an "easy, graceful swing." This startling but intriguing display was to be seen between Drummond and Stanley Streets — in the Victoria Skating Rink. Here the Fancy Dress Balls were held. They were displays of "beauty and magnificence" — better by far than any on ballroom floor, for the dancers glided over "a silvery floor of ice."

The Victoria Skating Rink had known glamor in its day. It was an imposing brick building with a rink 202 feet long by 80 wide — a surface of about 1600 square feet. Ornamental girders, rows of them, soared from the floor and swerved into vast arches, almost cathedral-like, reaching an overhead peak of some 50 feet. Around the borders of the ice ran a spectators' platform, a little over 10 feet wide. At one end was a balcony — a "directors' balcony." There admission was by invitation only, and the view was superb. The Victoria Rink was not an ordinary commercial venture. It was a social club, supported by its subscribers. Directors were socially eminent — such men as Edward Seaborne Clouston, later Sir Edward and vice-president of the Bank of Montreal; or Lieutenant-Colonel Frederic Clarence Henshaw, a director of several companies and commander of the Victoria Rifles.

Nights of the Fancy Dress Balls had undoubted magic. Such magic was heightened when electric light was installed — one of the earliest such installations in Montreal. To the spectators the wonder of this light was part of the dazzling display — so different from the dingy gas jets of earlier days (even though the Victoria Rink had had some 500 of them). This clear new light falling on the ice — the vacant ice before the ball began — favored the enchantment of expectation. The waiting audience had much to see. A centrepiece was always set up on the ice. For the Fancy Dress Ball of February 18, 1881 "an icy temple" had been built. Its octagonal columns gleamed in the electric light "with a thousand exquisite colors." Within the temple a fountain murmured pleasantly and sparkled. Also on the ice was a tall Maypole, with its long colored ribbons.

"Martial music" came with a startling crash from the band of the Victoria Rifles. The scene, until then so still, burst into color and movement. Skaters streamed onto the ice from either side of the entrance. They came in two lines — "one of the fair and the other of the sterner sex." They glided to the farthest end of the rink, then back to the centre. At a bugle blast all skated to the Maypole. They went dancing "in and out of the colored bands with exquisite precision." The dance over, they swirled round and round the big rink.

As they swept by they did more than display their costumes. The men acted their roles. Indians swung past brandishing tomakawks and scalping knives. Spaniards and Italians were "shooting love and jealousy from their piercing black eyes." Obese Dutchmen went by smoking their pipes.

At a Fancy Dress Ball at the Victoria Rink in 1873 Lady Dufferin, wife of the governor-general, was seated with her children on the observers' platform. She wrote in her journal: "... we were amused the whole evening watching the different characters as they came before us. There was one delightful old gentleman who passed us every round in some different way, acting capitally the whole time. There was an excellent and large monkey who performed for the children."

Montrealers taking part were put to the test every winter to find some new character to impersonate. As more than 100 were on the ice at the same time, duplication was hard to avoid. Often more than one Henry VIII appeared, more than one Viking, more than one Swiss peasant girl. Costumes varied in ingenuity. Customary among the "ladies' costumes" were the peasant girls— skaters in the peasant costumes of Normandy, Spain, Portugal, Greece, Poland, Russia, Italy, Turkey. Gypsy girls were never absent. Greater inventiveness was seen in impersonations of nature. Girls were costumed to represent Dawn, Twilight, Night, Starlight. There were girls costumed as Icicles, Snowflakes, Frost. Others were Butterflies. One appeared as a Chestnut.

Most impressive were costumes for characters in literature, history or folklore. To be expected were the perennial Little Bo-Peep and Little Red Ridinghood. Far more exacting were impersonations of a Lady of the Scottish Court of the Time of Charles II, or a Lady of the Court of Marie de Medicis. Vaguer as to type was "Ye Ladye of Ye Olden Time." The men's costumes at the Fancy Dress Balls were equally knowledgeable. On the ice of the Victoria Rink appeared Sir Walter Raleigh, Louis XIV, Richard Coeur de Lion, Oliver Cromwell. Two brothers appeared as "the Princes in the Tower" — Edward V and his brother, allegedly murdered by their uncle Richard III in 1483. One skater of classical tastes dashed about in the character of Archimedes, the Greek mathematician and inventor who died in 212 B.C.

Not all characterizations were quite so historical or so legendary. The contemporary influence of Gilbert and Sullivan was seen on the ice in Nanki-Poo from *The Mikado*, and one of the Pirates of Penzance. When it came to dancing on the ice these diverse characterizations joined as grotesque pairs. But the dances — The Lancers or Sir Roger de Coverley — were enchanting. Lady Dufferin wrote to her mother: "I think I have already told you how beautiful the Lancers are when skated, and you can imagine how the addition of costume increases their beauty: I never saw anything half so pretty."

But the Fancy Dress Balls at the Victoria Skating Rink faded away in the early years of the 20th century. The skating club sold the rink to J. William Shaw, the St. Catherine Street piano merchant. He planned to build a concert hall on the site. Costs of such a building, and uncertain prospects of an adequate return, led Shaw to sell the rink in 1925 to the Standard Realty Corporation. A garage went up where the old rink had stood.

Gone were the days when the Victoria Skating Rink had presented "one great kaleidoscope of brilliant coloring, a crazy quilt of odd designs, a living torrent of swaying, curving, gaily attired figures." All had vanished away, like Victorian ghosts, in the hard dawn of a new century.

Skating Carnival
Victoria Rink
1870

John Collins SKETCHBOOK From a Notman Photo

Sir William Van Horne: "A Dynamo Run by Dynamite"

Sir William Van Horne was gargantuan — a man larger than life. He was a massive, thick-set, bearded man. Colonel Allan Magee used to recall how Van Horne's presence could be felt even before he appeared. In the mornings, when Van Horne came down to his president's office at Windsor Station, you could hear him around the bend of the corridor before he came into sight: a heavy but determined footstep, a snuffle and grunt, a sense of an approaching presence.

Van Horne was imbued with superhuman energy. No one ever dared suggest to him that something was impossible; he delighted in impossibilities. He bore down on his problems like a locomotive at full steam, blowing a warning whistle, maybe, but still coming on fast, without applying brakes.

A Toronto journalist who went to interview him at his house on Sherbrooke Street described the singular sense of weight his presence seemed to give: "He had a head that on an average man would have looked toppling. But his body seemed almost too huge for his head. Not a fat man; just big, hard as a hammer, driving himself about with the exuberant energy of a young Indian."

"You don't seem to rest much," his interviewer remarked.

"I always rest," Van Horne replied. "I never worked in my life."

"Then whatever would you call it?"

"What interests a man can't be called work. I have always been interested. I have railroaded most of my life — because I liked railroading I don't call it work."

Van Horne turned night into day. "Time! What's time?" he would say. His vitality tended to overwhelm his guests. Professor James Mavor of the University of Toronto was invited to stay at his Sherbrooke Street house. He arrived in time for dinner. After dinner they had a talk in Van Horne's study. Van Horne showed him some of the works of art he had recently acquired, as well as some of his own sketches.

Professor Mavor later wrote: "His mental and bodily activities were alike amazing…. After looking at these drawings, we played a couple of games of chess. When these were finished the hour was already late, about one o'clock in the morning. 'Well, professor!' — Van Horne's usual mode of salutation — 'what do you say to a walk?' We walked out on Sherbrooke Street for a couple of miles…."

It was nothing for Van Horne to stay up almost all night. Once he was on a hurried journey to Ottawa. He started a game of chess before his train left Montreal shortly before eight o'clock in the evening. At three in the morning he was still at chess; by this time his car was on a siding in the Ottawa rail yards. He summoned the porter and asked for food. The car had not been stocked with food for so short a run. The porter could produce nothing more than a few hard biscuits and an unopened tin containing at least half-a-pound of caviar. Van Horne's opponent at chess could not face taking that much caviar on an empty stomach. Van Horne consumed the whole of it. He washed it down with neat whisky. The game of chess was resumed. It was kept up till five in the morning. Then Van Horne retired for a nap before starting a busy day in Ottawa.

Those who met Van Horne realized that they simply could not keep up with him. "To men of less robust physique," one observer commented, "thrown into close companionship with him, his vitality, in his prime, was overpowering. He taxed their physical resources so heavily and incessantly that they were fain to fall away and lie down by the wayside."

The importance of William Van Horne's more-than-life-sized energy is that it made Canadian history in the construction of the Canadian Pacific Railway. His part in the project was to be the builder — the man on the spot, who drove his gangs of workmen forward, as though commanding an advancing army. The prompt construction of the railway was imperative to open up the country and to attach remote British Columbia to the Canadian Confederation. If the railway collapsed, the hope for a nation might collapse with it. The work of construction, over every obstacle of terrain and space, was carried forward on Van Horne's energy. He and George Stephen (later Lord Mount Stephen) were a superb pair. Stephen, as the CPR's president, was the statesman of the project, the provider of financing; Van Horne, as general manager, was the construction man, roughing it on the site.

Van Horne had the stamina for his job. He rode the flat cars and the hand cars and in cabooses. Where rails had not yet been laid, he rode over the prairie in wagons or buckboards. He was ready to risk his bulk even where few would dare to tread. At the Mountain Creek trestle two men had gone down to death in a ravine, where a torrent swirled 160 feet below. Only a few days later Van Horne went over the same trestle. The engineer who went with him crawled across anxiously on hands and knees. Van

SKETCHBOOK

John Collins

VAN HORNE HOUSE

Horne crossed upright, on the two loose planks, inspected the work being done on the other side, and walked back again.

D. B. Hanna, in later years the first president of the Canadian National Railways, remembered those days. "He was astonishingly aggressive," said Hanna "...he laughed at men's impossibilities, and ordered them to be done — a dynamo run by dynamite." Van Horne was as impatient with the engineers planning the railway as with his gangs of laborers. Engineers were always raising difficulties, talking about problems. He disregarded difficulties and problems. He said what he wanted done. It was up to them to do it.

One of his engineers, J.H.E. Secretan, told what happened to him. Van Horne said he wanted 500 miles of tracks laid in the season of 1882. Secretan doubted it could be done. "... he scowled at me fiercely," Secretan says, "and before I left 'the presence' he informed me that nothing was *impossible* and if I could show him the road it was all he wanted and if I *couldn't* he would have my scalp. Thus ended a short but characteristic interview ...!" As a matter of fact, 480 miles of tracks were laid that season — very close to the mark.

The vitality of Sir William Van Horne was embodied in a very vital house on Sherbrooke Street. It was, as he said, "big and bulgy, like myself." He dominated that tremendous house, even as he dominated everything else. A visitor said that the carven images from the Orient in his collection "seemed to grin at him reverently as though he were some blustering genial god." Another glimpse pictures him: "Down in his art gallery two rampant Scotch collies leaped upon him like wolves. He wrestled them like children. The man should have had young lions to play with."

Stephen Leacock on the Platform

T he year was 1936. Stephen Leacock was on a lecture tour in the Canadian west. At Edmonton he addressed a joint meeting of the Canadian Club and the McGill Alumni.

He was referring to the recent defeat of Rt. Hon. R.B. Bennett and his Conservatives. While in office, Prime Minister Bennett had made a great point of stressing the Conservative policy of peace, order and good government. Fred V. Stone (who later became a vice-president of the CPR) was there. He recalled that Leacock began his speech by saying: "When I arrived in Alberta, I made inquiries for my old Tory friends. I was told there were no more Tories. They were all dead. Being like the man from Missouri, I determined to find out for myself. So I went out to the cemetery and sure enough I found them all there, lying row on row, enjoying the full benefits of peace, order and good government."

It was a typical Leacock opening. His audience had come prepared to laugh. He had them laughing at once. When they had finished laughing at that joke, they sat there anticipating the next one. He gave it to them — with good timing. As a public lecturer, Leacock was immensely successful. He lectured locally, nationally, internationally. Yet he hated lecturing. He called it a "dismal experience." Public speaking upset him. He tried to avoid eating anything before he spoke; if he did eat, he had indigestion. For the first few minutes of any address he was distressingly nervous, even if he never showed it. Somewhere in the audience he would pick out a particularly friendly face. To that face he would address all his remarks, until he began to feel better and could afford to look about. To encourage himself, and other speakers, he tried to adopt a feeling of boldness; the thing to do, he said, was to get up "and spit in their eye." But this sort of defiance never quite solved his own uneasiness.

Why did Stephen Leacock, if he hated lecturing so much, allow himself to become one of the most active public speakers of his generation? He had two primary motives. First of all, he was ambitious and had a lively sense of good publicity. He was an author. And he knew that an author must promote the sales of his books by making himself known as widely as possible. Leacock's other motive was the wish to make money. He liked money and admitted it. Calculating his earning power, year by year, was one of his pleasures. His salary of $5,000 as a McGill professor was not enough for him. His book royalties greatly augmented, and eventually exceeded it. And public lecturing not only boosted the sale of his books; it became a significant source of income in itself.

His fees for a single speech (as at a convention in the United States) might run as high as $1,000 (perhaps about $5,000 at the present value of money). For many other speeches he charged $500. These fees were often readily paid; a Leacock speech would make sure an event would be a success. Leacock, however, did not press too high for payment, if he sensed the money really wasn't there. He would rather settle for a lower fee than miss the opportunity for payment altogether. His maxim was: "Find out how much money they have and don't charge a cent more." Though he gave speeches of many kinds, before many groups, part of his public lecturing was professional. He engaged agents; they arranged tours. Yet he would also give speeches for nothing. For most his life he would charge nothing for speaking to audiences in Canada, while requiring substantial fees for speaking abroad. And he was freely available as a speaker to student and alumni groups at McGill.

In some of his earlier speeches he was more inclined to "ham" than in later years. Colonel H. Wyatt Johnston used to recall Leacock's appearance one year when Varsity was playing against McGill. Leacock (a Varsity graduate and a McGill professor) appeared at a smoker after the game. He had a few thoughts, he said. He had noted them down while on the long ride on a slow street car. Then he produced a roll of toilet paper. On this roll, he claimed, he had written a long poem in blank verse. While he held the roll with one hand, he kept letting the paper out on the floor with the other, pretending to read his composition.

In later years this sort of "hamming" was less prominent in Leacock's speeches. He became less the conscious lecturer than a man sharing funny reminiscences with his audience — more the raconteur than the performer. His style became easier, less forced or contrived. But in one respect Leacock's appearance remained eccentric. He wore clothes that had once been good in quality, but looked as though he had slept in them. Or, as his niece, Elizabeth Kimball, said, he looked at times like a teddy bear that had been left out in the rain overnight.

Audiences that knew Leacock as a humorist, and expected him to play the part, thought his appearance was just right. Occasionally he addressed audiences, outside Canada, that were less prepared for his appearance. It happened once in London. It was a grand occasion, in the main dining room of the Savoy Hotel. Everyone seemed to be there, even the Prince of Wales and the Archbishop of Canterbury. Well-cut Bond Street clothes were everywhere in evidence. Leacock and the head table guests were led into the room by an official in white wig, scarlet, gold-braided, velvet jacket, white neck ruffle, silken yellow breeches, and silver-buckled, squaretoed black shoes.

The audience stood and stared. A Canadian who was there felt his heart sink. In this grand procession Leacock walked, his hair tousled, his old blue suit rumpled, his coat collar half turned up, one sleeve part way to his elbow, his necktie half out of his collar. In the gathering voices could be heard, saying that something must be wrong. This couldn't be the speaker, Leacock. "Must be one of those damned reporters," someone was saying. After dinner, Leacock was introduced. He began to speak. His audience was indifferent, cool, even hostile. He seemed hopelessly miscast for the occasion. Then he stirred a chuckle, next a laugh. Soon they were sitting up, turning their chairs to see and hear better.

Leacock was saying, if he had known it would be this kind of party, he would have rented a proper suit for the occasion, as obviously the others had done. His wife made his suits. If one sleeve seemed longer than the other, that wasn't her fault. One of his arms was longer. This was the suit he would wear to church on Sunday. Though probably, like the Archbishop of Canterbury, he didn't go to church so much, now that he was older. The Leacock style of humor became irresistible. His audience, austere in the extreme, quickly succumbed to his "rugged, craggy happiness." When he quietly sat down, wiping his lips with his napkin, the audience clapped furiously, then cheered. One voice could be heard calling out: "Well played, Canada!"

John Collins SKETCHBOOK Stephen Leacock

The Man Who Brought Apartments to Montreal

The man credited with introducing apartment living to Montreal is Roswell C. Fisher. Back in the 1880s, Fisher believed the time had come for a new lifestyle for Montrealers. Instead of the struggle, trouble and expense of living in individual houses, Montrealers could live more comfortably, and as fashionably, in large, handsome apartment buildings. The inspiration for Fisher's idea was found by him in his English and continental travels. He had observed English clubs and Swiss hotels. He proposed to combine some of the features of both.

JOHN COLLINS SKETCHBOOK

SHERBROOKE STREET
AND THE APARTMENTS

Roswell Fisher was far from being the typical entrepreneur or developer. He was a scholar, a philosopher, thinking and writing on political economy and social problems. He was a well-educated man. Born in Montreal in 1844, of Scottish and New England descent, he attended Montreal High School, Rugby and Cambridge. Returning to Montreal, he entered McGill University, graduating in law. His articles on social questions appeared in the more intellectual journals. He was active in the Philosophical Society of Canada and was vice-president of the Good Government Association of Montreal. His idea of providing Montrealers with the option of apartment living was the outcome of his sociological and philosophical studies. He was not offering housing merely, but a whole new way of life.

For far too long, Fisher believed, people had been fretted and annoyed by the details of upkeep and repairs, of hiring cooks and housemaids, and all because they felt obliged to live in houses of their own. Fisher's idea was to provide gracious living without the cares and tribulations of householding. He would build elegant "co-operative mansions." The people who lived in these well-planned apartment houses could, by paying so much a year, settle, "at one stroke," their rent, taxes, gas, water and fuel. Fisher went so far as to plan for providing meals to the residents, so that "all trouble with cooks and marketing" could be disposed of as well.

His belief was that an apartment house, to be memorable in its impressiveness, should be an imposing building, at least five storeys high (a great height for those times). It should also be massive enough to cover a whole city block. In pursuit of his idea, he found a vacant block on the south side of Sherbrooke Street, between Crescent and Bishop. There he would build his apartment house in two stages. He would begin by erecting the first half at the corner of Crescent, then eventually complete his design with the second half at the corner of Bishop. Both apartments would be called "The Sherbrooke." When both had been completed, the first would be called "The Old Sherbrooke" and the second "The New Sherbrooke." He placed much importance on incorporating the name Sherbrooke in his venture. Sherbrooke was Montreal's most elegant street, known as "the Fifth Avenue of Canada." It was a street of mansions, many standing in large grounds. His aim was to provide fashionable living in apartments on Montreal's most fashionable street.

The first section at the corner of Crescent was built about 1888. It embodied many of his ideas. It was a high building, equipped with an elevator operated by steam power. Rooms were large, ceilings high. Though he gave up a plan to have a dining room for the residents, he nonetheless provided them with meals. These meals, cooked in a basement kitchen, arrived at each apartment on a dumb waiter — a small lift or elevator, with two shelves, worked by a rope-pulling arrangement below.

Proving his faith in this new lifestyle, Fisher himself moved into his building. He chose sunny rooms on the top floor, at the back. Eventually he added a penthouse, the first in the city. Certainly the entrance to his own apartment had impressive elegance. It ended in a conservatory, with a statue of Venus at the top of a flight of bronze steps. Water cascaded into a pool.

The apartment house was soon filled, especially with professors from McGill University, medical doctors, and well-to-do widows. In 1905, Roswell Fisher built the second section of his apartment house. In the meantime, this land at the corner of Bishop Street had lain vacant. He permitted a theatrical company to put up "hoardings" there — huge signs advertising its plays. In return, he was given tickets.

Though The New Sherbrooke adjoined the old, it differed in appearance. It was more ornamental in what was called the Renaissance style. The architect of The Old Sherbrooke is unknown; the architects of The New Sherbrooke were MacVicar and Heriot. In this new apartment house, Fisher returned to his original plan of providing meals. It had not worked in The Old Sherbrooke. Even his dumb waiter had to be abandoned. Kitchens had to be built in every suite. In the new building, a dining room was set up on the ground floor, in the same area where a restaurant was to be later.

By introducing the apartment house idea to Montreal, Roswell Fisher had been a social innovator. He had the satisfaction of seeing his idea widely adopted. The Grosvenor Apartments were built at the southwest corner of Sherbrooke and Guy in 1904; The Linton on the northwest corner of Sherbrooke and Simpson in 1907; the Maxwelton Apartments on the south side of Sherbrooke Street, opposite the McGill campus, in 1914.

Writing back in the 1880s to advance his idea of apartment living, Roswell Fisher had said that if what he was writing led to "the building and occupation" of one apartment house, he would "consider his advocacy amply... justified." His justification was seen in far more than one apartment house. Few men have had a greater influence on Montreal. He had introduced a lifestyle — revolutionary, perhaps, but inevitable and, for many, desirable.

Those Long, Long Skirts

When Victorian women came into an entrance porch they would seize their ground-length skirts in one hand. With a tight grip they would shake their skirts briskly. They wanted to rid them of mud and dirt gathered from the streets. This necessary procedure partly explains why many Victorian houses in Montreal have tile-lined porches. Tiles not only paved porch floors; they covered the walls, to a height of three or four feet. When Victorian women shook their skirts and sent the dirt flying, it would drop to the floor or spatter against tiled wall surfaces. Tiles could later be thoroughly washed.

Even for sports Victorian skirts were long. How long they were was observed by the governor general, Lord Dufferin. In the 1870s, when visiting Montreal, he often went skating at the Victoria Rink — the vast indoor rink between Drummond and Stanley Streets just west of the Windsor Hotel. While skating he had noticed something strange about the markings on the surface of the ice. Some of the marks were obviously made by the cutting edges of skate blades. But other, different marks puzzled him. He commented: "… when I was at the skating rink the other day I saw some peculiar tracks on the ice. I watched the skaters for some time to find out what made those tracks, and at last, would you believe it, I discovered they were tracks made by a lady's petticoats."

Victorian women on snowshoes swept the snow with their skirts, even as, on skates, they swept the ice. The Montreal artist, Henry Sandham, made many sketches of Victorian women on snowshoes. The costume they wore was attractive: a tasselled tuque, a long blanket coat descending well below the knees, a fringed sash (a sort of ceinture fléchée), and skirts down to the toes of their moccasins. Sandham's sketches show the sweeping depression left by the long and heavy skirts in the snow, especially when women were mounting a slope. Often it was wide and deep enough almost to obliterate the tracks made by their snowshoes.

It did not much matter what the sport might be, custom still dictated long skirts had to be worn. Women on the golf course wore skirts that brushed the grass. The Montreal Hunt club insisted on black riding habits for its lady members — habits with long skirts. On the hunting field they had to ride side-saddle. It was always an anxious spectacle when women, riding side-saddle, leaped hedges or fences. Such leaps would wrench them to and fro with such violence as to make onlookers wonder why their spines did not snap. Yet a woman riding astride would never have been tolerated.

In the Victorian era long skirts were required even for tennis — a sport demanding (perhaps more than any other) rapid changes of position and posture. Women tennis players, in every way, were overdressed. In the 1890s long skirts were worn with a tennis blouse having enormous balloon sleeves. Tennis hats were elaborate — beflowered, befeathered, sometimes even veiled.

The long Victorian era (from 1837 to 1901) knew no interval when skirts were shortened. Through all those 64 years they remained ankle-length, or lower. But the length of the skirts did not mean they were always worn in the same way. Long skirts were affected by fashions. These fashions frequently changed. When the era began, the long skirts were bell-shaped. By 1850 this shape was being emphasized by wearing a number of petticoats beneath the outer skirt — sometimes as many as six.

Ten years later the passion for the bell-shape went beyond wearing multiple petticoats. Crinolines were introduced. They were whalebone wire, on watch-spring hoops, suspended on strips of material. Here was the historic "hoop skirt". It was worn in Montreal even for skating. When a girl fell, she had difficulty getting up. In the meantime she made a spectacle for curious spectators. In the early 1860s crinolines had become so large two women could not enter a room together; no door was wide enough. Nor could two women sit side by side on a sofa; no sofa was so long.

By about 1865 skirts, though retaining their length, were changing their shape. The bell shape was modified. Skirts were becoming flatter in front, more extended in the rear. By 1870 the hoop skirt had almost disappeared. The bustle had made its appearance. At first it was only a pad or roll. By 1870, it became a shaped framework over which the long skirt was draped. Though the bustle seemed at first only a passing fad, it reasserted itself. By 1880 it had assumed an even more exaggerated form for the back of the skirts.

Mrs. Florence May Ramsden, a Montrealer, recalled in 1955 the bustle she had worn in the 1880s: "No. I never wore hoops but I did wear a bustle!… It was generally a small mattress-like affair stitched to my skirt, or a curious spiral contraption of two coils of wire attached to a stout piece of belting with a steel buckle, such as men have on their belts! The bustle was supposed to give a graceful sloping line to the long skirts, which were often four yards wide and faced (in the case of street dresses) with brush binding and bias velveteen — excellent carriers of dust and germs." By 1890 the bustle had gone. Skirts became increasingly simple and severe. By 1900 they were worn

John Collins SKETCHBOOK *Victorian Houses and Costumes*

tight over the hips and tight almost to the knees, when they flared to the ground sometimes with a slight train.

Skirts remained long even after the Victorian age ended. Even in sport, long skirts lingered. In the Montreal Hunt long-skirted black habits and side-saddles remained favored for lady members. The historian of the Montreal Hunt, Professor John Irwin Cooper, wrote: "There were still limits to emancipation.... Indeed, when in 1914 the daughter of a prominent citizen appeared on Sherbrooke Street riding astride she created a greater sensation (locally) than the news of the assassination of the Archduke at Sarajevo." Theodora Braidwood, a McGill B.A. of 1915, used to recall that in her day women students on the campus wore long tweed skirts below the ankles. She had snapshots to prove it. One snapshot was taken on the campus in 1914, showing three long-skirted students posed under the elms

with Professor Stephen Leacock. Theodora Braidwood even wore a long skirt when she played hockey in the girls team on the campus rink, or on the ice of the arena on Mount Royal Ave. Since hockey was an active sport, she had been permitted to shorten her skirt to one inch above the ankles.

Tennis skirts were worn long, even in international championship matches, until 1919. In that year Suzanne Lenglen shortened her tennis dress. But at least as late as 1922 her hemline had not risen above midcalf. Bicycling and skiing were doing much to bring about the revolution. Girls on bicycles were wearing bloomers of a sort; girls on skis began wearing breeches.

Emancipation was beginning to arrive. The drama of swaying skirts, four yards wide and down to the ground, was departing. But going, too, was the need to shake skirts free of mud and dirt in tiled entrance porches.

The Mysterious Dr. Ayers

On a summer's day in 1832 a crowd had surged into St. Jean Baptiste Street (the little street running from Commissioners northward to Notre Dame, a short distance to the east of Place d'Armes). Dr. Stephen Ayers had been seen entering one of the houses. The crowd, made up of rich and poor, milled about on the street. It was waiting for him to come out. All were anxious to see him; many wanted him to come to their houses, to visit those sick with the cholera. In that terrible Montreal summer of 1832, when one person in every eight died of the cholera, Dr. Stephen Ayers seemed the answer to prayers and fears. He had come with a sovereign remedy. If only Dr. Ayers could be persuaded to visit a cholera household, he might work one of his miracles.

The doctor was a weird character. He had been seen coming into Montreal by way of Notre Dame Street, riding one horse and leading another. Both were lean horses, rawboned. He was said to feed them on shavings. A Montrealer of the time described him: "He presented a very curious appearance; was careless and slovenly in dress; he wore a slouch hat and loose made clothes. His beard and hair were iron gray, which he allowed to grow long (an unusual thing at the time). In passing through the streets, on his rounds attending the stricken, he used to create quite a sensation by his extraordinary appearance. He carried a long staff and a leather bag or wallet."

Little in Dr. Stephen Ayers' appearance inspired confidence. He was said to look like a beggar or like an Indian fakir. His "rather handsome" face was spoiled by "a keen designing expression." At first he was ridiculed. He put up a plain cardboard notice, informing the public that he had an infallible remedy for the cholera, and would cure all who sent for him. The very wording of the notice was enough to make him sound like a quack. Yet he was not rapaciously mercenary, as most quacks were. He explained that he was actually a volunteer. He had heard that the cholera had struck Montreal, and had come north to be of help. All the evidence is that he charged no fees, though he would accept any payment offered. As his practice expanded, he had to hurry about town in a carriage, and charged his carriage costs.

A Montrealer who had seen Dr. Ayers treating several cholera patients decided to check on the results of the procedure. One patient was Antoine Letourneau, a spruce beer brewer. Letourneau had taken ill with cholera "in its most violent character." After treatment, he remained low and was not expected to live. The next morning, he was much improved, had no pain whatever, and was "confident of his ultimate recovery." This Montrealer visited two other cholera cases treated by Dr. Ayers. Both were men who worked for a grocer. One of them had suffered "excruciating spasms." The other felt "a dreadful sensation of burning in the stomach and chest." Next morning both had been able to get up. Another Montrealer, William Masterman, recalled in his old age how Dr. Ayers had saved the life of his mother. "My mother took the disease, and the doctor administered a dose of medicine …. It was an awful mixture, but it cured."

In the hysterical conditions of the time Dr. Ayers assumed almost supernatural proportions. Mrs. Susanna Moodie, who had just arrived as an immigrant, heard an excise officer in Montreal extolling Dr. Ayers: "Flesh and blood could never do what he has done — the hand of God is in it." Some of the French Canadian Roman Catholics thought he might be St. Antoine, the pious abbott of the fourth century, come back to earth in answer to prayers. St. Antoine had cured the plague-stricken in his time.

Support for his claims came from his patients. A lieutenant of the 45th Regiment in the British Army, in Montreal on a North American tour, saw how impressive these testimonials could be. "I saw a long letter addressed to him," he said, "signed by nearly 200 people whom he had attended, and who did not hesitate to say that they considered him as sent by Divine Power to their assistance."

Dr. Ayers left Montreal when the cholera came to an end with the cool September weather. He appeared in Kingston three years later. The Kingston *Chronicle and Gazette* reported: "That eccentric personage, Stephen Ayers, the 'Cholera Doctor,' who figured in Montreal in 1832, has made his appearance in Kingston. Having honored the vicinity of our printing office with a visit, … curiosity… was much excited by his long beard, leathery queue, and oddly assorted garments, which make him literally a thing of shreds and patches."

By 1837 Dr. Ayers was back again in Montreal. The town was not afflicted with the cholera that year, but he offered to cure a variety of other diseases and disorders. In his advertisements he "informs his friends that he proposes curing Consumption in its incipient stages, Typhus, Scarlet Fevers, Croup or Hives, Rheumatism and Gout, Influenza and Pleurisy, by methods considerably different from those used by other Doctors." The advertisements go on to explain why his methods are different. He had travelled among the Whites and the Blacks "in most parts of the United States, and carefully compared their habits and modes of living with those of several nations of Indians inhabiting the Mississippi, Missouri and some of their tributary streams.'' The knowledge gained by these travels had given him advantages ''few other practitioners'' possessed.

By nature an itinerant, he wandered off again. In later years advertisements for patent medicines appeared under his name. Either he had set himself up in business as a drug manufacturer, or some enterprising developers had seized upon his well-known name to exploit their products.

No doubt Dr. Stephen Ayers was some sort of quack. Despite his claim that he had credentials to show, he may not have been a doctor at all. But by some means he seemed able to restore some cholera patients to health. A possible explanation is that his mysterious arrival in Montreal, his vague origin, his strange appearance inspired in his patients a mystical faith. The belief that he could do something other physicians could not do may have been enough to tip the scales in favor of his patients' recovery.

In the midst of depression and despair Dr. Stephen Ayers brought faith and hope. Whoever he was, and whatever his qualifications or methods, he may have been a crude but effective practitioner of psychosomatic medicine.

When Louis Rubenstein Beat the World

In the winter of 1890 Louis Rubenstein set out from Montreal for Saint Petersburg, Russia. He was going to enter the contest with the best of all nations for the title of amateur figure skating champion of the world. The 28-year-old Rubenstein had already won the skating championship of North America. He was now reaching for the top.

When Rubenstein arrived in Saint Petersburg he put up at the Hotel d'Europe. His first visit was to the rink. What disturbed him was the different composition of the ice. It was harder, crisper than Montreal ice. His skates would

not take hold on it. He had four weeks for practice, and hoped he could get used to it in time.

Something far worse than differences in the ice came to haunt him. Rubenstein became aware he had arrived in a sinister, shadowed land. He was anxious when his passport was taken over by the hotel keeper. Then one day the police appeared. He was told to report at once at the police office. There, an official behind a desk sat silently for a time, looking him over. "You are a Jew?" he asked in good English. Rubenstein said he was. He was asked his age, where he was born. Rubenstein asked for

SKETCHBOOK

John Collins

RUBENSTEIN DRINKING FOUNTAIN

his passport. He was told he would get it in a few days. That was all; he could go. Rubenstein was anxious. Why all this mystery? Was there any trouble? There was no reply.

Two days later, while practising at the rink, he saw a strange figure approaching him. It was a uniformed official. He was told he was wanted again at the police office. This time he was given orders: "You cannot be permitted to stay in Saint Petersburg. You will be good enough to leave inside 24 hours."

"Why?" asked Rubenstein.

"You are a Jew, and there is no necessity to further discuss the matter. We cannot permit Jews to remain in Saint Petersburg."

Rubenstein then realized the risk he had taken in coming to Russia. Even in 1890 there was a sort of Iron Curtain. It was the era when pogroms against the Jews were bringing terror and death to the countryside.

He went out into the cold street. Then he remembered something that might help him. He had brought a letter from Canada. The letter had been given him by Lord Stanley, Canada's governor-general. It would introduce him to Sir Robert Morier, British ambassador in Saint Petersburg. Rubenstein went at once to the British embassy. Sir Robert, he said, "sympathized with me and got a little bit angry at the way I had been treated." He doubted that Rubenstein could get "a fair show" among the Russians. But he would do his best for him. "A British subject who comes to Russia," Sir Robert said, "to take part in an international match, will be allowed to stay, and you will stay until you compete, if the British Embassy has any influence in the Court."

Next morning Rubenstein was hoisted from his bed and taken to the Prefect of Police. The prefect was the wildest-looking Russian he had yet seen, with whiskers like wires. But he spoke mildly. At the special request of the British ambassador he would be permitted to stay in Saint Petersburg until the contest was over. Then he must get out immediately. His passport was handed to him.

For Louis Rubenstein, such experiences were hardly encouraging. Though permitted to stay, he was constantly shadowed by the police. "Oh, yes," he would say, in recounting his Russian experiences, "the police were very attentive and it seemed for a little while as if I was the only dangerous person in Saint Petersburg. I don't know what they thought I was going to do, whether I wanted to blow up the Winter Palace or set the Neva on fire. Anyway, they watched me closely enough to make me uneasy and dream of Siberia, but I got used to it after a while."

The February day of the figure skating competition arrived. The first test was for fancy skating, called by the Russians "diagram skating." Rubenstein saw that the Russian conception of skating was very different from his own. "The Russians," he said, "go in for acrobatic skating —

that is, making large energetic movements, jumping, etc., which while clever enough perhaps, are singularly ungraceful, and certainly would not be relished on this side."

Louis Rubenstein's turn came. His performance contrasted with his competitors. It had no violent, jumping gestures. All was graceful exactitude, and unfailing, accomplished precision. He could cut out a star, with all its points equal. He could make a figure eight on one foot, and loops or ringlets. He proved that he could do again what he had just done, and with as much finesse as the first time. He would go over his ice patterns, covering the same lines, without in the least blurring the edges.

The judges, prejudiced as some of them were, gazed. They found it hard to believe what they saw. Louis Rubenstein's little engraved skates swerved, flashed, twinkled. His almost mechanical perfection was nevertheless combined with artistic ease and elegance. The first prize was his. In fact, all margin for decision had been taken away from the judges. To have denied Louis Rubenstein the first prize would have been an international scandal.

Once he won his prize, his status in Saint Petersburg dramatically improved. He was able to stay in the city a number of days after the competition, well entertained by the skating committee. Then, with his prize, he set out on the long journey back to Montreal. "Well Done! Rubenstein!" ran the headlines in the papers as the champion returned. A crowd was at Bonaventure Station when he arrived by the Central Vermont train.

Rubenstein was active in many sports. For 18 years he was president of the Canadian Wheelmen's Association. He performed wonders on his unwieldy cycle of the old-fashioned type — a "Pennyfarthing" with the enormous wheel in front and the tiny wheel at the rear. Bowling was another of his sports; he became known as "the Father of Bowling in Canada." He was a swimmer, a curler. He presided for years over the Montreal Amateur Athletic Association. But figure skating held a particular appeal for him. It was supremely exacting.

Louis Rubenstein came, as he liked to say, of "one of the oldest Jewish families in the city." He entered the family business — Rubenstein Brothers, silver, gold and nickel platers and manufacturers. He also achieved prominence as an alderman. In 1914 he was elected alderman for Ward 5 (later known as St. Lawrence Ward). And he represented that ward until his death. He was responsible for the erection of the Rubenstein Baths for public use.

Over the years the graceful youth of 1890 developed into a portly presence, a man with a big moustache, pince-nez glasses, and observant, laughing eyes. He died on January 3, 1931. "No one ever heard a bitter word from him," said one of his colleagues on the City Council. "A good sport and a pleasant fellow." Today he is commemorated by a drinking fountain at the corner of Mount Royal Avenue and Park Avenue.

How Skiing Came to Montreal

Early in the year 1879 a Norwegian resident of Montreal, a Mr. A. Birch, appeared on skis. Montrealers had never seen skis before. They did not really recognize skis for what they were; they seemed only a variation of the snowshoe. In fact, Montrealers called them ''Norwegian snowshoes.''

To be sure, they were odd-looking snowshoes. One of Montreal's magazines, on February 8, 1879, ran a full-page woodcut of the skiing Norwegian.

Beneath the picture the caption read: ''Mr. A. Birch, a Norwegian gentleman of Montreal, has a pair of patent Norwegian snowshoes upon which he has taken a trip to Quebec starting Friday last. The snowshoes are entirely of wood, nine feet long, six inches wide, and have a foot-board and a toe-strap. He walks with the aid of a pole and crosses ice not buoyant enough to bear a good-sized dog, so buoyant are the shoes in action.''

''Norwegian snowshoes,'' though a novelty, made no lasting impact. Confidence in the superiority of the Canadian snowshoe was long unshaken. ''For the snowshoe no substitute has ever been proposed,'' said a writer in 1897. ''The Norwegian ski would not answer at all well in this country.''

One of the earliest Montrealers to acquire skis was James Ross (later a major-general and head of the accountancy firm P.S. Ross & Sons). In 1887, as a young man, he joined the exploring expedition in Yellowstone Park under Lieutenant Swatka of the U.S. Army. On that expedition he was introduced to skiing. He brought his skis back to Montreal and became one of the first to promote the sport in Canada.

Skis remained scarce in Montreal for a number of years. No one in Canada was manufacturing them. Retail shops did not stock them. Some had not even heard of them.

About that time, in 1899, skiing was being practised by three McGill professors: Percy E. Nobbs (later an Olympic fencer), J. B. Porter and R. J. Durley. Their skis came from Finland — ten feet long, narrow and light, turned up at both ends, fitted with a loose leather toe-strap and sealskin footpad.

In the evenings they skied down the hilly streets between Pine Avenue and Sherbrooke Street. As toe-straps were very loose, a ski easily came off and went flying downhill by itself. One runaway ski tranfixed a dog.

Sleighing parties on the hills encountered new dangers. One skier, shooting downhill and mismanaging direction, landed in the middle of a sleigh. His ski nearly put out the eye of the prettiest girl. Accidental romance resulted. Skier and girl married.

Montrealers, brought up on snowshoeing, knew nothing about skiing. Learning was hard, by trial and error. At first skis were used as if they were two narrow twin toboggans. Skiers simply pointed them downhill and shoved off.

No goggles were worn. Wind sent tears coursing down cheeks. At the bottom of the hill the tears had frozen into tiny icicles. Early skiers had only one pole, or none. Ski wax was unknown. Tallow candles were carried — sole remedy for sticky snow.

Many years passed before anything resembling a ski costume was defined. Skiers wore anything they thought best — anything they happened to have: long overcoats with a sash, short blanket coats of the snowshoers, mackinaws, high boots, riding breeches or heavy knickers. Always sweaters were worn; underwear was woollen; mitts might be fur gauntlets.

Nobody thought to dress lightly for skiing. All bundled themselves up against the cold. Results, when a group of skiers assembled, were grotesque.

Extreme amateurishness lingered for years. Novelty made the ski a toy — difficult, baffling, intriguing. Naive instructions were often issued, as in a publication for the Winter Carnival of 1909. Cozy, childlike, unsophisticated advice was offered, in a description of a skier trying to climb a hill:

''But in climbing a hill! Then it is that his patience is taxed to the uttermost, and he performs all sorts of gymnastic feats, slipping back, losing his balance, clinging to the points of his skis to straighten himself, or dipping his hands in the snow in a vain endeavor to obtain a steadying grip. Then, in despair, he decides to walk up-hill sideways, and this results in some woeful tangles, until he learns to balance himself on one foot, as it were, while he shoves the other carefully upward in a horizontal position, then draws the other to position beside it.''

Skiing by girls was still regarded by older women as too bold and rough, not fitting and rather bad manners. One of the girls, later Mrs. W. Melville Drennan, recalled cold looks from passing critics:

''Skiing, when the first ladies' ski school was the cynosure of all eyes on Mount Royal, was considered a very daring thing to do indeed. We sometimes received haughty looks

SKIERS ON MOUNT ROYAL

from ladies who were muffled in furs, and almost buried beneath muskox robes, when they drove past us, in their red cutters on the mountain.''

After the Montreal Ski Club was formed in 1904, its first event was a jumping competition on a small hill on Fletcher's Field. By 1910 the club had moved to a hill on Côte des Neiges.

At first Norwegians in Montreal easily took the first prizes. But some Canadians acquired skills rapidly. In the competitions for 1907-08 "there was very little difference, either in the style or distance." Huntley Drummond made a 76-foot leap one year — an astonishing achievement with the equipment and conditions of the time.

But after the First World War skiing shot ahead. By 1920 the Montreal Ski Club Annual, describing a winter's outing on Mount Royal, could say: "Gone are the days of snowshoes ... for skiing is now the king of winter sports in Montreal."

In 1921 the Montreal Ski Club acquired its first clubhouse. In that year H. Percy Douglas was president. Tobogganing had gone out of fashion; the house of the Park Toboggan Club stood empty. Douglas secured it for the Montreal Ski Club, rent free.

Mount Royal was still the centre of skiing. In the clubhouse on the mountain were a big sitting room, ski prints on the walls, open fireplace, a snack bar. Membership rose. Programs were varied: dances, Saturday trips around the mountain, moonlight ski parties, special events for junior members.

Mount Royal did not remain the centre of skiing for Montrealers. The sweep and variety of the Laurentians would soon be drawing Montreal's skiers northward, to some of the finest skiing country in the world. The change was symbolized by the closing of the Montreal Ski Club in 1933.

The Runaway Train at Windsor Station

The Boston & Maine Express was coming into Montreal a little after 8:30 on the morning of March 17, 1909. The tracks were on the downward grade, toward Windsor Station. But that morning the speed was not gradually reduced as the station was approached. The train was still thundering ahead at 50 or 55 miles an hour, even when it was as near Windsor Station as Guy Street. It was shooting past semaphores as though they did not exist.

A few stations back, at Highlands, a leak was noticed in the firebox. It did not seem serious. Nothing was done about it. Nothing could be done while the steam was at high pressure. At Highlands some trouble with the brakes had been repaired.

A passenger wished to get off at Westmount. Conductor Arthur H. Harvey signalled the engineer to stop. The train plunged by Westmount Station, unchanged in speed. Harvey just thought the engineer must have forgotten to stop. Then stranger things began to happen. At switch No. 7 the train gave an ugly lurch. It was tugging and straining at the tracks. It was aimed at Windsor Station like a rocket. The cabin of the locomotive, No. 12, was deserted. Fireman and engineer had both jumped out. The locomotive was roaring ahead with no one aboard. The throttle was wide open. The boiler had canted over to the left. A plug had been struck by the driving wheel. A gush of steam and water spurted into the cabin, on the fireman's side. "I heard a sudden terrific bang," said fireman Louis Craig, "and then steam and water struck me.... When there is an explosion like that and you do not know where it is, a man generally thinks first to save his life. I realized nothing but jumped right off."

Engineer Mark Cunningham stayed in the cabin for about another half mile. It could only be supposed he thought at first the mishap was less serious than it turned out to be. Steam and water were blowing on the side of the cabin away from him. Possibly he got down to see what he could do to fix it. Suddenly the full force of the scalding blast may have hit him in the face. He may have staggered back. Either he fell or jumped off the train.

Brakesman Joseph A. Dion realized something must have gone wrong; he had never seen a train racing eastward past Guy Street at 50 miles an hour. He signalled the engineer. No answer came. He jammed on the emergency brakes. The train jolted. Passengers were "thrown into each other's arms." A Pullman porter was tossed half the length of a coach; his face was ripped. The buffers in Windsor Station, at the end of the tracks, were now only about 1,600 feet away. The emergency brakes cut the speed

down to 25 miles an hour. But at 25 miles an hour the train burst down the tracks, under the canopy.

On the platform was a crowd waiting to meet friends arriving from Boston. The gateman at the station was Thomas Whalen (whose son Lawrence was to become Montreal's Auxiliary Bishop.) He saved lives. "I did not just know what happened for a moment or two," said Whalen. "I saw the train coming at a tremendous pace and tried to get the people back. I was still getting them away when the engine flew by me and a piece of wood hit me in the back. But the people on the platform got away without injury." The locomotive reached the buffers at the end of the tracks. It leapfrogged over them. The three passenger coaches "seemed to quiver and shake in agony." Those inside were tangled up like a football scrimmage. The coaches were wrenched free of the locomotive; they tumbled off the tracks. Passengers were shaken and shocked. None was hurt seriously.

The locomotive, followed by its tender and the baggage car, drove forward. It crashed through the wall of the Ladies' Waiting Room, then through two other brick walls. It knocked over a heavy stone pillar in the General Waiting Room, collided with a second pillar, then sank to the floor. There it lay, "panting like some monstrous animal brought to bay, steam escaping from its damaged boiler." Fortunately much of its steam had already escaped through the plug into the cabin, while the locomotive was still running on the tracks. If it had not, the boiler might have exploded on impact.

In 1909 Windsor Station was not the size it is today. Beginning at la Gauchetière, it ran down Windsor, now Peel, to Donegana, about halfway to St. Antoine Street. Donegana disappeared when Windsor Station was extended. As the locomotive crashed about indoors, it knocked out part of the southern wall; debris was scattered into Donegana Street. Before it stopped at the pillar, its nose had gone through a wall; the front part actually protruded outdoors. The massively constructed station rocked under the blow. Glass even tumbled out of windows over the main entrance on Osborne Street, opposite St. George's Church. Dust seemed thick as fog. The city, for blocks away, heard an explosion like dynamite, or the thunder of artillery. People rushed into the street. Montreal had recently been shaken by an earthquake; people wanted to know whether it had happened again. Inside the station, when the crashing echoes died down, groans and shrieks could be heard.

In the Ladies' Waiting Room, Mrs. W. J. Nixon was with her children — a daughter of 10, a son of 13. Nixon, train dispatcher at Medicine Hat in Alberta, had just heard that his job had been made permanent. He was coming home to close up his Montreal house and take his wife and children to Medicine Hat with him. Falling bricks and stone buried Mrs. Nixon and the children. A rescue party heard them groan. Long before they could be reached the groans ceased.

Also in the Ladies' Waiting Room were Mrs. Sarah Hughes of Moreau Street and her 12-year-old granddaughter, Elsie Villiers. Mrs. Hughes had come to see her friend, Mrs. Shoonmaker, off on the New York train. The two women were sitting on a bench, talking together. Elsie was a little distance away, examining the pictures on the wall. The locomotive roared through the room. The two women on the bench escaped injury. A piece of stone, knocked from a pillar, crushed Elsie Villiers's skull. Grief-stricken Mrs. Hughes waited until the body of her granddaughter was taken from the ruins. Then she went to the house of her daughter, Mrs. Villiers, on Marquette Street to break the news. The child had been staying at her grandmother's.

Mrs. Villiers had not seen her for a couple of weeks.

While the locomotive was crashing through Windsor Station the secretary of the CPR's special police service, William Bock, was at the desk in his office on the floor below the waiting rooms. Right over his head the floor gave way beneath the locomotive's tender. It spilled down on him, a shower of plaster and beams. Two hours passed before they could get him out.

Cunningham, the engineer, never recovered from his leap from the locomotive cabin. Fireman Craig had landed in a snowbank, and rolled into the ditch. He was able to get out and walk down the track some way before another train picked him up. The coroner's inquest found no blame. The locomotive had been in good condition when it was sent out. Nor did the jury have fault to find with the engineer. "We are of the opinion," they said, "that Cunningham acted heroically and properly under the circumstances, and stayed on the engine as long as he could." His scalded hands were evidence of his courage.

John Collins SKETCHBOOK

WINDSOR STATION

"Morning Calls" in the Afternoon

"**M**orning calls" were one of the most rigorous social obligations of Victorian Montreal. And the odd thing about such "morning calls" was that they were customarily made in the afternoon between 3 and 5 o'clock — late enough for the household to be finished with lunch, yet early enough not to interfere with dinner. "Morning calls" were not in the least casual. Strict obligations of etiquette and decorum regulated alike the callers and those called upon. Everything had to be done according to the rules.

How strict these rules were may be seen in a Montreal magazine, *The Saturday Reader.* In the issue for September 29, 1866, appeared an article: "ETIQUETTE FOR LADIES: MORNING CALLS." The article emphasized such calls were not to be left to choice or inclination. They were required under a long list of social circumstances.

For her part, "the lady of the house" was free not to receive a caller. She could resort to the "not at home" procedure. The servant who answered the door would be

John Collins Sketchbook "Calls" in Victorian Montreal

instructed before 3 o'clock to say that the lady of the house was ''not at home.'' This need not mean that she was out, only that she was not receiving that afternoon. If she wished, of course, she could instruct her servant to admit certain visitors and say ''not at home'' to others. Convention required that a ''not at home'' announcement from a servant was always to be accepted as though it were true. Most Victorian women avoided any difficulty by fixing a regular visiting day — an ''at home'' day. It might be the first and third Wednesday, or the second and fourth Thursday in the month. On these days she would be at home to receive her callers.

''At home'' calls had to be brief. A few minutes would be enough. As part of the convention of the brief visit a lady caller never removed her bonnet or took off her gloves. Her muff or parasol was carried with her into the drawing room (often known as ''the parlor''). Only an umbrella (because in wet weather it might be dripping) could be left in the hall stand. Gentleman callers entered the drawing room carrying their hats and gloves.

The art of prompt departure was made easier during an ''at home.'' Arrival of other callers provided fitting opportunities for leaving. The hostess stood to receive each new visitor. Social deportment required that a caller make his brief visit as interesting as possible. Conversation should not begin with the weather; some brighter topic should be found. Callers were expected to be keen and ''animated.'' On the other hand, the caller must not allow a sparkling conversation to prolong a ''morning call'' beyond its customary brevity. An appropriate moment must be seized to bring it to a graceful but definite end. A caller need not always come alone. If a lady had a lady friend staying with her, she had the social right to take her to make visits. The lady of the house was ''bound to receive the latter with precisely the same amount of politeness and friendliness which she displays towards the former.'' But there were limits placed on callers. Never were they to arrive with very young children, or with dogs or other pets.

Among the calls considered obligatory was the one that had to be made three or four days after a dinner or evening party. Here, again, rules were strict for visitor and visited. The lady of the house should not express a hope that her guest had enjoyed herself at the party. Such a remark could not elicit anything but a compliment; compliments should never be ''fished for.'' The caller should never criticize any guest met at a party. If the hostess asked her what she thought of somebody who was there, the reply should be guarded. Critical answers might be repeated. They would be certain to make ''enemies of those persons so commented on.''

Victorian calls, though frequently required by etiquette, did not always mean that the caller had to enter the house. Convention permitted the leaving of calling cards. Such cards, however, had to be personally delivered. Cards should not be sent through a servant. Only one exception

was admitted. Servants could be sent to deliver cards for a lady in acknowledgment of inquiries made at her house during her own illness or the illness of someone in her household.

Rules dictated what sort of cards and how many should be taken or sent to a friend's house, in lieu of entering for a visit. All cards had to be engraved. A mother with her daughter or daughters, calling upon a lady, should leave only one card. If the house called at had grown-up daughters, or lady visitors known to the caller, two cards should be left. Where lady visitors were staying at the house, but were not acquaintances of the caller, two cards should be left, or the corner of one card should be turned down. If a caller went to a house where the lady had married sons or daughters staying with her, she should leave two cards, with the names of the married couple written in pencil on one of them. If a lady were leaving home for some considerable time she was expected to make a round of visits. It would never do simply to disappear. When a card was handed to the servant at the door, the letters P.P.C. (pour prendre congé — to take leave) should be written on it. If, however, the lady were leaving the neighborhood permanently, the initials should be P.D.A. (pour dire adieu — to say farewell).

One of the most difficult questions in etiquette — and the most severe of all the rules — concerned visits of gentlemen to ladies. Calls of ladies on gentlemen, of course, were not to be thought of. Even when a lady called upon a married couple, the visit was always to the wife. But visits of gentlemen to ladies were permissible, if the rules were observed. Married ladies or widows might receive calls from gentlemen. So might ''single ladies of a certain age.'' But even in these cases caution had to be exercised to avoid any rumor of scandal; ''great care should be taken to admit only those gentlemen who are of excellent reputation.''

Certainly, where there was only one daughter in the family, and she young and unmarried, it would be shocking if she were to have gentleman visitors during her mother's absence or illness. But if there were two or more sisters, they might ''collectively occupy their mother's place,'' to the extent of receiving those gentlemen who were well known to the family and well approved. Even in such cases, however, ''care should be taken by the sisters never to leave one alone in the drawing-room but to remain together until the visitor has taken his departure.''

All such rules were part of the highly regulated life of the period. They were considered indispensable, if a civilized society were to endure. As one 19th-century writer said: ''Many unthinking persons consider the observance of etiquette to be nonsensical and unfriendly, as consisting of meaningless forms, practised only by the silly and the idle; an opinion which arises from their not having reflected on the reasons that have caused certain rules to be established, indispensable to the well-being of society, and without which, it would inevitably fall to pieces, and be destroyed.''

Sliding Down Steep Streets

Côte des Neiges Road (Chemin de la Côte-des-Neiges) as it comes down to Sherbrooke was once the best hill in town for tobogganing and bobsledding. Back in Victorian times traffic was no problem. Côte des Neiges was a country road. Snow lay where it fell on the hill all winter long. With a little push a sled would start, gathering speed as it descended. Only a few habitants would be encountered slowly hauling their loads of manure home from the city's many stables. The sleds whizzed across Sherbrooke Street, down Guy, across St. Catherine, slowed a little before Dorchester, and then plunged down the steep lower Guy Street hill, passed under the Canadian Pacific tracks and ended the run at the tracks of the Grand Trunk.

The traffic that streams up and down Côte des Neiges today, on this first road west of Mount Royal, had then no existence, and no reason to exist. Even sleighs in winter found the hill difficult. On snowing nights it might be even disastrous. On the wild night of March 10, 1869, in a storm of sleet and snow, the men of the Montreal Snow Shoe Club, tramping on the hill, came upon an abandoned horse and sleigh, the horse quite dead. Montrealers who had fine country houses on Côte des Neiges (mansions, some of them) generally used them in summer only, retreating downtown for the winter. When winter travel had such difficulties, it is not surprising that a hill so long, so steep as Côte des Neiges was left to the toboggans and the bobsleds, with no interruption, except from an occasional farmer going or coming from Côte des Neiges village.

But even the occasional farmer might get in the way. Dr. W. George Beers, the muscular dentist who was a leader in Montreal's sports, once had the experience of shooting down Côte des Neiges, when the hill was glazed by ice, and seeing a parked horse right in his path, on Sherbrooke Street. "I remember coming down Côte des Neiges Hill," he wrote, "when at the bottom standing square in the way of crossing the street, was a *habitant's* horse and sleigh. A man stood on the road with his back to the hill, talking to the farmer. Two of us were on the toboggan, and within a few yards of the horse; the road was smooth ice. We both laid back our heads and like a flash shot under the belly of the horse between his legs. All we heard was a fierce neigh of fright from the horse."

The first great sliding hill had been McTavish Street. In 1922, when in his 82nd year, Henry Birks, the founder of Henry Birks & Sons Limited, recalled sliding down McTavish Street when a schoolboy. The ruined house of Simon McTavish, the fur trader, was still standing at the head of the street, just below Pine. It was known as "the Haunted House." Some said that even the ghost of Simon McTavish joined the fun. He had been seen sliding down McTavish hill on the lid of his coffin. From McTavish Street the tobogganers and bobsledders had been driven by encroaching traffic to Côte des Neiges. And by the 1870s some were being driven still farther west to Brehaut's Hill, in Côte St. Antoine. Brehaut's Hill made a fierce slide, steeper even than Côte des Neiges. Today it is Mountain Avenue in Westmount.

Sliding on hills abrupt as Brehaut's had all the excitement of danger. And Brehaut's was the scene of the great toboggan tragedy of the winter of 1873. The victim was John Anderson, a commercial traveller for the firm of J. P. Clark & Co., dry goods merchants. He was a well-trained athlete, a snowshoer with the Montreal Snow Shoe Club, as well as a tobogganer. They described him as "a most genial young fellow, in the prime of life, and with a fine prospect opening before him." Anderson and his friends had gone to Brehaut's Hill on a Saturday afternoon in February. The hill had a bad name among the prudent; several accidents had already happened there. But it was the most exciting hill for tobogganers.

Anderson and his friends went down several times. He said they had been "going like the wind." Then Anderson and one of his party went down together. The toboggan began swerving from the direct course. It struck against a small snow heap. Anderson's companion shot into the air. He fell head foremost, shocked but not injured. Anderson was found with his feet still in the hood of the toboggan. He was on his side, unable to move arms or legs.

His friends laid him on a toboggan. They covered him with fur robes and dragged the toboggan along Sherbrooke Street. On the way they met a crowd coming back from watching snowshoe races. It was a grim encounter. "While the blithesome spectators of the Snow Shoe Races on Saturday were wending their way homewards," wrote an eyewitness, "a mournful procession pursued its way along Sherbrooke Street on its way to the Montreal General Hospital. The party dragged a toboggan bearing an unhappy looking bundle enveloped in buffalo robes. The bundle was a human being, the toboggan, the instrument whereby a lithe, active young man, had in a moment been transformed into a mere wreck, broken, bruised, and paralysed."

At the hospital, members of the Montreal Snow Shoe Club (the "Tuques Bleues") and Masons from his lodge (the Royal Albert) took turns "in keeping the poor fellow company through the long hours of his nights of

JOHN COLLINS SKETCHBOOK

SHERBROOKE and COTE DES NEIGES

suffering.'' On April 28 John Anderson died. Anderson's death cast a gloom over hill sliding in Montreal. But the redoubtable Dr. Beers, while deploring Anderson's death, refused to allow it to drive the tobogganers away from the hills.

Dr. Beers would be asked the anxious question: ''Is there any real risk in tobogganing?'' And he would answer at once: ''Of course there is, and that's half the vim of it; but accidents happen in the best regulated sports.... You'll get jolted and jerked, and covered with snow from head to toe, but that's healthy. But you'll get many a fascinating and thrilling ride without a single upset, and scarcely a joggle. It all depends on the condition of the hill, and the character of your steerer.'' Dr. Beers had been one of those who used to slide down Côte des Neiges. The increase of traffic had driven him to Brehaut's Hill. He loved flashing down it like a comet. There might be risks on the hills, but it was likely to be so much healthier than being fainthearted and ''moping around the stove in winter.''

Sparrows Are Immigrants

It may seem surprising that the house sparrow, now the most familiar of Montreal's all-the-year-round birds, was once unknown on this island. Back in 1839, for instance, a list of Montreal's birds was drawn up by Dr. Archibald Hall. He was an eminent physician of the time, one of the earliest doctors on the staff of the Montreal General Hospital. Apart from his work in medicine, he was distinguished as a naturalist. Dr. Hall catalogued 208 species of birds observed at that time in the neighborhood. The house sparrow was not among them. It had never been seen here.

Importing the English house sparrow seemed at first to have little to recommend it. A drab little creature, it had no song at all, only a monotonous cheep. It was known as ''that nondescript little bird.'' When at last the English house sparrow began to be imported by North America it was only that it might be put to work. It would be useful as an industrious devourer of insects. Other birds ate insects, but were absent much of the year. If the sparrow could be made a winterer, it would be on hand in the later winter and early spring, when most other birds were still away but when the attack on insects should begin.

The need to wage war on insects became imperative in the 1850s. Trees in city streets and squares were being killed by ''the ravages of insects and particularly of caterpillars.'' Little could then be done to save the trees. One of the few deterrents was to girdle them with tin troughs. Filling these troughs with oil, or other liquids, might retard the infestation. At this time the first attempts were made to import the English house sparrow. The exact date of the earliest acclimatization is difficult to set with precision. As early as 1851 the Brooklyn Institute is said to have imported and released eight pairs of house sparrows. They did not survive. In 1852 the Institute raised a fund of $200. With this sum it brought in 100 more sparrows. The very fact that this species was not native, but alien, made its acclimatization hazardous.

One of the most determined and influential importers of English house sparrows was Colonel William Rhodes of Quebec. In 1854 he set six loose in Portland, Maine, and about as many more in Quebec. On freeing the birds in Portland, he wrote a letter to the Portland *Advertiser*, recommending the English sparrow as an insect destroyer. ''This idea of picking off insects with birds commended itself to the municipal authorities in Boston and other large cities,'' he said, ''who made large importations of sparrows, with the result of saving their ornamental trees from destruction.'' It was one thing to import and release English sparrows in the comparatively mild climate of most cities in the United States. It proved far harder to domesticate them in the winters of Quebec.

None survived from Colonel Rhodes's first importations. But in the winter of 1868-69 he seemed to be having greater success. His experiments in Quebec were being closely followed in Montreal. At the end of February 1869, *The Gazette* reproduced an item from the Quebec *Chronicle*. The *Chronicle* had reported that about 20 sparrows had somehow managed to live through the stormy winter. They could be seen daily, fluttering about the Quebec Artillery Barracks. ''The sparrows,'' said the *Chronicle*, ''appear to acknowledge St. Valentine's Day, even in this cold climate, as many of the birds are already paired and may be seen peering into holes in the walls with a view to finding secure nesting places. We observe that some of our citizens are erecting little sparrow houses.... We report favorably of Mr. Sparrow as a Colonist, as he is doing well and thriving.''

These colonists were already demonstrating their usefulness as insect eaters. The reporter of the Quebec *Chronicle* had seen them busily at work: ''Their utility is more particularly observable at this season of the year; the hot sun vivifies insect life several hours of the day, when from their semi-torpid state they become an easy prey to birds; the eggs, too, of the caterpillar tribes are approaching maturity. Little birds, such as the sparrow ... can commit great havoc among what will become insects at a late period.''

Encouraged no doubt by what Col. Rhodes was doing in Quebec, English house sparrows began to be imported into Montreal. A Montreal Sparrow Fund was established. It was aided by the Allan Steamship Line, which offered to bring the birds over the Atlantic free of freight charges. In 1871 this item appeared in *The Gazette*: ''ENGLISH SPARROWS. Many applications have been received by the gentleman who is introducing sparrows from England, to import a supply for other places. The subscriptions are made especially for Montreal streets and squares, and the Corporation have contributed a large proportion, besides which the Messrs. Allan have generously given free freight for the birds.

''Under these circumstances it is impossible to send the sparrows intended for Montreal to other places. Those desirous of importing sparrows are referred to Mr. E. Carpenter, 61 Lime Street, Liverpool, who has furnished sparrows for Quebec and several cities in the States. The order sent from Montreal is for 600 birds, which are to be delivered here in good condition in the month of May. Any one desiring to subscribe to the Montreal Sparrow Fund can send in their names to Mr. Cotte of the Jacques Cartier Bank.''

Though at first an alien, the English house sparrow eventually settled down so well as to become almost typically Canadian in its robustness. It retained, however, something of cockney impudence. More, perhaps, than any other wild bird, it its ready to live close to mankind. It is not really a bird for countryside or the forest. Its preference is for city life. The Canadian naturalist Thomas McIlwraith wrote in 1893: ''In winter they cling more to the centre of cities where they can be seen nestling around the sunny side of the house chimneys, grimy and sooty, but full of life and ready at any time for a fight.'' In the province of Quebec the sparrow used to be called the most religious of birds, because it was so often seen around religious buildings, such as churches or convents.

The house sparrow's name in Latin is especially descriptive. It is *Passer Domesticus*. In Latin *passer* is the word for sparrow. *Domesticus* is defined in Cassell's Latin Dictionary as ''belonging to the house or family ... a friend of the house.'' This emigrant has come to seem an old friend in his new land. The Quebec antiquarian and ornithologist Sir James M. LeMoine wrote about 100 years ago: ''The house sparrow has indeed multiplied amazingly, and though an emigrant, and not *un enfant du sol*, has found a hearty welcome.'' It had become hard to think that there was once a time in Montreal when the house sparrow was not chattering in the eaves, or leaving his footprints in the snow by the doorstep.

IF YOU PUT OUT A BIRD-FEEDER HOPING TO ATTRACT CHEERFUL CHICKADEES OR THE COLORFUL JAYS OR CARDINALS YOU ARE SURE TO GET THE DRAB HOUSE SPARROW

THE HAPPIEST TIME FOR THIS IMMIGRANT FROM ENGLAND MUST HAVE BEEN THE DAYS OF HORSES ON MONTREAL STREETS

John Collins

SKETCHBOOK

P. T. Barnum Presents Tom Thumb

"The most Wonderful Curiosity the World ever produced," P.T. Barnum declared in presenting Gen. Tom Thumb to Montreal in 1843. "The Public are respectfully informed," his announcement went on, "that the Wonderful and Astonishing DWARF, GENERAL TOM THUMB, the smallest and best proportioned man that ever walked alone, may be seen for a few days only, at ORR'S HOTEL, Notre Dame Street."

The Montrealers who crowded into Orr's Hotel on Notre Dame Street (rue Notre-Dame) in 1843 saw a real male no bigger than a doll. Tom Thumb stood 25 inches tall; he weighed 15 pounds; his feet were only three inches long; he did not come above Barnum's knee. Though Barnum presented Tom Thumb as a dwarf, he was not a dwarf but a midget.

OTTAWA
BUILDING

Barnum was only beginning his exploitation of Tom Thumb when he brought him to Montreal in the summer of 1843. He had seen him for the first time nine months before, while on a visit to Bridgeport, Connecticut. The midget's name was Charles Stratton. "After seeing him and talking to him," he said, "I at once determined to secure his services from his parents to exhibit him in public."

At that time the child was five years old. But since he was six months old he had ceased to grow. Barnum believed in making the most of his exhibits, even if he had to stretch the truth. He advertised the five-year-old child as being 11. The greater age would make his tiny size seem all the more marvellous. For publicity purposes the midget needed a name. "Charles Stratton" had no particular appeal. He renamed him Tom Thumb. Barnum borrowed the name from the legend of King Arthur's knights. Sir Tom Thumb, one of the knights, had dwelt in a golden palace with a door one inch wide; he rode in a coach drawn by white mice. Barnum took "Tom Thumb" and dropped the "Sir" for "General." The absurdity of a 25-inch general made the title irresistible. So it was as "General Tom Thumb" that Charles Stratton was brought to Montreal in 1843.

Tom Thumb, on that first visit to Montreal, was not much more than an exhibit, like a sideshow at a circus. He could be seen from 9 in the morning until 10 at night. Barnum, however, soon began to develop Tom Thumb's many talents. No longer was he on display for such long hours. He was appearing for two performances a day. He sang. He danced. He impersonated famous personages, especially Napoleon. He appeared as Cupid and shot harmless little arrows among the ladies in the audience. He posed as classical statues. He strutted about the stage, quick with puns and patter, at times quite saucy and not a little contemptuous.

The genius of Barnum as showman was seen in the way he brought Tom Thumb into the courts of Europe. In 1844 Barnum took his midget to London. He realized nothing could do as much for Tom Thumb's fame as the patronage of royalty. He persuaded the American minister to the Court of St. James's to seek an audience with Queen Victoria. The Queen commanded Tom Thumb's appearance at Buckingham Palace. He and Barnum were ushered into the royal picture gallery. The Queen was there, with Prince Albert, and her mother the Duchess of Kent, and two dozen members of the nobility.

Tom Thumb, looking "like a wax doll gifted with power of locomotion" advanced boldly to the queen, and bowed. "Good evening, ladies and gentlemen," he said in his piping voice. The salutation was well received — with hilarity. He was there for an hour. He sang, danced, gave imitations. He was witty and piquant. Barnum then took Tom Thumb to the continent. He was received by King Louis Philippe of France. In Spain he was invited to sit beside Queen Isabella to watch a bull fight. In Brussels his presence was commanded by King Leopold, Queen Victoria's uncle. Barnum and Tom Thumb returned to the United States in 1847. Both were rich.

In 1861 Barnum brought Gen. Tom Thumb back to Montreal. This time he appeared in the hall of the Mechanics' Institute on St. James Street (rue Saint-Jacques) at the corner of St. Peter (rue St-Pierre) where the Royal Bank stands today. The years between the first Montreal visit of 1843 and the return in 1861 had made an immense difference to the status of Tom Thumb. He was no longer exhibited almost like a freak in a sideshow. The reflected glitter of royalty was now upon him. As evidence of his triumphal progress "The General's Magnificent Presents received from Royalty" were placed on view in the Hall.

The Ottawa Hotel, where Tom Thumb stayed, is still there. It is on the south side of St. James Street, a little way east of McGill. Today it is shops and offices. The old name survives, as the Ottawa Building.

Gen. Tom Thumb had himself changed, between his first Montreal visit and his second. He was no longer the babylike child. He was now a little man of the world, sophisticated, educated, arrogant. He had grown, from 25 inches to 35. His weight was up from 15 pounds to 52. He wore a moustache.

This was not the last of Tom Thumb's visits. He came to Montreal again in the autumn of 1863. Barnum had something new to offer this time. The general had become a married man. Earlier in the year he had married Lavinia Warren, another midget in Barnum's troupe. Their wedding, in Grace Church in New York, had been the wedding of the year. Two thousand guests were invited. Some persons, not invited, were offering $60 for a pew.

Montrealers did not have to wait long to see Tom Thumb's bride. Only eight months after the wedding Barnum rented Nordheimer's Hall on St. James Street. There he presented "General Tom Thumb and his beautiful little wife." One Montrealer, Fred T. Claxton (uncle of Hon. Brooke Claxton) set down his memories of that visit of 1863. "There were always three or four boys and girls invited to the stage," he wrote, "to stand beside the midgets for comparison in heights, and I was among the number the day I was there, dressed in the kilt. Of course I was a head taller than the General. They had the daintiest coach and equipment I have ever seen. It was patterned after one of the royal coaches of England. On the box sat a coachman in a wig and cocked hat, while on the footboard was a footman, similarly attired. A pair of tiny Shetland ponies were at the pole, and you may be sure that there was a crowd of small boys running alongside through the streets."

Tom and Lavinia had 20 years of happy married life. The General grew portly and pompous, and a big spender, with his yacht, pedigreed horses, expensive cigars. He died of apoplexy, at the age of 45, on July 15, 1883. Ten thousand attended his funeral. Barnum certainly had not neglected Montreal down through the years when he was presenting the most profitable of all his finds — "the most Wonderful Curiosity the World ever produced."

The Way Montreal Used to Sound

When a city is transformed by time, people most often speak of "the changing scene," and of how different the city looks from what it used to be. But the sounds of a city change as much as its appearance. A city comes not only to look different, but to sound different. Every generation of Montrealers has had its own sounds; the sounds of yesterday are heard only in the memory. The wistfulness felt in recalling old sounds may have little to do with whether they were harmonious or harsh. Echoing from the past, all become nostalgic.

When the English actor Sir John Martin-Harvey (who regularly brought his company to Montreal) was writing his reminiscences, he took pleasure in recalling a very dull sound. On his winter visits he stayed in the Ritz-Carlton on Sherbrooke Street. There he could hear metal striking metal, as broken tire chains struck the mudguards every time the wheels turned. Another unmusical sound that some Montrealers remember nostalgically was the rattle of the coins in the metal change dispenser that used to hang beside the fare box, near the bus driver's right hand. The rougher the road, the louder the rattle. Early in 1975 the Montreal Transportation Commission ended change-making on its buses. Even if a bus is jolted by a pothole today, no coins rattle.

Summer used to bring the haunting, immemorial, wailing of the ragman. It was a wail most often heard in the lanes behind the houses, where he might be closer to the back doors and the cellars. When offered anything, he bargained grimly, shaking his head and parting painfully with as few coins as he could. Some of the ragmen came around with potted plants, often ferns, a little dusty. These were offered as payment. As he dealt almost always with the housewives, potted plants, in those days, were good for barter.

While the ragmen dealt almost entirely with housewives, another category of street pedlars dealt only with children. The corn vendor rang a handbell. It was much like the one used by men of the Montreal Waterworks to signal a turning off of the water supply. Then in a one-note tenor or baritone he would yell out: "Blé d'Inde! Blé d'Inde!" Children would come on the run. For a few cents each they would be handed, wrapped in grease-resistant paper, a hot, buttered, salted ear of corn. They could retire to the nearest curb or doorstep to enjoy it. The corn vendor had a charcoal stove in a two-wheel cart (like a dump-cart).

Other street vendors catered to children with ice cream, or some sort of taffy. But of all such street vendors the one who lasted longest was the seller of French fried potatoes

and popcorn. He drove about in a specially constructed horse-cart. It was roofed and had four all-glass sides. Against these glass sides popcorn was stacked. What added a distinctive note to Montreal's street sounds was his steam whistle. It had a continual, high-pitched, piercing, far-carrying note. This whistle attracted the children. For five cents, French fried potatoes or popcorn was handed out in a stiff paper cone.

Still other street sounds were made by two other kinds of street vendors: the breadman and the iceman. The sound made by the breadman was the slamming of the doors. These little doors were at the back of their closed-in wagons and on both sides. By opening one or another, the breadmen were able to draw out the different kinds of bread, buns or cakes they would carry in a basket to show the housewives. The doors were always swung shut. The breadmen (employees of the principal bakeries) slammed their way from street to street.

The icemen made a chipping sound. Their wagons were covered to shut out the melting sun. Inside were huge slabs of ice — often natural ice cut in winter from the river. With a large ice pick the iceman would chip up these slabs into blocks of approximately 25 or 50 pounds. These were delivered to customers along the route for their refrigerators. The customers had printed cards with big numbers on them to indicate how much they wanted, and these cards were put up in the front windows. The sound of chipping the ice drew the children of the neighborhood. As soon as the iceman, in his rubber apron, left his wagon to carry a block in his tongs to one of his customers, the children would scramble into the cavern-like interior of the wagon. They would snatch up chipped fragments. Sucked on a hot day, these chips were almost a substitute for ice cream. As the ice had been cut in winter from a river as yet unpolluted, the sucked fragments did no harm.

Other sounds that echo in memory are far more musical. The sound of the sleigh bells seemed to dance upon the air. It was cheerful, enlivening. Even the horses seemed to enjoy it and stepped out all the quicker. The memory of the sleigh bells is in the reminiscences of Mrs. Evelyn Cartier Springett (Mrs. Arthur Richard Springett), a grand-daughter of the famous old Montreal merchant John Torrance. "After a heavy snow," she wrote, "everything was as lovely as an enchanted forest, and the crisp, frosty air was full of the jingle of sleigh bells. Their music is now a thing of the past, but in those days it was against the law to drive in winter without them, because the soft, deep snow muffled the sound of approaching horses' hoofs. The bells were generally arranged on a strap around the

SKETCHBOOK
John Collins

SLEIGHBELLS
ON
MOUNT ROYAL

horse's belly or on the shafts of the sleigh; the smarter outfits had silver ornaments on the saddle and sometimes there were gay colored tassels under the horse's chin and a coronet of bells on his head.''

Of all sounds of the past none was so wistful as the music of the organ-grinders. Montreal had many of them; they numbered 50 in 1900. Heard too near, the street organ might have too much of grunt and wheeze. But heard a block away, through an open window, *Rigoletto* or *The*

Last Rose of Summer might have the echo of remote romance. The last of Montreal's organ-grinders seems to have died away sometime before the end of the 1950s. Arthur Lachapelle, the small old man with the long white hair, wearing a brown hat with a turned-down brim — he lasted nearly to the end. But he knew that the days of the organ-grinders, as well as his own, were almost done. ''Today people have music in their homes,'' he said in 1954. ''There is no need to go far for what they like.''

Winters of Hectic Idleness

There was a time when Montreal used to be in wintry isolation half the year. Before railways, that isolation was deep and firm. When the port closed in the autumn, contact with the outer world dwindled. The town had to live unto itself. It had little to do but seek local amusements, until that day came late in the spring when "the first fair wind" brought the first white sail from over the sea. Then business would revive. The town went back to work. It worked hard till late autumn, when the last ship sailed and the ice closed in again. It was a sign of those times that *The Gazette* became a daily for the summer months long before it became a daily all the year round. Summer was the season of action and news; winter was the season when little was being done and little was new.

In many ways winter's isolation had its charms. It created a vacuum only pleasure could fill. Such winter pleasure was not a recreation from work; it was a distraction from idleness. Even the imprisoning ice on the river, no longer serving the needs of commerce, was made to serve the needs of amusement. It provided rinks for skating, or for curling. And every winter the ice provided a ring. A "deputation of gentlemen" called on the commanding officer of the Royal Engineers in the Montreal garrison. These gentlemen asked him if he would graciously give them the benefit of his professional skill. Would he mark out on the river ice a ring exactly one mile in circumference?

During the winter, Montrealers could challenge one another to sleigh races around the ring. As each time around would be precisely one mile, they could make their bets on any number of miles they chose. The ring could also serve as a winter's "mall." It would be a place where Montrealers could drive or walk around and meet one another. After the officer of the Royal Engineers had traced out a circular mile, it would be marked by planting young fir trees in the ice. The president-elect of the ring would then invite the officer "with great ceremony" to dinner. The "remainder of the day would be passed in great conviviality."

In those isolated Montreal winters "great conviviality" became a way of life. No one need feel he was spending too much time in amusing himself. There was little else for him to do. He would not be neglecting his work, for there was little work. Giving dinners or dining out occupied much of every day. How rapidly dinner followed dinner appears in a private diary kept from 1806 to 1810 by the fur trader Joseph Frobisher, whose big mansion, Beaver Hall, stood on the slope still known as Beaver Hall Hill. This record he appropriately named the "Diary of my

dinners." Almost every entry in that diary concerns a dinner. When he was giving dinners at home, he listed his guests. These guests numbered from seven to as many as some two dozen. When not offering such winter's hospitality, he was dining out at the Beaver Club, or the Bachelors' Club (though he was no bachelor), or as a guest at the officers' mess of the 100th Regiment, or at the house of a friend.

Repeated entries concern "country parties." A country party of February 10, 1808, proved too much for him. He fell and hurt his side while trying to pull off his boots. For several days he unhappily stayed at home, painful and weak, unable to have friends in or to dine out. But as soon as he recovered, the dining was resumed with vigor. On the first day he dined at the Bachelors' Club; on the second he went on a country party; on the third he gave a dinner at home to ten guests. For country parties, friends would gather in their sleighs at some meeting place, often Place d'Armes. They would set out in procession for a drive, often to some inn in the country, or to a farmhouse where the parlor had been rented for the day. Food and wine were brought in hampers. After the rural revels, the friends drove home, often by starlight or the light of the moon.

Not only those of wealth and position enjoyed these long months of winter idleness and pleasure in the isolation of ice-bound Montreal. Clerks and mechanics were idle too. They enjoyed themselves in their own way. Thomas Storrow Brown, who came to Montreal as a young man in 1818, wrote of those winter days: "We had a six months' holiday in trade.... There were no railroads or telegraphs to keep merchants and their clerks under whip and spur all the time. Mechanics waited for spring to work. On the other hand, there being no care and little occupation during winter, all would devote themselves to frolic and jollity...."

Montreal's long winter holiday in the ice-bound era, delightful as it may have been in many ways, had one serious drawback. "Great conviviality" for so many months on end took its toll of even the toughest constitution. Joseph Frobisher's diary of his dinners is interspersed with hints of penalty. Not only did he fall and hurt his side while trying to pull off his boots after a country party; there is also an ominous reference on March 2, 1806: "Confined to the house with a slight gout in my foot."

Not even young men could stand pleasure's furious pace in those idle winters. Thomas Storrow Brown wrote: "Winter was, I have said, an idle season given to carousing.... With men, drinking was too much the great pastime. Those young men who could stand the most liquor were often the most thought of by their employers. At some dinner parties all were expected to get drunk, and lest any should be delinquents, the door would be locked to keep them from escaping.''

Such sustained indulgence made Montreal's winters a season of debilitation. In 1870, when in old age, Brown remarked on how few of the young men he had known in his own youth had survived such rigorous pleasures: ''Merchants' clerks indulged so freely that I at this moment remember less than six of all the young men and lads I then knew, who have survived the consequences. Theirs was a short and merry life, ending too often before the age of 30....''

Signs of spring heralded the end of Montreal's isolation and its rather hectic idleness. The ice of the river, weakened by the noonday sun, lost its grip. Then, always suddenly, the ice broke. The break-up was never noiseless. Sounds from huge blocks, as they rose and heaved, and battled with one another, echoed over the Montreal waterfront like ''the discharge of distant artillery.'' Perhaps some Montrealers regretted the end of the snug winter isolation, when the outer world seemed remote and the cares of work were suspended. But probably, for most, the glint of the sun on the open water brought a feeling of liberation, as they began looking downstream for a glimpse of the first white sail from over the sea. The hard-working season of Montreal's summer was about to begin. But there may have been a sense of relief from the ultimate weariness of too much ''frolic and jollity.''

John Collins SKETCHBOOK
The First Sail of Spring

The Indians of Westmount

On July 22, 1898, a gardener was digging in the grounds of the St. George's Snowshoe Club at the northeast corner of the Boulevard and Aberdeen Avenue in Westmount. When the gardener had dug down about 2-1/2 feet his spade struck bones. He dug farther. A whole skeleton was uncovered, then a second, then a third. Police Chief Harrison of Westmount was summoned. The Police Chief was taking no legal chances. He claimed the skeletons. They were deposited in the Westmount morgue.

The Westmount citizen best fitted to appraise the find was W. D. Lighthall, the lawyer who was also a historian, archeologist, and ethnologist. But he was out of town, holidaying at a seaside resort in the United States. He first heard of the skeletons when he read a brief item in his Montreal newspaper. At once he took action, even at a distance. He was in a position to act with authority, as he was Chairman of Health on the Westmount town council (and later Westmount's Mayor). He sent instructions to Police Chief Harrison. At no time were the bones to be

SKETCHBOOK

John Collins

ABERDEEN AVE

GROUNDS OF ST. GEORGE'S

discarded; they must be kept carefully for scientific purposes. The Police Chief was asked to gather any information he could about other discoveries of bones in Westmount.

When he was back in Westmount, W. D. Lighthall collected all the information and studied it. It turned out that this was by no means the first discovery. Evidences of Westmount's Indians had come to light previously. All had been unearthed in an area of about 600 by 300 yards — roughly bounded by Argyle, Montrose and Aberdeen Avenues and the Boulevard. A number of years earlier a skeleton had been uncovered, near the surface, when the cutting was being made on Argyle Avenue, a little west of the house of Mr. Earle. Some boys had gone off with the skull. They were kicking it about as a football. Earle secured it. Roots of grass interlaced the skull, showing how near the surface it had been buried.

Earlier still a skeleton had been found, also near the surface, just east of John Macfarlane's house on Montrose Avenue. It came to light when a gardener named Latter was digging a flowerbed in Macfarlane's garden. It was an impressive skeleton, over six feet long. After it was exposed a few days, Macfarlace ordered Latter to bury it again at the same spot. The flowerbed was planted on top of it. Some time afterward Latter was to find a skeleton in his own garden, at the head of Aberdeen Avenue, just opposite the St. George's Snowshoe Clubhouse. He also put it back in the earth where he had discovered it. From all this evidence W. D. Lighthall was convinced that the Indians must have had a cemetery on the slope of the mountain in Westmount. Possibly, they had a village nearby.

The site, he noted, would have been ideal for a village. It was on a plateau, about half way up the mountain. The higher ground behind it would provide shelter from prevailing winds. As the mountain was an isolated rise in the great plain of the St. Lawrence, the plateau was most favorably placed for a look-out. It was also well placed for defence; any enemies would have the disadvantage of having to mount the slope, against defenders already in a superior position to fight them off. As a village site there were other advantages. The good light soil would be suitable for the Indian crops of corn and beans. Excellent water supplies were near at hand. A fine perennial spring was only about 100 yards to the west. A little farther away was another known traditionally in Westmount as "the old Indian well," having been used by Indians at a later period.

Lighthall decided that if Indian remains had been uncovered by accident in the area, perhaps others could be uncovered by systematic excavation. The Town of Westmount granted him the services of two laborers. On Saturday, September 10, 1898, he went with them to the grounds of the St. George's Club. He chose a spot at the edge. The laborers cut a trench, about two feet deep. They reached a spot ten

feet southward from where the gardener had found the three skeletons in July. There the pickaxes struck two large stones. These stones had been placed in the form of a reversed "V," Lighthall had the stones pulled up.

Beneath them the skeleton of a tall young man lay on his right side, with face down, head toward the west, knees drawn up. The bones were covered with the nearly dry whitish earth of the locality, to a depth of about 2-1/2 feet. Two good photographs were taken before the skeleton was moved. Then the bones were examined. The form of the skull was similar to the others found in the grounds in July. The teeth were fine — all perfect except a grinder lost years before. One armbone had once been broken but had healed. The earth was searched for any hand–made objects. None was found.

Seven days later Lighthall returned to the clubhouse grounds for further excavations. Again the laborers went to work with pickaxes and shovels. They did not have far to go. Only about four or five feet north of the grave of the young man found on September 10 they again struck stones. They knew they had found a grave; the big stones had been placed in the form of the reversed "V." The stones were raised. Beneath lay the skeleton of a young girl. It was in the same crouching position as the others, though the bones were more closely bunched together. The top of the head had been laid toward the north, looking partly downward.

This skeleton was frail and slender. The skull was of a more refined type than the others: the intelligence had been higher. Evidences of youth were varied; among other things, the third molars had not erupted in either jaw. Her age must have been between 18 and 20. The search for some hand-made object, frustrated in all the other graves, was at last successful. In the girl's grave was found a single bead of white wampum. "As white wampum was the gift of a lover," commented W. D. Lighthall, "this sole ornament tells the pathetic story of early love and death."

In the 1890s W. D. Lighthall supposed that these Indians had been Mohawks. By 1922 he had come to believe they were more likely to have been Algonkins. In an address to the Royal Society of Canada he said that further research into the evidence suggested that they were Algonkins of an early tribe. This tribe was different in customs to the Algonkins found on the St. Lawrence and the Ottawa by the European settlers. It was allied to earlier Algonkin tribes in Missouri, Alabama, Kentucky, Tennessee and southwestern New York.

Lighthall's conclusion was that an early tribe of Algonkins must have been living, sometime before the year 1400, on that plateau on the mountain, near where the Boulevard was later built. As they had come to Westmount more than five centuries ago, they would certainly rank as Westmount's earliest inhabitants.

Disturbances in Church

It was a Sunday evening in April 1833. Rev. Stephen Davis, a minister from Ireland, was preaching in Montreal's Baptist Church on Ste. Hélène Street. In the midst of his sermon he could see the attention of his congregation being drawn away to the church's windows. Fire had broken out a few blocks away. And it was a spectacular fire. The British American Hotel on St. Paul Street was in flames.

Rev. Stephen Davis did his best to go on with his sermon. The fire was now his lively competitor. One or two people got up and left. He expected before long he would be preaching to empty pews. But except for the one or two deserters, his congregation stayed with him until the service was over. He marvelled at their self-restraint. He had had an earlier experience of trying to preach while a fire raged in the distance "Upon one occasion," he recalled, "though the fire was at a considerable distance, the place became so deserted, and the agitation of those who lingered so manifest, that I was obliged to break off the discourse abruptly."

A clergyman in his pulpit generally feels secure from interruption, perhaps more secure from interruption than any other public speaker can ever hope to be. He speaks in a sacred precinct, to an audience bound to observe decorum. In his pulpit he is high and lifted up.

Rev. Jacob Ellegood never expected to be interrupted when he began his sermon on the Sunday evening of April 14, 1861, in St. Stephen's Anglican Church, then on Dalhousie Street, not far from the waterfront. In the middle of his sermon a very strange thing happened — something that had never happened before. He was interrupted while he spoke; and he was interrupted by (of all people) the sexton. The sexton came right up into the pulpit and whispered in his ear. The sexton told the preacher that St. Stephen's Church had been suddenly surrounded by water. The water was running in the streets, four to six feet deep. Rev. Jacob Ellegood made no attempt to complete his sermon. He broke off at once and ended the service. When he went to the church door he found what the sexton had told him was true. Water was swirling by; formidable chunks of ice were being carried along with it. The congregation was marooned, unless someone was ready to plunge into the stream, struggle to dry ground, and bring help. Rev. Jacob Ellegood volunteered.

All his life he was a "muscular Christian," an athlete and an advocate of outdoor exercise. Not even the icy water discouraged him. His curate was ready to take his chances also. That night the spring ice, carried downstream by the current, had jammed in the river. The river had backed up behind the blocked ice, as behind a dam. Then it had overflown the banks into the city. Ellegood and his curate together waded into the flood, the curate carrying his little son on his shoulders. They both had trouble keeping their footing. The water was swift; floating ice bombarded them. But they floundered northward until they got above flood level.

Ellegood, dripping wet, ran for aid along St. Antoine Street to the southwest corner of Guy. There (where the Salvation Army Men's Hostel stands today) was the house of Montreal's mayor, Charles Séraphin Rodier. Ellegood pounded the door. The mayor's head appeared at an upper window. The mayor was bald, but his baldness was seldom seen. He made a point of wearing a wig; he had a cabinet of them. Ellegood shouted to him to come down, wigged or wigless. The mayor opened the door. Ellegood asked for a document he could take to the police, ordering them to go to St. Stephen's in boats to rescue the congregation. The mayor wrote out the order and signed it. With this authority Ellegood ran to the nearest police station and handed it in. He then ran through the April chill to his own home and into a tub of hot water.

Church services in Montreal have not been interrupted only by fire and flood. On some occasions (though they have been rare) someone has stood up in a pew and denounced the sermon. These dissidents have broken the unwritten law that a sermon must always be heard in silence, whatever the listener's disagreement might be. A young Anglican preacher, Rev. John Garth, was expressing his advanced views in a sermon at Trinity Chapel at Ste. Agathe des Monts in the Laurentians, on the Sunday morning of August 27, 1899. In this sermon he declared that the Bible was full of mistakes, that God had given infallibility to no person or book in this world, that such stories as Adam and Eve and Jonah and the whale were only myths or legends. He went on to say that the inspiration of Shakespeare and Browning differed only in degree from that of Isaiah and Paul.

His congregation consisted mostly of Montrealers who had summer places in Ste. Agathe. Among them was R. Wilson Smith, a prominent financier and a former mayor of Montreal. He did not interrupt the preacher, but the moment the sermon was over Smith, a large, heavy man, stood up in his pew. He could not, he said, refrain from declaring his disagreement from the extraordinary statements the preacher had just been making. For his part, he believed absolutely in the Bible as the Word of God. Sufficient of the prophecies had already been fulfilled to prove the infallibility of the whole. He simply could not sit

John Collins SKETCHBOOK Rue Ste. Hélène

silent and hear attacks on the Bible from a Christian pulpit. No reply was made by the preacher. He gave out the closing hymn. Then he retired to the vestry. The hymn over, the congregation sat for a time awaiting his reappearance. When he did not come out of the vestry, the congregation "slowly filed out to discuss the unusual service in which they had participated."

Not many preachers have had to contend with such aggressive interruptions. Minor interruptions occurred in many church services. The minister might be interrupted by people arriving late and causing some disturbance as they make their way into a pew. Another interruption might come when members of the congregation fell asleep, especially if they began a rhythmic snore. Most preachers learned to put up with such interruptions. They accepted them as among the minor, perhaps inevitable weaknesses of human nature. But at least one Montreal preacher regarded latecomers or sleepers as interrupters. He dealt with them accordingly.

This preacher was Rev. Donald Fraser, the Scottish minister in the 1850s at the Côté Street Presbyterian Church. A member of his congregation wrote: "He was very impatient of any interruption, and I have seen him, when a person came in late, stop in the middle of the Psalm he was reading — in the middle of a verse even — and wait, with a disapproving look on his face, till the belated comer had dropped blushing into his seat. He was also very summary in dealing with any unfortunate wight who might have been overtaken by slumber during the sermon. He would stop and look steadily at the spot until some neighbor nudged the culprit into startled wakefulness. Mr. Fraser, after this significant pause, would resume his discourse with the words, "As I was saying when I was interrupted." The anticipation of being made the centre of interest in this way had certainly a salutary effect in ensuring punctuality as well as a wakeful attention."

Billy Eckstein: Montreal's "Mr. Fingers"

For many years, back in the First World War and long afterward, the west wall of the Strand Theatre, at St. Catherine and Mansfield, was covered by an enormous painting. It depicted a man at a piano. Beneath were the words: "The World's Greatest Motion Picture Interpreter."

The "Interpreter" was Billy Eckstein. As scene followed scene on the silent screen in the Strand, Billy provided appropriate theme music. His repertoire was endless. Everything from honky-tonk to the classics. He played for hours on end, adapting his theme music to the film's changing scenes.

Though the Strand was a movie house, Billy Eckstein was its star performer. Every day, before the showing commenced, an attendant would come with a fresh handkerchief in his hand. He would shake it loose from its laundered folds. Then he would sweep the handkerchief across the ivory keyboard, removing any fleck of dust. Eckstein would appear, acknowledge the applause, seat himself at the keyboard, the lights were dimmed, the curtains parted. Movie and music began.

In his way Billy Eckstein was a virtuoso. His fingers ran, danced, swooped and leaped up and down the keyboard. Rachmaninoff, one of the greatest pianists of all time, had learned about Billy Eckstein. One day, while in Montreal, he came to the Strand to hear him. He stood in silence, listening and watching. He shook his head in disbelief, as he turned away. "Impossible!" he said. "I don't believe it."

Billy Eckstein was born in Point St. Charles on December 6, 1888, one of 14 children. His father was a German furrier, George Hugo Eckstein. His mother was Swedish. As a musician, Billy began as an "Infant Wonder" and became a "Child Prodigy." He first played in public at the age of three. At 11 he was drawing sidewalk crowds while he played in a piano dealer's window in Toronto. For two summers he performed at the Canadian National Exhibition.

At the age of 12 Billy won a scholarship at the new McGill Conservatory of Music. He went overseas to study — in Sweden and Germany. His musical education was classical; his entire career might have been that of a classical performer. But, when he returned, a department store owner in New York made him an offer to perform there. The money seemed too large to turn down. An American agency took him up and booked appearances for him all over the United States. Prospects seemed best if he continued as a "Child Prodigy" — "The Boy Paderewski."

Billy was growing up. Keeping a childlike look became a problem. Fortunately he remained small, never more than four feet and 11 inches. He was dressed in a Little Lord Fauntleroy suit. When he sprouted a beard, he had to shave twice a day. He got away with it, even in the White House, where he performed on the famous Gold Piano for President Theodore Roosevelt. The illusion could not be kept up forever. Once the act began to seem a hoax, bookings collapsed. Eckstein gave up and came home to Montreal.

Billy Eckstein was a young man embarking on a second career at a time in life when most young men were only beginning their first. He was now the "Cinema Interpreter." At first he played at the Lyric Hall, on St. Catherine, at the corner of Stanley. In 1912 Billy moved to the Strand with his movie interpretations. He was to be at the Strand for 20 years — until the talkies really began to talk.

When the Strand no longer had any role for him to play, Billy Eckstein found himself to be a displaced person — a victim of the technological revolution. But he realized that nostalgia was a marketable product. The night clubs needed live performers. And they were sentimental places, quite ready for his evocative way of bringing back the days that were no more. Just because he was so thoroughly outdated, he became a novelty. No musician of a later generation had fingers that could dance about the keys the way his could. There was his new presentation — he was now "Mr. Fingers."

Billy found his new location at the Château Ste. Rose. There he performed for another 20 years, as long as he had at the Strand. For intervals he played at the Lido Club, at the Clover Cafe in midtown Montreal, and in the Piano Top Lounge at the Berkeley Hotel.

He had other interests. Composing was combined with performing. He collaborated with Gene Buck on the song *Goodbye Sunshine, Hello Moon.* Ziegfeld made it one of his chief songs for his 1919 Follies. Billy was a great little patriot. Turned down for military service for being too small, he boosted the Victory Loan campaigns with his own songs. *"Lest You Forget"* was one for the First World War. In the Second World War he came through with a whole series. At the height of one of the war-loan campaigns, people on St. Catherine Street were astonished to hear a piano playing in the midst of the traffic. It was Billy on a flat truck, complete with an upright, playing patriotic airs as he went by.

He had a spiritual side. Though born a Presbyterian, he

later belonged to no church. Yet every day he went for ten minutes to a Roman Catholic Church near his home. And every day he walked for three miles on Mount Royal, for the sake of the quietude and the outdoors and the sense of nature. He made himself Mount Royal's watchdog. Letters to the editor went at once, if he saw anything being done that might spoil the Mountain.

Time was moving on for Billy Eckstein. But he was to go down in a blaze of glory. On May 27, 1963, the old Her Majesty's Theatre on Guy Street presented its own farewell performance. The theatre was to be closed and demolished. A special program, featuring theatrical personalities, was arranged. Billy Eckstein was to play. But in the weeks before that night Billy was not feeling well. At 74, the years had suddenly caught up with him. He just made it to the theatre. It was the very end of the program, the last act. Billy was brought on stage by Phil Maurice, of Consolidated Theatres, the owners of Her Majesty's. He was presented with a scroll and bouquet of red roses. Phil

Maurice then withdrew to the wings. Billy was left alone at the centre of the stage, to receive his acclaim.

Billy's old followers were out in force. Many of them were only boys when they came to hear him at the Strand. They now gave him the applause he loved, greater and longer than he had ever had before. When it died down, Billy spoke a few words. "I'm sorry," he apologized, "I'm not able to do some of the stuff I could do when I was younger. But I'll be back with bells on." The applause started up again. Wally Newman's orchestra struck up *Auld Lang Syne*. The asbestos curtain came down to end the evening.

The emotions and excitements of that evening proved too much for Billy Eckstein. The next day he collapsed. They hurried him to the hospital. He never regained his health. On September 23, 1963 he died. "When I can't play any longer," he used to say, "I don't want to be around any more."

SKETCHBOOK

John Collins

THE OLD STRAND

Sir Edward Beatty: McGill's Aggressive Chancellor

In 1921, when the governors of McGill chose Sir Edward Beatty, president of the Canadian Pacific Railway, to be chancellor of the university, they found themselves with an extraordinarily lively figurehead. Sir Edward was stocky. He stood erect, resolute, often with his elbows bent outwards, as if ready to do battle. His hat was definitely tilted to one side.

The new chancellor knew his own mind; he wanted his own way. Tommy Matthews, McGill's registrar, had many opportunities to see Sir Edward in action. He remarked: "Sir Edward was Irish and naturally pugnacious.... At meetings a little opposition brought a sparkle of enjoyment to his eyes, but he had won so often that he naturally rather expected to win again, and continued opposition to what he wanted was difficult for him to understand."

Beatty was determined to keep himself in shape to handle his workload. He had played soccer in college days. Now he hired a physical trainer, named Jacobi. From his house

JOHN SKETCHBOOK
Collins Beatty Memorial Hall

at 1266 Pine Avenue West (later Beatty Memorial Hall) he had easy access to Mount Royal Park. Every evening (unless impossible weather or some exceptional obligation prevented him) he would run around the mountain, dressed in an old sweater, rumpled trousers, with a peaked cap pulled to one side of his head. He also kept in shape by boxing with his trainer. Evening invitations to his house were usually for 9 o'clock, after he had been through his physical workouts.

Though taking on the role of a university chancellor, Sir Edward, with characteristic forthrightness, made no attempt to pretend he had scholarly attainments or literary inclinations. In his address to McGill he said: "Lest … there should be any doubt about it, I may as well admit frankly and publicly that I was not selected because of academic distinction or a profound knowledge of the classics. The dead languages are very dead to me."

He knew, however, he had a role to play. McGill was then a private institution, without (or almost without) government aid. It had to find the means of paying its own way. To finance McGill as a private institution large private donations were needed. By his own position, and his wide, strong contacts in the world of business, Sir Edward was able to round up subscriptions. He loved cheerful givers, but he was quite prepared to pressure the reluctant. The chancellor, at the same time, was more than a financial provider — far more. He developed a deep devotion to the university. Next to the CPR, it was the most absorbing interest of his life. He came to believe that a practical man has his place in the general management of a university. He may impart a healthy tone of reality to those who may be inclined to move among abstractions, and feed on theories.

Soon he became a dominating presence, even among McGill's governors. For many years the governors of McGill University held their meetings in the board room of the Canadian Pacific Railway. This was an odd place for university gatherings. But it suited the convenience and temperament of McGill's chancellor. Sir Edward's private office adjoined the board room; a door led from one to the other. Sir Edward could be occupied with CPR business until exactly the minute the McGill governors' meeting was due to begin (generally at 4 o'clock in the afternoon). He would step quickly through the connecting door from one room to the other carrying with him three pipes already loaded with tobacco. Meanwhile the McGill governors had been standing about chatting among themselves "Good afternoon," said Sir Edward. He had no other words for anybody, but walked at once to his position at the head of the board room table. The governors abruptly broke off their chatting, even leaving sentences unfinished. They scurried to the table to take their seats.

In those years the graduating students assembled on the campus on convocation day, then walked in procession to Loew's Theatre on St. Catherine Street, where the ceremonies took place. Chancellor Beatty stood at one side of the campus avenue, his arms akimbo, staring, even glaring, at the graduating classes as they moved by. He seemed to be trying to appraise what sort of crop McGill had produced that year. The scrutiny was disconcerting.

The chancellor's wishes were hard to withstand. He had come to believe that the man needed as dean of the Arts Faculty was the professor of classics, Dr. W. D. Woodhead, always known as "Woodie." Dr. Woodhead was entirely devoted to teaching and scholarship; he had an aversion to administration. He went to his interview with the chancellor, determined to decline the offered appointment. He came back from the interview, shamefaced and hangdogged. He had become the dean of arts. "Sir Edward," he remarked ruefully, "was in a very forceful mood today." During his chancellorship the office of principal stood vacant for a number of years. He seemed to feel no urgency in filling it. His energy and prominent association with the university led to repeated rumors that he was thinking of giving up the CPR and becoming principal himself. He had to issue public denials.

One of his last important decisions was to appoint Dr. F. Cyril James as principal and vice-chancellor in 1939. The offer was made with characteristic bluntness. "In normal circumstances," he told Dr. James, "McGill would search for a really distinguished successor in Canada and the United Kingdom, but at the present time all such people are being absorbed into the war effort. The Board of Governors would therefore like you to take on the job."

Though the chancellor's natural tendency to take charge, and have his own way, was at times resented and deplored, he won wide recognition for his zeal for McGill's interests, his own generosity, his private and secret acts of helpfulness, his graciousness as host at splendid dinners, his courage and loyalty. In the end the chancellor's strong grip had to relax. Illnesses were crowding in upon him. On March 17, 1941, he slumped in his chair with a stroke. He was wrecked in body. Impaired speech made him reluctant to preside at meetings, or even to attend them.

The long Beatty regime at McGill was drawing quietly to its close. In the last years Chancellor Beatty's stockiness was gone; he looked frail; he spoke little. But the old magnetism, the sense of his immense powers of leadership seemed to return with his death in 1943. Memory made the old Chancellor seem once more a dominating presence. "A deep silence … settled over the crowded station" as his bronze coffin was taken for the last journey, and "hats were doffed and heads bowed." And Principal James said: "We must go forward, lonelier than before, toward the goals which seemed so much nearer when he marched by our side."

Early Skiing in the Laurentians

Skiing came to Montreal for many years before the movement toward the Laurentians began. Mount Royal at first met all the skiers' needs. Skiers at first followed the traditions and habits of the snowshoers. Mount Royal was the centre of snowshoeing; it became the centre of skiing. In wintertime the Laurentians were almost closed to Montrealers. They had discovered what the region might mean for sport. But the sporting season was really from spring till autumn. The Laurentians were marvellous for hunting, fishing, swimming, boating. Most Montrealers got out before the ice formed; they did not return until the ice broke. Through the long winter months snow gathered over the Laurentian mountains, hills and trails but skiers knew little about them or made little use of them.

Some settlement had taken place in that north country, largely under the leadership of Rev. François-Xavier-Antoine Labelle. Emigration of French Canadians to the United States, he hoped, might be checked by vigorous Laurentian colonization. Father Labelle's northward settlements were to prove valuable to early skiers. French-Canadian farmhouses were almost the only accommodation many pioneering skiers from Montreal found.

One dollar was the charge for being put up for the night, meals included. Pea soup in a big pot was always at the back of the kitchen stove. Pork was also served, with boiled potatoes. Dessert was apple pie with maple syrup, and wretched coffee, or boiled black tea. Such plain and ready fare went down well after a cold day's skiing. Skiers were even tired enough to sleep in the beds, on thin mattresses (stuffed, they often thought, with something like corn husks). Such mattresses slumped in the middle. Quebec heaters made the rooms warm through the evening, but, fed with wood, they went out long before dawn. Cotton blankets or quilts had little warmth in them. Skiers learned to turn in with all their clothes on. One from New York woke up to find nose and cheeks frozen. Such farmhouse accommodation was hardship. But skiing in those early days was never thought of as an elegant luxury of the beautiful people. It was rugged. Much of its attraction lay in the challenge, the struggle, the endurance. The exhilaration of pioneering a new sport in a new region turned hardship into adventure.

Earliest skiers found the Laurentians a winter wonderland, but also a wilderness. No maps of direction or distance guided the skier through the miles of snowy expanse. Once they left the few little settlements, they slid into the awesome unknown. Laurentian trails were mapped for the first time by Tom Drummond (cousin of another early skiing enthusiast, Huntley Drummond). Tom Drummond was a civil engineer. At Mrs. Marshall's boarding house in Shawbridge he set up his headquarters. From Mrs. Marshall's he set out to trace ski trails through the bush, over hills, through valleys, across frozen lakes and rivers — all the way to Ste. Agathe.

Tom Drummond's maps were no amateurish sketches, the sort of thing somebody might trace out in skeleton lines on the back of an envelope. His maps were drawn with scientific exactitude. Those who have seen Tom Drummond's Laurentian maps remark how "beautifully done they were." For years they decorated the walls of Mrs. Marshall's boarding house. Long ago they disappeared.

Railway trains were the only means of reaching the Laurentians in the 1920s, when skiers began heading northward. They were slow, rarely on time, and struggled with hills. Skiers, so far from enjoying privileges, were severely regulated. Skis could not be brought into the coaches. All had to be checked at the station for 25 cents. On arrival skiers themselves had to go to the baggage car to take them off.

As the number of skiers increased, they demanded better service. In 1928 H. Percy Douglas, prominent in the Montreal Ski Club, went to see Sir Henry Thornton, president of the Canadian National Railways. He persuaded Sir Henry to inaugurate the first ski train to the Laurentians. The CPR soon followed. Percy Douglas described the mood on these excursions: "These early ski trains were great fun and on a bright Sunday morning all the 'regulars' would turn up. Everyone seemed to know everyone else, and the aisles were full of friends visiting up and down the train. Trips were arranged and gossip exchanged. There were bridge games and accordions, and everyone carried some kind of a pack or ruck-sack for the midday lunch — a big family party.... The costumes, especially those of the pretty girls, are most amusing to look at in old photographs."

As more and more skiers came into the Laurentians, lodges and hotels were established and developed, along with ski-tows, skijoring, and other facilities. Before long the Laurentians were dotted with skiing centres. Many were commercial hotels; others were the lodges of clubs, such as the Laurentian Lodge Club at Shawbridge; McGill's Red Birds Ski Club at St. Sauveur; or the ski chalet of the Penguin Ski Club (the women's ski club) in the St. Sauveur valley. Houses of Montrealers in the Laurentians ceased to be summer houses only. More and more Montrealers owned winterized weekend houses in the north.

SKETCHBOOK

John Collins

LAURENTIAN FARM HOUSE —

The supreme link between the old days and the new was the almost mythological figure — Herman (''Jackrabbit'') Smith-Johannsen. Living well over 100 years, he became skiing's living legend. A Norwegian engineer, he had become a salesman of engineering equipment for a company in Cleveland. After 1915 he worked in Montreal, with his weekend place at Lake Placid. The Great Depression gave him in middle age what he needed most — a justification for giving up salesmanship and heading into the north country.

In the Laurentians, Jackrabbit became a trailblazer. Mont Tremblant's highest summit today bears his name; he opened its ski runs. Trails were cut by Jackrabbit connecting many mountain villages. Trailblazing was more than mapping; he cut down trees and bushes to clear the skiers' pathways, using what he cut for firewood. When asked the secret of his stamina, he always replied that it lay in natural living.

The massive winter invasion of the Laurentians, beginning in the 1920s, expanded in the 1930s, and reached increasing sophistication after the Second World War. Communication with the Laurentians by road in winter became so easy that the skiers' specials on the railways were discontinued for want of passengers. At the many skiing resorts, skiers were emancipated from the farmhouse hardships of early days; they spent their weekends in city-like luxury.

The comfort and ease of modern Laurentian visits, while removing primitive discomforts, also ended many of the Laurentians' untouched charms. The skiers of the 1920s never heard a snowmobile. Often they could ski all day without coming upon tracks left by other skiers. Some who had known the early days in the Laurentians sometimes wondered whether they had not, after all, been the best.

Strathcona and the Regiment He Raised

The monument to the Strathcona's Horse in Dominion Square commemorates a cavalry regiment unique in Canada's military history. It was a regiment raised, mounted, equipped and transported at the expense of one man. No wonder *The Times* in London commented: "There are not many countries in the world where individual citizens are to be found able and ready to prove their patriotism on so splendid a scale."

The offer to raise this regiment came from Lord Strathcona early in the year 1900. The British government was waging its war against the Boers in South Africa — a war that was staggering badly, from disaster to disaster. In Canada the Liberal government under Sir Wilfrid Laurier had raised and dispatched one contingent and was about to dispatch a second. Just at this time came the surprising

offer from Lord Strathcona, then the Canadian High Commissioner in London, to raise and dispatch a regiment without cost to the government. Huge gifts from Lord Strathcona were not unusual. As a Montrealer he gave McGill University the Royal Victoria College and (with his cousin, Lord Mount Stephen) he gave Montreal the Royal Victoria Hospital. He had been a rich man for many years — governor of the Hudson's Bay Company, president of the Bank of Montreal, and one of the chief financiers of the Canadian Pacific Railway.

Strathcona planned the regiment carefully. Time did not allow for training men who did not know how to ride. He wanted the regiment to be recruited among men well-used to the saddle. He gave his instructions: "My proposal is that four hundred men should be recruited in Manitoba, the North-West, and British Columbia, unmarried and expert

STRATHCONA and the MONUMENT

horsemen, at home in the saddle, and thoroughly efficient as rough-riders and scouts.'' The commander of Strathcona's Horse was a man with a singularly appropriate background in frontier warfare and horsemanship: Colonel Samuel Benfield Steele of the North West Mounted Police (later Sir Samuel). They were ready to leave for embarkation at a moment's notice — all in less than two months from the date of Lord Strathcona's cable to the Canadian Government. The regiment was larger than the 400 that Lord Strathcona had at first proposed. Twenty-eight officers and 512 other ranks went over to South Africa, and reinforcements followed.

The sea journey from Halifax to Cape Town had its misfortunes. Pneumonia broke out among the 599 horses aboard. Accustomed to the high, dry atmosphere of the prairies, they could not stand an ocean voyage in winter. The spread of the pneumonia could not be checked. Scores of horses had to be thrown overboard. When the ship reached the warmer latitudes, the dorsal fins of sharks could be seen cutting the water in the wake, waiting for the carcasses. The losses were made good after they arrived.

The regiment had an undoubted western look, different from any other regiment in the war. Sir Arthur Conan Doyle, serving in South Africa as a medical officer, described them as ''a fine body of Canadian troopers … distinguished by their fine physique, and by the lassoes, cowboy stirrups, and large spurs of the North-Western plains.'' Lord Strathcona told Colonel Steele to buy anything that might be needed. ''During these strenuous days,'' Steele recalled, ''I had much encouragement from Lord Strathcona, who wrote me several kindly letters, impressing upon me that I was to spare no expense in providing for the comfort of the men and the efficiency of the regiment…. I am sure it would have been impossible to find a better equipped corps in the world.''

Strathcona's Horse was a regiment uniquely suited to special duties in scouting. It did not serve in South Africa as regular cavalry in the larger battles, but in probing and testing the Boer positions. The Boers were experienced and skilful raiders. Strathcona's Horse were depended on to feel them out, to reconnoitre kopje and donga, and discover the enemy before he struck. This type of service generally involving small detachments of Strathcona's Horse, rather than the regiment as a whole, brought with it unusual opportunities for self-reliant, quick-thinking, direct fighting — a few men fighting against a few men.

One day at Clocolan two of the Strathconas, Corporal K. C. Macdonnell and Private W. H. Ingram, both from the Canadian west, were sent to cover a ridge several miles away. When they came up to the top of the ridge they found themselves face to face with eight Boers who were coming up from the other side. The Boers had rifles; the men of the Strathcona's Horse had only revolvers. But they shot it out, until three of the Boers were killed, and two wounded. Ingram was killed. Macdonnell, though he had

been shot through the body, somehow made his way back over the four miles to Clocolan.

One of the recruits from the North West Mounted Police, Sergeant A. H. L. Richardson, won the Victoria Cross in service with Strathcona's Horse. There had been hard fighting in the village of Wolvespruit. The odds were heavily against the Strathcona's Horse. They were ordered to withdraw. Private Alex McArthur, wounded at close range in arm and thigh, was riding off when his horse was shot and rolled over upon him. Sergeant Richardson went to his rescue. His own horse had been wounded and could only drag itself along. To reach McArthur, Sergeant Richardson had to ride through ''a terrific cross-fire.'' He dismounted, drew McArthur out from under the horse, all within 300 yards of the Boers. He then pulled McArthur up beside him, and rode slowly back on his own limping horse.

The men of Strathcona's Horse had enlisted for a year's service. At the end of the year it was the general impression that the war was almost at an end. Word came to the regiment at Viljoen's Drift that they were to embark for Canada. They were praised for what they had done. ''I have never served with a nobler, braver or more serviceable body of men,'' said General Sir Redvers Buller. ''It shall be my privilege when I meet my friend, Lord Strathcona, to tell him what a magnificent body of men bear his name.'' Lord Strathcona welcomed them to London, provided comfortable quarters and a round of entertainment. He made arrangements with Buckingham Palace for the regiment to be reviewed inside the grounds. King Edward VII himself presented the men with their medals.

The monument in Dominion Square honors both Lord Strathcona for his ''patriotism and public service'' and the regiment he raised. The north side of the monument has an oval bas-relief of Strathcona. Surmounting the pedestal is the dramatic bronze figure of a trooper of the regiment grasping the bridle of a rearing charger. The sculptor came from the Eastern Townships — George W. Hill. He was a competent sculptor, trained in Paris: among his other statues are the Cartier memorial in Fletcher's Field, the War Memorial in Westmount, and the memorials to George Brown and Thomas D'Arcy McGee in Ottawa. The monument was unveiled on May 24, 1907. The ceremony was marked by one of the most massive military displays Montreal had ever seen.

The idea of the sculptor in depicting a Strathcona Horseman restraining his charger by the bridle was something more than an artist's fancy. The men in the regiment had spirited horses but knew how to handle them. When the regiment turned its horses over to General French's cavalry, they went out of control. Colonel Sam Steele says that several of them bucked so badly that he had, ''at the request of the remount officer, to send some of the men over to remind them that they had to behave themselves.''

Sir John A. Almost Fought a Duel in Montreal

Among the most curious stories about Sir John A., and one of the least known, is that he once came near to fighting a duel in Montreal. At the time when Macdonald came to Montreal, back in the 1840s, he was a young man in his early thirties. He was described as "wearing a long-tailed coat and baggy trousers, with a loose necktie somewhat of the Byronic style. His face was smoothly shaven, as it always was, and he had the appearance of an actor."

This young man's features, however, were far from fine. He had a homely face, with an unusually large and inelegant nose. Some of his movements were oddly birdlike. Like a bird, he had a quick, all-comprehending glance, and birdlike jerking of the head. The resemblance was confirmed by the way he moved to a chair; he seemed to be alighting in a hesitating way from a flight. He was not handsome, certainly, but he was obviously clever, and agreeably jaunty.

The YOUNG JOHN A. and The old Sir JOHN

Torchlight Procession in Montreal 1877

John Collins

SKETCHBOOK Canada's First Prime Minister

Macdonald had come to Montreal in 1844 because the city had been chosen as the new capital of Canada (though the word "Canada" applied only to the present provinces of Ontario and Quebec, at that time united under a single government — the beginning of the union that was eventually to extend from coast to coast). As the recently elected member for Kingston he had come to take his place in the parliament building (converted from the old St. Ann's Market). The building stood in what today is Montreal's Place Youville. Macdonald wished to live as near as he could to the parliament building. He rented a room only two blocks away. It was over Henderson's grocery store, at the corner of St. Maurice and St. Henri.

The Montreal *Gazette* took notice of Macdonald's maiden speech in parliament. The session was scarcely three weeks old when this new member entered a debate. *The Gazette* saw him as inexperienced, but still a young man of undoubted promise. "Mr. Macdonald ... is evidently not used to parliamentary debate," *The Gazette* commented, "but he evidently has the stuff in him. He gathered up the strands of argument with great dexterity...."

The question of fighting a duel came in 1849. The Tory government had been defeated. The Reform Party, led jointly by Robert Baldwin and Louis-Hippolyte LaFontaine, was in power. It introduced the Rebellion Losses Bill — a bill to recompense those whose property had been damaged during the Rebellion of 1837-38. Tories, as the parliamentary opposition, attacked the bill with fury. They denounced the Baldwin-LaFontaine government for making no adequate distinction between those who had remained loyal during the rebellion and those who had been the rebels. By publicly compensating rebels who had suffered losses the government would be making the rebellion seem legitimate.

Debate in the parliament building on Youville Square grew frenzied. Prominent among those taunting the Tories was a member of the Reform cabinet, William Hume Blake. One of his comments outraged the Tory leader, the old stout, inflexible, redoubtable Sir Allan MacNab. The Tories demanded a retraction. "Never!" cried Blake. Tories screamed at their opponents across the floor of the house, shaking their fists. Disorder spread to the spectators in the public galleries of the house. They took up the fight. Fisticuffs were exchanged, and blows from walking sticks. Nothing could be done but to adjourn the sitting. Members left their places. Little by little the crowd was urged out of the galleries. Its shouts echoed only from corridors and vestibule.

Next day, debate on the Rebellion Losses Bill was resumed. Blake spoke. He was reading extracts from documents. Apparently he was adapting these documents to his purpose; he was dropping out inconvenient words or passages. Macdonald interrupted him on a point of order. "I should feel obliged," he remarked, "by the honorable member reading all the words." Blake demanded: "What

does the honorable member mean?" Macdonald defined what he meant: "I want the honorable member to read the whole of it. I shall do it for him myself, if he wishes. Is it parliamentary, in reading documents, to leave out whole sentences and parts of sentences?" Old Sir Allan MacNab arose at once to support the young Tory member. In the parliament at Westminster, he said, such an unreliable reading from documents would certainly be considered irregular. Blake looked at MacNab and Macdonald with absolute scorn. He turned back to his speech with the words: "I shall read any part I like."

John A. Macdonald, being in his early thirties, did not have the caution and prudence that later political experience developed in him. The long, hot debate bred rashness. Macdonald, angered beyond endurance, sent a message, probably in writing, across the floor of the house to Blake. It was a challenge to a duel. Until recently duels had been an accepted, if not honored, custom in Canada. They were regarded as the only civilized means of defending honor, or exacting redress, in circumstances when no other recourse was possible. But a revulsion of public feeling against duelling had set in. Duels, so far from being allowed to take place as private affairs not to be interfered with, were being interrupted and prevented whenever they could be.

Macdonald and Blake were seen to leave the house. No one remarked upon it until the speaker himself astonished the members by ordering again the public galleries be cleared of all spectators, all reporters. When none remained in the house except members and officials, the speaker, Augustin Norbert Morin, announced he had been informed that Macdonald and Blake had left to fight a duel. No time must be lost. The sergeant at arms should go at once to find the two and tell them they must return to their places in the house without delay. As the symbol of his irresistible authority, the sergeant at arms was to take the mace with him. It was an extraordinary procedure. The mace, the revered symbol of Parliament, rarely, if ever, left the house.

The house was now tense with curiosity and expectation. Macdonald entered and took his place. The sergeant at arms informed the speaker he had been unable to find Blake. The speaker then commanded that Blake again be sought, arrested if found, and brought back to the house under guard. At next Monday's sitting Blake, under guard, was brought in. He and Macdonald declared in turn that they submitted to the will of the house. They gave assurances that no duel would be fought. The house, satisfied with these declarations, ordered Blake to be set free. If the speaker had not intervened in 1849, if Macdonald had fought his duel with Blake and killed or been killed, or even if he had acquired the intemperate reputation of a duellist when duels were on the wane, his whole great career in Canada's political history might have abruptly impaired, or even ended before it had really begun.

The Happy Illusion of Money

If a visitor to Montreal in the 1850s or 1860s wished to put up at the best hotel in town — one known throughout the continent — the charge would be about $2.50 a night. Such was the charge at the St. Lawrence Hall, Henry Hogan's famous hotel on St. James Street, on the north side, just west of St. François Xavier. Such a price may be contrasted with what a visitor would pay today at one of Montreal's principal hotels. It is a striking example of what inflation has done to the value of money.

Just what the St. Lawrence Hall in the 1860s was offering for $2.50 was described by a sophisticated English tourist, George Tuthill Borrett, a Fellow of King's College, Cambridge. He found "a fine handsome house, after the style of the new hotels in London and Paris, with a noble entrance-hall." The dining room was "an elegant room... entered by splendidly wide passages and corridors." Bedrooms were "large, light, and airy, and the ventilation of the building perfect."

In that Victorian age, before the clutch of modern inflation was felt, a great deal, evidently, could be offered for $2.50. This may be seen, most of all, in the meals that were included in the charge. Borrett described the overwhelming breakfast: "I found myself in about two minutes surrounded by a multitude of little oval dishes, on which were fish, steaks, chops, ham, chicken, turkey, rissoles, potatoes (boiled, roast and fried), cabbage, corn, cheese, onions, and pickles, besides plates of hot rolls, buns, crumpets, toast and biscuits, flanked by a great jug full of milk and an enormous vessel of coffee...."

"Luncheon is served on the same liberal scale, dinner, tea, and supper, ditto. It is no use trying to shirk a dish; the waiters will insist on your trying everything, so your only course is to try. Everybody tries every dish; no one feels any compunction at leaving untouched what has been brought to him; waste is immaterial, for meat is dirt-cheap, vegetables and fruit abundant." Such was pre-inflationary life at Montreal's leading hotel in mid-Victorian days. It was a time when a guest was literally being offered too much for his money — an age in which meat could be spoken of as "dirt-cheap."

Housekeeping was on an inexpensive scale. Bonsecours (in what today is Old Montreal) was the chief retail market. Here, again, cheapness and abundance prevailed. The report on prices in the Bonsecours retail market for December 10, 1890, shows how little inflation was felt, even toward the close of the Victorian era. A brace of spring chickens could be had for 80 to 90 cents. Turkeys

were 90 cents to $1.25 each. A brace of partridges was 65 to 70 cents. Among the vegetables, cabbages were 20 to 25 cents a dozen. Big hubbard squash was 10 to 15 cents each, pumpkins 10 to 20 cents. Potatos were 90 cents to $1 a bag.

Dairy products were available at comparable prices. Good dairy butter was 19 to 20 cents a pound, fresh eggs 25 to 28 cents a dozen. Among meats, choice beef was selling for 12 to 18 cents a pound, mutton from 12 to 15 cents, pork from 12 to 14 cents. As for fish, trout was 10 cents a pound, halibut 12 to 15 cents, finnan haddies were 8 to 10 cents each.

The novelist H. G. Wells, who had known the late Victorian period in London in his youth, once remarked that it was then possible to live "in the habitual enjoyment of such a widely diffused plenty and cheapness ... as no man living will ever see again." Conditions in Victorian Montreal suggest he may have been right.

It now seems surprising how well many people could live in Victorian times on what now seem very moderate incomes. In the 1880s, for example, the congregation of St. Paul's Presbyterian Church on Dorchester Street was prepared to make a really generous offer to obtain a distinguished minister from Scotland. The congregation sent a call to Rev. James Barclay, one of Scotland's eminent ministers, famous for his preaching at St. Cuthbert's in Edinburgh, and one of the Scottish chaplains to Queen Victoria. St. Paul's in Montreal was so anxious to have him come that they offered him a stipend apparently unprecedented in the city for any gentleman of the cloth. It was a stipend of $7,500.

Not all members of St. Paul's believed in extravagance on this scale. Most of them, being Scots, were likely to be outspoken in disagreement. Among them was an eccentric character, John Morrison. Rev. James Barclay, having accepted the generous offer from Montreal, preached his first two sermons in St. Paul's on a Sunday in 1883. Congregations were large. The evening service had come to its close. Morrison, like others, stood up to put on his overcoat. His Scottish voice echoed down the church, as he commented: "A verra fine deescourse, a verra fine deescourse — but no' worth $7,500 a year!" And he stalked out.

This stipend, though apparently beyond anything being paid in any other church in Montreal in the 1880s, would today be reckoned as very restrictive for a married man with children, even if he may have had a free manse. So has inflation drained money of its value. Victorian Montrealers

The
St. Lawrence Hall
of the
last
century

JOHN SKETCHBOOK
Collins St. James and St. Francois-Xavier

were living under a happy illusion. They had faith in the stable value of money.

Such faith is seen in John Donegani. He was an important Montrealer — landowner, alderman, magistrate, hotel proprietor. Among other properties, he owned an orchard. It comprised the land between Bleury and St. Alexander Streets. One evening the superior of the Jesuits, Rev. Felix Martin, and the Roman Catholic Bishop of Montreal, Mgr. Ignace Bourget, called upon him. They spoke of the need of a site for the Jesuit college — St. Mary's College. His apple orchard would be just the spot needed. Donegani agreed in 1846 to sell the orchard at a price far below its true value. He realized that this act of generosity would deprive his heirs of part of their natural inheritance. For this reason he inserted a stipulation in the deed of sale. If, at any time in the future, the land ceased to be used for the college, his heirs would receive due recompense. He set

the figure at £12,500 sterling, about $58,000 at that time. For more than a century and a quarter, St. Mary's College continued its work on the site of the orchard. But in 1976 the building was demolished. The heirs were then in a position to be paid the $58,000. But times had changed. The figure of $58,000, calculated according to the conditions of 1846, had been drastically drained of its value by 1976. Moreover, what had once had been an orchard was now near the heart of Montreal's modern office district. But John Donegani, wishing to guarantee the future of his heirs, had made a hard and fast agreement.

Montreal's Victorians were not modern men with "inflationary expectations." For them the stable value of money was the cornerstone of their lives. They would almost have lost faith in life itself, if called upon to believe that money would one day become the most perishable of all commodities.

The Worst Train Wreck

The doorbell rang violently at 2.30 in the morning of June 29, 1864. It was at the Dorchester Street house of Henry Bailey, local superintendent of traffic in the Eastern Division of the Grand Trunk Railway. Bailey was startled from sleep. As a railway superintendent, he knew such a summons at such an hour could mean only one thing: a catastrophe somewhere on the line.

He ran down to the door. A messenger was there. By the light of the messenger's lamp he read his instructions. He was to go at once by special train to Beloeil. A train had run off the bridge. A locomotive and about a dozen cars had tumbled into the Richelieu River.

Bailey went first to Sherbrooke Street — to the house of Charles J. Brydges, general manager of GTR. He found Brydges already informed and ready to set out. By a special train they, and other GTR officials, journeyed the 21 miles to Beloeil station. On that grim journey through the night, Brydges could surmise, even before he saw the wreck, what had probably happened. Between St. Hilaire and Beloeil the Richelieu River was spanned by a bridge, some 1,100 or 1,200 feet long. It was a drawbridge. Near Beloeil a section of the bridge could be swung to one side to allow masted boats to pass by on the river below. Brydges had always been anxious about that arrangement. "There was no doubt," he said later, "a drawbridge was the most dangerous thing that could exist on the main line of a railway."

From the Beloeil station, the GTR officials hurried to the river bank. The night was clear and starlit. As Brydges had feared, the drawbridge was open. In the gap below, railway cars lay in a heap, like a handful of matches tossed upon a floor. Cars lay at all angles — some this way, some that; some flat, others pointed end-up. They had crashed on to barges passing below at the time.

It was an unnerving sight. Out of the water stuck "the stark, stiff hands and feet of the dead." From the wreckage voices cried out. They were unintelligible. They shouted in an unknown tongue. The smashed train was an "emigrant special." Its passengers were nearly all Germans. They had set out from Hamburg about May 18. From Quebec they were being sent by the GTR to Upper Canada, travelling in grain cars, or in cattle cars.

The GTR sent crowded messages over its telegraph line to Montreal. Orders were sent for more special trains to be dispatched to Beloeil. Medical supplies, blankets, food — must arrive as promptly as possible. Before long they would need coffins, stacks of them. Appeals went to the Montreal General Hospital and to the Hôtel Dieu. Doctors responded. Local doctors worked with those from Montreal. GTR trains were being converted into hospital trains, to bring the injured into the city. Some patients needed immediate attention. Surgical operations had to be performed in the sheds. This was the worst railway accident in Canada's history. The final death toll rose to 99.

Horror was deepened by mystery. How could such an accident happen? A coroner's jury (including some of Montreal's principal citizens) was appointed to find out. It met for many days.

On the night of the catastrophe Henry Bailey, the Grand Trunk Railway superintendent, had spoken to the engine driver, William Burnie. He found that Burnie had survived the wreck and was sitting in the stationmaster's kitchen. Bailey testified: "He was sitting in front of the stove.... He was leaning forward and seemed overwhelmed with grief. ... I asked him how the accident happened. He said the train was on the bridge before he saw the light...." Bailey asked Burnie if he knew he was required by Regulation 24 to stop before beginning to cross the bridge. He said he knew. Then Bailey exclaimed: "Good God, how could you run into destruction in this way?" Burnie replied: "I didn't know the road, and there was no time to do anything."

As the coroner's inquiry went on the possibility emerged more and more clearly: when Burnie drove his train toward the bridge he may really not have known where he was. He had been appointed an engine driver only nine days before the accident. Except, perhaps, for one trip over the bridge, he had been driving only between Durham and Acton.

The practice of the Grand Trunk Railway was to promote firemen to be engine drivers. This was done on the theory that an experienced fireman came, by observation, to learn how a train was run. Thomas King, GTR foreman at Richmond, said William Burnie had been advanced from fireman to engine driver without any formal examination of his qualifications: "There is no board of examiners.... I did not inquire if he had any knowledge of the signals at the bridge. I give a driver charge of a train for the first time without putting a superintendent over him."

This system was criticized by Walter Shanley, one of Canada's leading civil engineers, who had been Montreal manager of the GTR from 1858 until 1862. "It is a rather short apprenticeship," he said, "to place an engineman, only nine days employed as such, over a road that he had only gone over once before."

On the tragic trip in June 1864, Burnie was uncertain of his knowledge of the road. He had no confidence in himself. He even went so far as to ask the brakeman to come into the cabin of the locomotive with him. For a brakeman to ride in the cabin with the engine driver was against the company's rules. A brakeman's place was in the cars behind. He should be ready to apply the emergency brakes, if signalled by whistle by the engine driver. The brakeman, however, felt he had to help Burnie, who did not seem to know enough about the route to run the train safely. He stayed in the cabin with Burnie as far as the St. Hilaire station. There the conductor ordered him to the rear car to attend to the tail light.

From St. Hilaire onward, Burnie did not seem aware that the approach to the bridge was on a downgrade — a downgrade that would increase the engine's speed by momentum. Burnie may not have realized he was nearing a drawbridge. He did not bring the train to a stop before entering on the bridge, as Regulation 24 required him to do. He ran right upon it. He did not even see the warning signal on the Beloeil side until he was about halfway across. He then reversed power and whistled the brakeman. But by then all was too late.

After the weeks of testimony, Coroner Jones addressed the jury on July 22, 1864. "I think it is beyond doubt," he said, "that if the rule, No. 24, had been observed, and the unfortunate train stopped, Burnie could not fail to see the danger signal...."

By 1 o'clock the next morning, the jury had reached its verdict: "It is the opinion of the undersigned that the said engine and the train were... precipitated by the gross carelessness of William Burnie, the driver." Burnie alone had been singled out by the jury for criminal responsibility. The management of the Grand Trunk Railway was only reprimanded for insufficient supervision and control.

At once controversy broke out. Critics insisted the verdict was a cover up. The "higher ups" in the GTR were being allowed to escape, while Burnie was being made the scapegoat.

William Burnie was later sentenced to ten years in prison. He did not serve his full term, but was released when the furore had died down. He was seen walking the streets of Montreal, broken physically and mentally, and pointed out as the engineer of the fatal train. Yet not everyone was convinced that Burnie deserved all the criminal responsibility for the carelessness that lost 99 lives in the worst train wreck in Canadian history.

JOHN COLLINS SKETCHBOOK
Monument to the German Immigrants
MOUNT ROYAL CEMETERY

O God! O Montreal!

An owl had its part in inspiring a poem — the best-known poem ever written about Montreal, with its refrain, "O God! O Montreal!" This owl was being stuffed in 1875 in a back room of the Montreal Natural History Society. The remarkable society, founded as far back as 1827, was a group of naturalists, nearly all amateurs. It occupied a large and imposing brick building, with a classical-columned portico, at the northwest corner of University Street and Cathcart. Many older Montrealers remember this building in its later years, when it had become the Kearns auction rooms. On the site today is the Station "B" post office.

In this building the Montreal Natural History Society had its museum. To prepare specimens of wild life for display in its cases, the society employed an old Cornishman, Samuel W. Passmore. He had the official title of "Taxidermist to the Montreal Natural History Society." Passmore took much pride in his brother, a London printer in partnership with a man with the extraordinary name of Alabaster. The firm of Passmore and Alabaster had been guaranteed prominence and prosperity by being awarded the contract to print and publish all the numerous works of one of London's most popular preachers, Rev. Charles H. Spurgeon of the Metropolitan Temple.

One day in 1875, Samuel Passmore, while stuffing an owl in the Montreal Natural History Society's museum, was surprised by an intrusive visitor. This visitor really had no business coming into Passmore's room. It was a "back room," such as every museum has, where the work of preparing exhibits goes on unseen by the public. This visitor was the Englishman Samuel Butler, the singularly talented dilettante, of moderate but adequate income, who dabbled cleverly in many things — in literature, philosophy, science and art.

Butler was in Montreal for the time being because he had been dabbling in business. He had invested in the Canada Tanning Extract Company. The company was doing badly. Butler believed, mistakenly, that if he came out to Montreal he might set everything right. As he had scientific interests, among many others, he was naturally attracted to the Natural History Society's museum. As he went about, looking at the exhibits, he happened to come upon the back room. Curiosity (always strong in him) prompted him to see what was going on there. In this room he saw Passmore stuffing the owl.

As he glanced about the room he noticed, hidden away where the public would never see them, plaster casts of several of the masterpieces of ancient Greek sculpture. Among them was a cast of one of the most admired of all Greek statues: the Discobolus (the Discus Thrower). He was scarcely surprised to see the Discobolus banished to gather dust and cobwebs. He had already found Montrealers were "as yet too busy with commerce to care greatly" about art.

"Ah," said Butler, "so you have some antiques here; why don't you put them where people can see them?"

"Well, sir," answered Passmore, "you see they are rather vulgar." The Discobolus had no pants. Butler says Passmore "talked a great deal and said his brother did all Mr. Spurgeon's printing."

Butler, with a mind essentially satirical, saw in this situation the makings of a poem. He took poet's licence to reshape the facts a little. To him it seemed more effective for his purposes to change Passmore's brother into a brother-in-law, and to make him Mr. Spurgeon's haberdasher instead of his printer.

That day's encounter with old Passmore stuffing the owl resulted in Butler's poem *A Psalm of Montreal*. In the fifth verse Butler has Passmore say:

> *"The Discobolus is put here because he is vulgar —*
> *He has neither vest nor pants with which to cover his limbs;*
> *I, Sir, am a person of most respectable connections —*
> *My brother-in-law is haberdasher to Mr. Spurgeon."*
> *O God! O Montreal!*

Butler's poem was not published for three years. On May 18, 1878, it appeared in London in *The Spectator*. It was not long in reaching Montreal. Exactly two weeks later it was reprinted in the Montreal magazine *The Canadian Spectator*. The Montreal Natural History Society bitterly resented Butler's ridicule of Samuel Passmore, respected and devoted taxidermist.

The Society felt Butler had not been understanding or fair about why it had removed the Discobolus to the back room. This cast had been donated to the Society in the early 1830s by a London benefactor, Nathaniel Gould. It was one of several. All had been so damaged in transit "as to lead to the supposition that they were irrevocably lost." At that time the Society had welcomed these gifts. Two of its members, working patiently, were able to restore them. The casts were placed on exhibition. But as the Society's collections grew, and space became limited, priority had to be given to specimens of natural history. After all, it was the Museum of the Montreal Natural History Society. Plaster casts of Greek statues, while suitable for an art gallery, were somewhat irrelevant in a museum of natural history.

Tex Dawson

A post office stands on the site of the Montreal Natural History Society museum.

When the Discobolus, and the other statues, were withdrawn from exhibition, they were not thrown out, even though they were only plaster casts and not in good condition. They were kept for the day when Montreal would have a museum of fine arts. That day came. In 1881 the Society presented these plaster casts to the Montreal Art Association, which had built a museum for fine arts on the east side of Phillips Square. There they were suitably displayed. When the young English poet Rupert Brooke visited Montreal in 1913 he made a point of finding out what had happened to the Discobolus of Butler's poem. "I made my investigations in Montreal," he said. "I have to

report that the Discobolus is very well, and, nowadays, looks the whole world in the face, almost unabashed."

To Samuel Butler, however, the banished Discobolus, gathering dust and cobwebs in the back room of the Natural History Society in 1875, seemed to symbolize Montreal's cultural backwardness, its Philistine outlook. He had found other instances of it. "A man, a true Montrealer," he wrote in his notebook, "told me he had a yearning to get away from civilization; I said we were all of us given to discontent, and seldom knew when we had got what we wanted. He did not see it, and I did not mean that he should, but I felt better for having said it."

Man and Horse — A Team

Driver and horse formed a team, partners in a common effort. The driver of an automobile, whatever his pretensions, was only a glorified mechanic. Even the drivers of carts developed a companionship with their horses. Some carters might be harsh and cruel, in the same way some motorists might be irresponsible and dangerous. But the good carter, a true teamster, felt he really was a member of a team.

How deep the bond could be was seen in the case of Télésphore Leduc. He was a teamster with the Canadian Cartage and Storage Company — the company handling freight deliveries for the Canadian National Railways. In 1927, though 74, he was still driving a team, as he had every working day for 47 years. "I like horses, love them in fact," said Leduc, "and I have never beaten a horse. Whipping is unnecessary. Gain their confidence and they will do anything they can to aid you. A horse has brains and he has feelings. He will prove to be your best friend — if you will only let him."

Télésphore Leduc was only one of many teamsters in the company who lived in friendship with their horses. An observer remarked: "It is a common sight on the city streets to see Canadian National horses nuzzle their drivers as they return from delivering an express package, or whinny when they approach, and try to search their pockets for a sweet or an apple, which they know is being carried for them. They are not afraid of the driver, nor stand in painful anticipation of a blow. To them the driver is their best friend and protector and their quiet air of confidence and well-being as they trot along the city streets is the best evidence of the care with which they are treated."

In Montreal the public had an affection for the horse that a mechanical age could not provide. This sentiment led to Montreal's great horse parades. The first of them took place in the autumn of 1926. Thousands of people would line the route from the Forum to the reviewing stand (the steps of the civic library opposite Lafontaine Park).

All companies with horse wagons had their entries: the cartage companies, the breweries, the milk companies, the laundries, the department stores, the coal companies, the bakeries. Fire horses were there, too, even cab horses. Massive draught horses were always a feature of the parade. Among them were Clydesdales, Suffolks, Shires and the grey Percherons. The sheer pride and pleasure of driving such splendid horses brought a Montreal clergyman into the parade. Rev. Edward Bushell, of St. Matthias Anglican Church of Westmount, in his clerical attire, drove a CNR wagon drawn by three huge horses abreast. "Your

vehicle," one of the judges told him later, "should have been labelled 'the Chariot of Ben Hur'."

Flags and banners fluttered along the route. Bands played lively airs as the well-groomed horses went by. The crowds cheered. The mayor awarded prizes. Aged horses, still working, had a category of their own, with special prizes. In 1927 the top prize went to Ratta of the Guaranteed Pure Milk Co. Ratta was 21 years old. Télésphore Leduc was there that day. He was awarded the shield of the League of Justice for Animals, as recognition of his long record of humane treatment. At these Horse Parades the mayor of Montreal, Médéric Martin, presided. "We see today for ourselves," he would declare, "that Montreal has horses as fine as those of any other city."

The deep understanding between driver and horse had been seen in its most dashing way in the turn-outs of the Montreal Tandem Club in late Victorian and in Edwardian days. In their displays the subtlety and sensitiveness of the partnership had reached its height of development. When members of the Tandem Club assembled on Dominion Square to begin their regular Saturday afternoon drives, hundreds of Montrealers would endure the winter cold just to witness the sophisticated spectacle of style and elegance — superb sleighs, quality harness, silver bells, deep robes and, above all, the spirited horses.

The horses did not have to be urged on. They were eager to be off. It was their occasion, as much as that of the drivers and their guests. Contemporary accounts dwell on the impression given by these horses — an impression that they were not merely animals in servitude but sharers of the excitement. It is in an account of 1876: "Then comes a stunner — a skeleton sleigh, red as fire, drawn by a trotter black as coal, which steps out grandly, chomping at his bit, swinging his head loftily, eager to be off and away on a mile stretch and with minutes to cover it. The driver sits erect in his tiny seat, clad in bearskin, looking very important."

Another writer depicts a similar scene, in 1881: " ... and how our noble animals enjoy the winter season when the roads are hard and dry and the air bracing. You see them prancing along in their handsome harness trappings....
There is no need for the whip, the music of the bells is as inspiriting to the animal as it is pleasing to the occupants of the sleigh, who sit embowered in luxurious sables." No wonder those who had known the days of transportation as a living partnership of man and beast could not be reconciled to the encroachments of mechanization. By 1911 the Montreal Tandem Club was gone. One who had known it longed for the era when the club had represented all that

was most skilful in the art of driving. Men had then "vied with one another in the smartness of their equippage and the beauty of their horses." They had known what it was to feel the tug and pull of the reins, and to relish the partnership in motion.

In earlier days the streets of Montreal had been alive. "Only a rider or driver can appreciate," he said, "the feeling of pride in the control of a high-spirited creature, born to be wild yet amenable to all the laws of civilization. That sensitive, vain, aristocratic, capricious animal that waits your pleasure, that serves your convenience, that companion of hours spent in intimate association ... that graceful, strong, lithe beast that bears you swiftly from one point to another with as much pleasure in the going and action as you yourself...

"And with all this there is the link of sympathy."

When motor vehicles got stuck the horses rode by.

From "Sairey Gamps" to Professional Nurses

An elderly woman, scarcely sober, entered the jewellery store of Richard Hemsley on Notre Dame Street one day in 1885. She had a gold watch with her and handed it to Hemsley, wanting to know how much it was worth. Hemsley examined it. Certainly it was "a beautiful gold watch." He asked her where she got it. The woman explained. She had been nursing a gentleman who had smallpox — the worst kind, known as "black smallpox." He had kept the watch beside his bed and wound it every night. When he died, his widow gave the watch to her. In that year Montreal was being swept by a smallpox epidemic. More than 3,000 died. Hemsley lost no time in giving her back the watch. He washed his hands at once with carbolic.

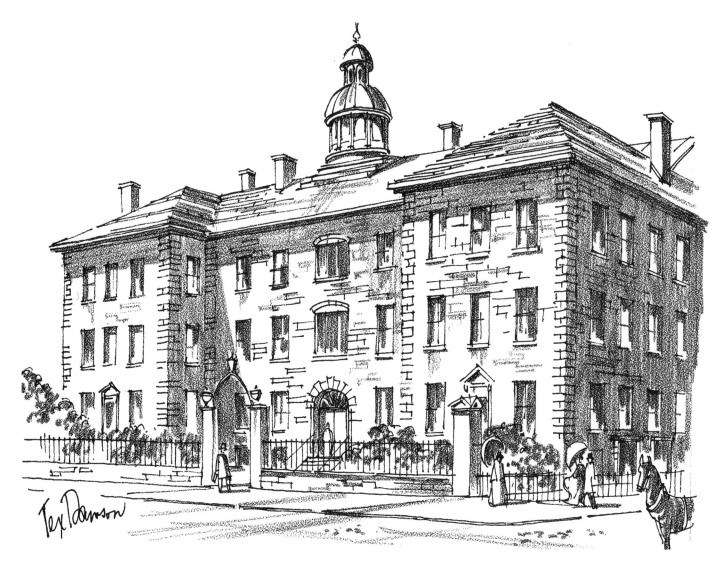

The old Montreal General Hospital on Dorchester.

In telling the story in his old age Hemsley remarked, "At that time nursing was done by a class of women quite different from what they are today." Then they were called "Sairey Gamps," after the frowsy, tippling old nurse in Charles Dickens's novel *Martin Chuzzlewit*, who used to fill her teapot with gin. These old women were rough and tough. Obstreperous or delirious patients were no problem to them. If such patients disturbed the ward, the nurse in charge would toss them flat on the bed, and strap them down, unaided. If a patient was noisy, she put a gag in his mouth. Dr. H.S. Birkett, in his student days at the Montreal General, learned how rough these nurses could be. One day he was sitting on the side of a bed, talking to the patient. From the end of the ward the nurse bellowed, "Get off that bed!" He ignored her at first; he could not believe the uncouth command was meant for him. The shout from the end of the ward was repeated. This time she added, "or I'll throw you off!" He looked around and saw the nurse was shouting at him. "Come and try!" he called back, never thinking that she might do it.

In a moment, however, she bustled down the ward and grabbed him. He thought it would be fun to wrestle a bit with her. Soon it became a wilder struggle than he had expected. Patients were delighted with this unexpected entertainment. Bets were placed, mostly on the doctor. He was slim; she had the advantage of weight. Weight counted in the end. He was floored.

Nurses in that era were in no sense professionals. They were regarded as servants and treated as servants. Night nurses were known as "watchers" — a name that suggested their limited role. Often they were hospital servants of one kind or another who were assigned to be nurses. In the 1860s, perhaps even later, they had to combine nursing with charring. They had to clean windows, wash dishes. Often they were only casual labor; the turn-over was rapid. Despite their Sairey Gamp reputation, some of these early nurses developed into reliable women, who had learned much the hard way. Dr. William Osler (the Sir William of later years) always had a respectful memory of one old woman, a Sairey Gamp in appearance, who was "equal to the best" in her devotion and skill. Such good types, however, were rare.

Patients who needed nursing care in their homes often looked to members of their families or to friends to take care of them. One Montrealer, Mrs. F.P. Shearwood, recalled that "it was not unusual for any society matron or the wives of the city clergy to be called upon to sit up at night with a patient of whom she had never heard. It was supposed to be the right and mission of women to give their fellow citizens such free nursing services." One of the reasons for trying to find some respectable person to care for the patient at home was that those who were ill dreaded the idea of going to the hospital. "In those days," said Dr. Francis J. Shepherd, "it was with the greatest difficulty patients could be induced to go into a hospital. It was the popular belief that if they went, they would never come out alive."

Conditions at the Montreal General Hospital were then so primitive that only nurses of the Sairey Gamp type would have been ready to work in them. Cockroaches were everywhere. So were the rats. Floors were worn, even worn through. Patients lay on straw mattresses. Nurses slept in cold and draughty cubicles. On winter mornings snow covered their beds.

By the 1870s the Montreal General Hospital realized the need for professionally trained nurses and a training school. Several attempts to make the necessary changes failed, or were only partially successful. Then Dr. Shepherd found exactly the person the hospital needed — Nora Livingston. The Shepherd and the Livingston families were neighbors at Como. Francis Shepherd graduated as a doctor from McGill; Nora Livingston graduated from the New York Hospital's training school. In 1890 he persuaded her to apply for the post of head nurse and director of the nurses' school at the Montreal General.

Though Nora Livingston had no experience in organizing such a school, she was an immediate success. She was a large woman, stately, with a notable resemblance to Queen Victoria. Her presence was formidable, her requirements strict, yet she could be very understanding of a nurse's problems. She saw everything, though she never attempted to spy. She believed that in a hospital everything sooner or later is found out. Around her waist she wore a gold chain with keys on it. She would rattle the keys as she walked, to give warning to the nurses of her approach. And she said "they were fools if they did not take it." She taught her students the dignity of their profession. They must let everyone know that the trained nurse was utterly different from the Sairey Gamp of other days. She also stressed that the patient had to receive devoted and skillful care: "The *patient* — always the patient first."

Every day Dr. Shepherd dropped into Miss Livingston's office for a chat. They both began to grow old. One day he said to her: "My operating days are over. I can't see now." Not long afterward, in 1919, she suffered a stroke and went back to live in Como. Even in her active years at the hospital she had always tried to go to Como on Saturdays. Mrs. H.C. Winch of Cowansville had lived in Como as a child. She recalled: "To most people who knew her, her name stood for dignity, duty and discipline, the qualities by means of which she had brought the General Hospital School of Nursing to such perfection. I, however, was privileged to know her more human side, to listen to her softly modulated voice in friendly conversations, to be with her in the meadow picking daisies, for which task she protected her hands in long white gloves lest any stain should impair their Monday morning perfection."

Strength Gone Wild! The Runaway Horse

One of Old Montreal's most terrifying sights was the runaway horse. People screamed, ran, tried to hide. Runaway horses had everything needed to intimidate — size, weight, strength, frenzy and pounding hoofs. Almost the only way a runaway horse could be brought to a standstill was to leap for the bridle; the horse's head had to be dragged down. Getting close enough to a galloping horse to seize its bridle was hard enough. Even if the bridle could be seized, immense strength was needed to pull the head down and to hold it down. A horse could rear, throw its head up. In the struggle a man could be tossed about, thrown off, then trampled. Most runaway horses in Montreal were dragged to a halt by carters or cabmen. They had learned the moods of horses and how to handle them if they went wild.

On one afternoon in December 1875, two runaway horses were stopped by cabmen or carters coming to one another's help. The first of these incidents took place in Place d'Armes. A cabby was driving his sleigh from the Place d'Armes stand. The horse was startled. The driver, thrown from his seat, tumbled backwards into the sleigh. He struggled to get up but was entangled in the fur robes. By the time he got to his feet the horse was running away. "In the nick of time," said *The Gazette's* reporter, "two carters who saw his predicament, with great presence of mind, sprang for the horse's head and prevented what would doubtless have resulted in a serious accident."

In this case, two men together were able to pull down the horse's head. One man, even if an experienced driver, might not be enough. This was demonstrated in the second runaway that December afternoon.

A cabby was sitting in his sleigh at the stand in front of one of the city's hotels — the Montreal House on Custom House Square (now La Place Royale). Some unexpected sight or sound threw the horse into a panic. It galloped off, until it struck a lamppost. The driver was jolted into the street. Though severely shaken, he still got up and laid hold of the bridle. But the horse reared and whirled him about, and was getting the better of him. Again carters came to the rescue. They, too, seized the horse's head. Only their combined strength could bring the horse under control and lead him, subdued, back to the stand in Custom House Square.

When a horse ran wild anyone in the vehicle behind faced two choices, both appalling. He could just hang on and hope for the best, or he could jump out, with the certainty of injury.

These choices confronted W. R. Baker, secretary of the CPR, on April 2, 1912. He was in his carriage, being driven down Peel Street, from St. Catherine. The horse bolted. It went galloping down the street. The lurching carriage swung past the Windsor Hotel. Baker was alarmed. The driver seemed to have lost all control. To escape an oncoming smashup, Baker jumped out. He landed heavily on the road. An ambulance carried him off to the Royal Victoria Hospital. There he was found to have suffered a discolated hip, as well as severe cuts and bruises about the head. Soon after he jumped from his carriage his driver managed to pull the horse to a halt. Baker had made the wrong decision.

At times some bystander, neither cabby nor carter, came forward as a volunteer to battle alone a runaway horse, other bystanders being too scared to share the risks. It happened at the Winter Carnival of 1884. Dominion Square was jammed by the crowd that gathered for the carnival's last night, its grand climax. Montrealers in thousands mingled with thousands of visitors, mostly Americans, drawn by a display unique in the world. On that last night the Ice Palace on Dominion Square was defended by some snowshoers, attacked by others. Fireworks were the weapons. The crowd on Dominion Square saw the attackers coming down Mount Royal, a line of torches in the dark of the winter's night. These attackers marched into the square, singing and cheering. Their arrival was the signal for battle.

Fireworks burst skyward from the battlements of the Ice Palace. The attackers replied with fireworks of their own. Shafts of flame and showers of sparks soared over "the old grey city," in a dazzling uproar. Around the edges of the square sleighs were drawn up, filled with spectators who preferred to watch the display seated in warmer comfort under the robes. Sleigh horses, however, were not accustomed to the blazing noise. On that carnival night of 1884 one of the horses panicked. It reared up, beating the air with its raised hoofs, ready to plunge into the crowd. The crowd, densely packed, could not clear out of the way.

Nearby was an American visitor. He grabbed the bridle. The horse gained new strength from its rising fears. As the carnival's display in the square rose to its climax the fireworks blazed brighter, the roar grew louder, the horse grew wilder. Though the American was leaning on the bridle with all his weight and strength, the horse, trying to shake him loose, was flinging him about. It was a sensational battle between man and beast. If the beast won, there would be a disaster in the crowded square. At last the fireworks faded out of the sky; the roar echoed away; the

Pulling on reins rarely stopped a runaway.

horse subsided. The American visitor was cheered — the hero of the carnival.

In later years, after the Boy Scouts had been established in Montreal, scout masters told the boys about the scout spirit, and brave deeds in time of danger. Inspired by these talks a Montreal Boy Scout saved two children from a runaway horse in 1913. Scout Albert Marchand was in a store at the corner of des Carrières and Drolet. Screams were heard from outside. He ran to the door of the shop.

A runaway horse was dragging a swerving coal wagon at the gallop down des Carrières Street.

At the corner, in the path of the horse, were two little girls. One was about four years old, the other about two. They did not move. Either they had not seen the horse, or fear paralysed them. Marchand dashed into the street. He swung one of the children aside, then turned back for the other. He snatched her away, just before a wheel of the coal wagon rolled over the spot where she had been.

Crime and Merriment

In Montreal in the 1870s, one of the best-known faces in police circles was the face of Ellen Collins. On the morning of June 4, 1879, Ellen Collins "was arrested for the hundredth time (approximately)." At 11 a.m. she was brought before the Recorder's Court "in a highly jubilant state." The Recorder asked her whether she was guilty of being drunk. "I'm always drunk, your honor," Ellen replied. Then, winking at the constable who had arrested her, she remarked, "But you couldn't steal a kiss though I was drunk, you thief." The Recorder asked her whether she was married or single. Her reply was pompous, "Single at present." The Recorder came to believe he was unlikely to get any serious answers from her. She was remanded (sent back to jail). There she was to be kept until in a fit condition "to answer questions properly."

The Recordre's Court, being concerned primarily with minor crimes, mostly infringements of the civic bylaws, was not accommodated in the Court House on Notre Dame Street, but, appropriately, in City Hall itself. Later it was moved to the City Hall Annex on Gosford Street.

Victorian Montrealers had a lively relish for stories from the Recorder's Court, as reported in the newpapers. They found amusement in the antics of criminals — not serious criminals, but the strays, vagrants, topers, petty thieves. Much of the fun came from the presences of the accused, the quaint naivety of their alibis and explanations. Such simplicity in crime had a kind of innocence — not that the accused were often innocent, though their excuses were.

The police who paraded them before the Recorder's Court were part of the comedy. These lordly representatives of the law always seemed comic when they appeared with their insignificant quarry – a girl, an old woman, a tattered old man.

The month of June in 1864 was particularly rich in comic criminality in Montreal. A tavern keeper was brought to court for being open on a Sunday. When the police raided his tavern the customers escaped through a rear door. The keeper himself was apprehended. He explained in court he had only gone to his tavern on Sunday because a barrel was leaking. He had to attend to it and had struck a light to see what he was doing. The police had seen the light through his window and had burst in upon his innocent occupation. A constable remarked that the leaking barrel must have been at the counter of the bar, judging by the number of customers seen standing there when the police entered. The tavern keeper was fined, with jail as an alternative if he did not pay.

One day in 1864 a woman named Bridget Best appeared in the Recorder's Court in Montreal. She laid a charge of assault against Private John Waugh of the 30th Regiment. Bridget had visited Private Waugh in his room. There she accused him of being a married man. The private, for whatever reason, resented being so described. They quarelled. In court "she bore the evidence of not having been caressed very tenderly, in the form of a black eye." Private Waugh produced witnesses. His sergeant testified he was a soldier of good character. Moreover, he had been sober on the day in question. Then the defence produced the really decisive evidence: Bridget already had two black eyes, before she entered the private's room. Court dismissed the case with costs.

Women figured rather conspicuously at the Recorder's Court. On March 20, 1867, a constable presented two women — Mrs. Mary Hayden and Mrs. Mary McGowan. The constable explained to the Recorder why he had arrested them. While walking his beat along la Gauchetière Street, he noticed a crowd in front of a saloon door. A crowd in front of a saloon meant only one thing — a fight. He pressed his way to the centre. What he saw surprised him. The combatants were two women.

The Recorder called on Mrs. Hayden to explain what had happened. She told the court that her husband had "centred his affections" on Mary McGowan. If Mrs. McGowan did not encourage his approaches, she did nothing to rebuff them. Mary Hayden then told Mary McGowan to bring the affair to an end. The response from Mary McGowan was unsatisfactory.

Since her appeal had failed, Mary Hayden resorted to sterner measures. She challenged Mary McGowan to "fight it out." This time the response was positive. The fight was on, with the indignant Mary Hayden getting the better of it. The arrival of the policeman "put an end to further bickering." As both women, in his view, were guilty of street fighting, he arrested the two of them. The Recorder, J.P. Saxton, fined both 10 shillings or 15 days in jail. Neither had 10 shillings. Both had 15 days in jail to cool their anger.

Usually the police had little difficulty in making their arrests for the sort of cases that came before the Recorder's Court. But making arrests in Griffintown, even for minor offences, might be another matter. The Irish of that community had a traditional antipathy to the constabulary, whom they called the "polissmen." If there was any trouble in Griffintown, the Irish felt quite capable of dealing with it themselves. They needed no outside help from the police.

On June 17, 1864, two constables were struggling to arrest a Griffintown Irishman for some minor crime. Almost at once a crowd gathered. The constables were then struggling not only with a powerful Irishman, but against the combined fury of dozens of local citizens. With the aid of a third policeman (a member of a federal force) they somehow held on to their prisoner and brought him in. But an account of the time states that this was not accomplished until the constables had ''suffered ... destruction of their clothes.'' In this case, the sentence was unusually severe for a Recorder's Court. The accused was fined $20 or two months in jail.

As Gilbert and Sullivan's policemen sang in chorus in *The Pirates of Penzance*: ''When constabulary duty's to be done. The policeman's lot is not a happy one.'' Certainly the policemen's lot was not a happy one in Montreal, when constabulary duty had to be done in Griffintown — even if it were only a case for the Recorder's Court. It was not funny for the constables involved, but it was for the readers of Victorian newpapers.

This Recorder's Court was located in the City Hall.

Was Dr. James Barry a Woman?

In 1865 *The Gazette* ran a curious story. It was a report from overseas that Dr. James Barry, one of the highest-ranking officers in the medical corps of the British Army, had been discovered after his death to be a woman. The strange case of Dr. James Barry became the talk of many a town. It became the talk of Montreal. He had been in Montreal much of the time

between 1857 and 1859, in the high post of Inspector-General of Hospitals for the British garrisons in Upper and Lower Canada. The claim that Dr. Barry was a female was made by the charwoman who had been engaged to lay out the body for burial. She declared Barry was a perfect woman. More than that, the doctor in earlier life had given birth to a child. The charwoman said she could tell by

Annex to Montreal City Hall stands near where Dr. Barry attended chapel.

marks on the body. She ought to know; she had had nine children herself.

Dr. Barry had tried to compensate as best he could for his unmilitary appearance. His boots had false soles three inches thick, and heels higher than customary. He made much of his elaborate uniform, with its cocked hat, big epaulettes and enormous sword. All these efforts did little for him. They only made him appear more incongruous than ever in his military role.

Dr. Barry, while in Montreal, attended services at St. John's Chapel on the upper part of Gosford Street. St. John's Chapel was serving as the Anglican cathedral. The old Christ Church Cathedral on Notre Dame Street had been destroyed by fire in 1856. Today's cathedral on St. Catherine Street was still under construction.

Among those who remembered Dr. Barry entering the chapel was John Reade, later a poet and an editorial writer at *The Gazette*. Often Reade had looked up from his prayer book to see the doctor coming in dramatically late. "We can well remember," he recalled, "the sensation which was caused when the puny Inspector-General, with her military uniform and a sword almost as large as herself, marched up the aisle of St. John's Chapel … and took her seat with the air of an emperor."

Dr. Barry occupied a house at or near the corner of Durocher and Sherbrooke Streets. He lived in style. He went about town in a covered sleigh, built to shelter him from wind and snow. It was a stunning sleigh, with red paint, musk ox robes, silver bells. In Montreal it was one of the few sleighs with both a coachman and a footman. The doctor evidently had an income over and above his army pay. He took his place in Montreal's society. John Reade used to recall the entertainments over which he presided in the house on Durocher.

Montrealers became aware of Dr. Barry's eccentricities. He was a food faddist who never ate meat. His diet was restricted to fruit, vegetables, and goat's milk. He kept a goat to assure his supply. John Reade had heard that he took the milk directly from the goat's udders. The goat was raised on a bench or table to give him easy access. Dr. Barry's vegetables had to be prepared according to his habits. He was a difficult guest to have to dinner. One Montreal hostess, having heard that he fancied boiled turnips, served a dish of mashed turnips and cream. The sight of the cream revolted him. He rejected the dish as indigestible. Whatever his personal peculiarities may have been, Dr. Barry was a skillful and progressive surgeon. He tried always to reform the military hospitals. In Canada he found conditions in these hospitals deplorable. He submitted a series of sharply worded recommendations for reform.

In his own illnesses Dr. Barry was reluctant to seek help from any other doctor. He was afraid of a medical examination. In a severe attack of bronchitis, he felt compelled to send for Dr. George W. Campbell, later dean of McGill's Medical Faculty. Dr. Campbell did not detect his patient's sex. In later years, lecturing to medical students, he used his own experience as a warning to be observant. "Gentlemen," he would say, "if I had not stood in some awe of Inspector-General Barry's rank and medical attainments, I would have examined him — that is, her — far more thoroughly. Because I did not, and because his — confound it, her — bedroom was always in almost total darkness when I paid my calls, this, ah, crucial point, escaped me." Possibly in his last illness in London, at the age of 71, Dr. Barry died without any doctor's attention. His death certificate was signed by Staff-Surgeon Major D.R. McKinnon. But it is doubtful if Dr. McKinnon had ever attended him. He later admitted: "Whether Dr. Barry was male, female, or hermaphrodite I do not know."

Reports in the press at the time of Dr. Barry's death stated army surgeons were sent to perform an autopsy on the body. They submitted an official report that the body was indeed that of a woman. The existence of this report was later confirmed by an army officer, Lt.-Col. E. Rogers. In the 1870s he was planning to write a historical novel based on Barry's life. He first wished to ascertain the facts. He was given access to the official files. He said that he read with his own eyes the autopsy report, certifying that Barry was a woman. This report, if it really existed, has since disappeared. Its alleged disappearance adds still another mystery to the Barry story.

Though he lived and was buried under the name of James Barry, no one was ever able to find out who he really was. Rumors provided suggestions. Some said his father was a Scottish earl. Others went so far as to say he was the illegitimate child of King George IV (an uncle of Queen Victoria). Some such illustrious and influential ancestry seemed needed to explain how so mysterious a person could have been protected from his enemies and advanced so far.

The clue to Dr. James Barry's life may have been contained in a small box he always had with him. While stationed in Jamaica in the 1830s he fell gravely ill. He sent for his friend, John McCrindle, chemist and druggist. Barry asked him, in case the illness proved fatal, to secure the black box and keep it carefully until it "was sent for." Barry probably had that box with him years later, while he was in Montreal. It was in his London quarters on Margaret Street where he died in 1865. On the day after his death a nobleman's footman in livery arrived and went away with the black box. Very likely the secret of Dr. Barry went with it — nobody knows where.

Indian Customs at the Beaver Club

In the winter of 1785 the Beaver Club was founded by the Nor'Westers, the fur traders of Montreal. All members had the special camaraderie of veterans. One of the original conditions of membership was that no one could be admitted who had not spent at least one winter in the wilderness of the Northwest, known as the *pays d'en haut*. All members had experienced the adventures of that merciless region. They had taken their chances of being lost, of drowning, of freezing to death, of starving, of encountering hostile Indians.

They had been toughened by hardships. Now, safe and rich in Montreal, they took all the more satisfaction in recalling together at the club's meetings that they had acquired their wealth in the hazardous way, at the risk of their lives. The motto of the club sufficiently expressed their common courage. It was engraved on the gold medal each member wore on a ribbon about his neck. The motto was: "Fortitude in distress." The customs of the Beaver Club called back memories of the members' wilderness days. Many were customs derived from the Indians.

One of these customs was giving the Indian war whoop. It demanded considerable skill, if it was to be well done — the screech that curdled the blood. As one of the club's rituals, a member would stand, a paddle in his hands, to sing a voyageur's song. An effective rendition of the war whoop brought these songs to a sensational close. A master of this performance was Hon. James McGill, the founder of McGill University. He was described as "singing a voyageur's song with accurate ear and sonorous voice, imitating, paddle in hand, the action of a bow-man of a 'North Canoe.' " He never failed, at the end, to scream the war whoop like a native.

Perhaps the most accomplished rendition of the whoop was given by William McGillivray, a pre-eminent figure at the Beaver Club, being the chief director of the Northwest Company, and the member who gave his name to Fort William (now part of Thunder Bay). McGillivray's rendition of songs and whoops was given not only at the Beaver Club's meetings but at social gatherings in his own Montreal mansion, St. Antoine House. After dinner, at his mansion, he would seat himself at the piano. With one hand he played a wild voyageur tune, *Le premier jour de mai*, singing to his own accompaniment. A guest, describing his performance, revealed how such a song must have sounded at the Beaver Club. "His practised voice", said the guest, "enabled him to give us the various swells and falls of sound upon the waters, driven about by the winds, dispersed and softened in the wider expanses, or

brought close again to the ear by neighboring rocks. He finished, as is usual, with the piercing Indian shriek."

The Indian war whoop was heard at the Beaver Club in another regular procedure. All members had to stand, kneel or sit in line. Each had a walking stick, a poker, or some other substitute for a paddle. All sang a voyageur's song in unison, as the hardy voyageurs were wont to do when descending a rapid, stemming a current, or skimming the still bosom of a romantic lake. All together gave the war whoop as the climax.

The war whoop was only one of the Indian customs at the Beaver Club. At every meeting the Indian calumet, the pipe of peace, made its appearance — the tobacco pipe with its long, ornamented stem, used by the Indians in such ceremonies as the ratification of treaties. At the Beaver Club it was passed around the table. Each guest was required to take a puff from it as a gesture of his fellowship and good will. While the calumet was making its round, a member of the club appeared, dressed in Indian costume. He made a speech, often in an Indian language.

A special Indian performance was prepared for the visit of Lord Dalhousie, the Governor-in-Chief. That meeting took place in May 1824. The club had previously moved about, from one hotel to another. Then it had settled, not unnaturally, at the best hotel in town, the Mansion House. It stood on St. Paul Street, just across the narrow side street from Bonsecours Church. Today that corner is occupied by the eastern end of the old Bonsecours Market, now civic offices.

At that meeting in 1824, the appearance of a member dressed as an Indian had more than the customary glamor. This member wore the costume of an Indian chief. After "a complimentary speech," he "threw down at his Lordship's feet a rich full Indian costume, saying 'father take that.' " It was a "magnificent" costume made of whole skins, exquisitely embroidered with stained porcupine quills, and "ornamented with the claws, teeth, and tails, of the rarest and most ferocious animals of the far interior of this vast continent." The headdress was made up from the "most beautiful feathers of birds." The whole costume, with its weapons, was valued at $500. The old account of the ceremony continues: "... and, what is more remarkable, the tribe for whom it had been produced were so far removed from the haunts of civilized men, that they had never seen a European, nor communicated with one, until a few adventurous traders had stumbled upon them in exploring those remote regions."

East end of Bonsecours Market covers site where Beaver Club met.

That gesture of presenting the "magnificent" Indian costume to the governor was one of the last of the Beaver Club's Indian ceremonies. The club was waning. There were intervals when it did not meet at all. An attempt to revive it was made in 1827. It did not — perhaps could not — succeed. Many of the Nor'Westers were gone. Their fur trading company had been absorbed by the Hudson's Bay Company, its great rival. Washington Irving, the American author who had been a guest of the club when a young

man, now wrote of the change: "... the lords of the lakes and forests have passed away; and the hospitable magnates of Montreal — where are they?"

About the Beaver Club there had always been the romance of the wilderness — the cruel region that yet had riches to yield to the adventurous. The club's Indian rituals had brought the glamor of the far Indian country even into an elegant banquet hall of Montreal's most sophisticated hotel.

Greatness and Madness on the Stage

On an August evening in 1826 a crowd blocked St. Paul Street. It pressed around the doors of the Theatre Royal (where Bonsecours Market now stands). Impatiently, it knocked on doors with sticks and rattled latches. The performance in the theatre was not due to begin for an hour. Far before opening time Montrealers gathered. They wanted to be sure to get in.

That evening they would have a chance to see and hear Edmund Kean, one of the most dazzling of English actors. He was to appear in one of his most famous Shakespearean roles — in Richard III. His acting had a strange abrupt vehemence, bursts of passion, such as no other actor seemed able to attain. The poet Byron said that seeing Kean on stage was like reading Shakespeare by flashes of lightning.

When the doors of the Theatre Royal opened the crowd burst in. For awhile it was jammed at the entrance. When it broke through it filled the theatre in a few minutes.

Montrealers' urge to seen Kean came not only from his past triumphs but from his present misfortunes. He was, in a sense, a fugitive — a man driven from his own country. At the pinnacle of his fame he had wrecked it all. He drank heavily and may also have taken drugs. His reputation was deformed by botched performances, breakdowns on stage, even failures to appear. A sex scandal was added. In 1825 he was taken to court by Albion Cox, a London alderman. Cox sued him for seducing his wife. He was awarded £800.

At Drury Lane Theatre audiences hooted Kean into silence. Other managers, fearing riots, were reluctant to have him in their theatres. Forced out of his own country, he turned to North America, hoping to re-establish his reputation. In the United States his reception was unpredictable. Some audiences applauded, others jeered. There was a riot in Boston, much trouble in New York. When Kean came north to Montreal in the late summer of 1826. He did not know what to expect. Frederick Barnes, as manager of the Theatre Royal, announced that Kean had been engaged to give citizens an opportunity to see him in his celebrated Shakespean roles — as Richard III, Shylock, Brutus, Othello, Lear.

Montrealers did not feel like kicking a great man when he was down. They waned to give him a chance to prove himself, and to encourage him to make a comeback from his disordered life. When the curtain went up on his first Montreal appearance he was greeted "with a thundering acclamation that lasted several minutes and at last seemed to cease only from eagerness to see his performance."

Kean was taking no chances. He was depending on familiar parts and old experience to carry him through. They did. He was even able to recapture at times something of the outbursts of passion, the flashes of fury, that had made him incomparable in his prime. A Montreal critic made a comment similar to Byron's many years before. He thought Kean's outbursts were like rockets at night — "sudden, soaring, explosive and radiant." All the while, however, Kean was tottering near a breakdown.

One Canadian observer, who had known Kean in England, was in a position to judge how far he had gone downhill: "I had not seen him since 1819. He had lost his former bounding elasticity of step; his little vigorous frame ... was now rather bowed down.... I had not conversed long before I saw that ... a still greater change of mind had occurred. His conversation was unsettled: he flew from one subject to another."

On the evening of August 22, "a party of respectable citizens" gave Kean "a splendid dinner" at the Masonic Hall — the Hotel on St. Paul Street, near the theatre. It was his moment of triumph and he spoke freely. He had been driven out of England, he said, by indignities and persecutions. But in Montreal his self-respect had been restored. But the abyss was still near. Before his stay in Montreal was over, he slid into it. For his last week or so he was "indisposed." With Kean "indisposition" meant only one thing. He had relapsed into old faults and habits.

Kean went on to Quebec. There he had a triumph in Shakespeare's Richard III, followed by periods of wild madness. By October he returned to Montreal and appeared again in the Theatre Royal.

Kean was in worse condition than on his first visit to Montreal, two months earlier. His voice was hoarse. Disaster came in his performance of *Macbeth*. Kean lost control of himself on stage. While speaking to King Duncan, whom he was plotting to murder, Kean burst out laughing. He could not get hold of himself. This boisterous laughter was no part of Shakespeare's play.

Then came the murder. King Duncan had retired to his room to sleep. Macbeth kills him in his bed, then emerges on stage. Kean's remorseful expression after the deed had always been one of his stunning achievements. But on this Montreal stage "the propensity to laugh" got the better of him again. A laughing murderer turned tragedy to farce. To make matters worse, a dog had somehow got onto the stage. He looked up at Kean and barked. Members of the audience began imitating dog barks. Kean gave up all attempts at self-control. He walked off the stage, laughing all the way.

This crazy performance of *Macbeth* was more than even Montreal's tolerance could accept. A drama critic at the play let Kean have it in his review. "On Wednesday," he wrote, "the tragedy of Macbeth was murdered at our Theatre, and we are sorry to say that Mr. Kean was one of the principal perpetrators of the 'horrid deed.' Never did we see a play worse performed.... Through the whole piece he was inferior."

After such a calamity, Edmund Kean left Montreal for New York, to take a ship back to England. There he still hoped to pick up the pieces of his shattered career. In his last attempt, Kean went back to another old role — *Othello.* His son was in the supporting cast. In the midst of the play, Kean had just spoken the words: "Farewell the tranquil mind." He suddenly collapsed on his son's shoulder. "I'm dying," he moaned.

When Kean was dead an application was made to the Dean of Westminster. His friends wished to bury him in the Abbey, a fitting resting place for a man who had once been the glory of the English stage. The dean rejected the application. It was the final act in the tragedy of Edmund Kean. Nobody seemed to want him, living or dead.

Edmund Kean disgraced himself on the Montreal stage.

Strange Experiences of Colonel Ham

One night about 1916 Col. George H. Ham, head of publicity for the CPR, was awakened in his house in Montreal. He heard a voice. It was just outside his bedroom door. That voice kept saying, "George Ham, George Ham, George H. Ham of the CPR." He recognized it as the voice of his old friend Reggie Graves. For some time it kept repeating the same words. They seemed a plea for help, a cry of distress. In the background he recognized the voice of another friend, Brent MacNab.

George H. Ham had an office in Windsor Station.

George Ham knew he was hearing something very strange. Reggie Graves and Brent MacNab could not be in the hallway of his home at that hour — 2 o'clock in the morning. When he turned on the light the voices ceased. When he turned it off, Reggie Graves could be heard repeating the same words. At first Ham supposed he must be dreaming. He pinched himself to see if he was awake. He was. After half an hour of silence, Ham fell asleep.

The next night he was awakened again. The hour was the same — 2 o'clock. Again the voice ceased when he turned on the light; it was heard again as soon as it was turned off. After a while Ham lit a cigarette. He smoked part of it, then stubbed it out in an ash tray beside his bed. If it were there in the morning, he would know he had not been dreaming. When he awakened in the morning he turned at once to the ash tray. The partly burned cigarette was exactly where he had put it during the night — objective evidence that he had not been asleep and dreaming when the voices were heard.

Three or four days later Reggie Graves and Brent MacNab dropped in to see him. He described to them what he had heard. Reggie Graves told him that he had been suffering at that time from a painful illness. "It's true," exclaimed Reggie, "it's true — I was in great distress and bodily pain and you were my only sheet anchor and I called out to you both nights." Reggie Graves's home was at Ste. Rose, 17 miles from where Ham lived.

George H. Ham appeared to be the last man in the world who would have an occult or mystical experience. He was a huge man, with the big, droopy moustache of the late Victorians — a man who had roughed it in the early days of the Canadian West. He seemed to be the total extrovert, an astute, no-nonsense man, looking outward rather than inward, a very practical man of the world. Sir William Van Horne had hired him in 1891 as the publicity man for the CPR. Ham's role was to get to know as many people as possible across Canada, and to get to know them by their first names. He was to publicize the railway, win friends for it, and soothe the complainers.

By a sort of contradiction in terms, George Ham was a mystical extrovert. Hearing Reggie Graves, crying out to him in the middle of the night from 17 miles away, was only one of the unearthly experiences that kept occurring throughout his long life. On another night he was awakened in his house at 4 o'clock. He could hear women's voices. While he could not make out what they were saying, he could easily distinguish one of them. It was the voice of someone he knew.

The next day he checked on the reality of what he had heard. He phoned the woman whose voice he had recognized, and told her she had been up that night till 4 o'clock, talking to other women. She said he was quite right. A neighbor had fallen ill. She had gone to see her, and had stayed with her until that late hour. The sick woman's house in Montreal was more than a mile away from George Ham's.

Other strange experiences took the form of premonitions. One spring, about 1917, Ham was in Los Angeles. He could not sleep, disturbed by a feeling of impending misfortune. Next morning he hurried to the local CPR office. Two telegrams informed him of the serious illness of one of his best friends, William Stitt, general passenger agent of the CPR. The second telegram announced that William Stitt had died that morning.

Another of George Ham's inexplicable experiences was in a haunted house. It was back in the 1870s, while he was living in Winnipeg. He and his wife rented this little house, just south of old Grace Church on Winnipeg's Main Street. During the first night in the house noises were heard. The stove in the next room "rattled like mad." They investigated. They could find nothing to cause such a racket. At other times a door would slam. When examined, it was found wide open. One night they were startled by a clatter in the kitchen, as if some tinware had crashed to the floor. They hurried downstairs. Nothing had fallen. Ham spoke to his landlord. But he only laughed. "You're hearing those noises, too," he said. "Well, I won't raise the rent anyway on that account." Ham heard of an old tradition, that the house stood on ground at one time an Indian burial place. But whether the unseen intruders were the spirits of Indians he could never know. He and his wife became accustomed to their presence. Ham said, "They didn't disturb us at all, and we got rather proud of our ghostly guests."

With his sense of mysterious forces lying below the surface of life, George Ham had reverence for the mystical element in religion. He was never a skeptic regarding the miracle-working tradition. With this attitude he became, though an Anglican, a supporter of Brother André and his shrine to St. Joseph on the side of Mount Royal. He had been impressed by what had happened there to an employee of the CPR, Martin Hannon of Quebec. This employee's legs and feet had been "terribly crushed" in an accident in 1908. Heavy marble blocks had fallen on them. He could only hobble on crutches.

According to Ham, in 1910 Hannon visited the shrine on the mountainside. Brother André rubbed his mangled limbs with oil, prayed over him, then declared him cured. From that moment, Hannon walked. He did not even need a cane. George Ham became a voluntary publicist for Brother André and the shrine. He wrote a book, *The Miracle Man of Montreal*. It sold widely in the United States, and drew many visitors and pilgrims to the shrine.

When George Ham neared the end of his days he wrote, "And now the curtain is rolling down.... With free one-way transportation to the Great Beyond ... we shall fearlessly face the great overshadowing problem: 'Where do we go from here?' The answer will come from the unknown world."

Appraising Comments on Montreal's Women

One of the earliest descriptions of the women of Montreal was written in 1749, back in the time when the city was part of New France. The commentator was a travelling Swedish scientist, Peter Kalm. He found Montreal's women vivacious, fun-loving, piquant. Kalm wrote: "One of the first questions they put to a stranger is whether he is married; the next, how he likes the ladies in the country, and whether he thinks them handsomer than those in his own country; and third, whether he will take one home with him." Kalm added: "... nobody can say that they lack either wit or charm."

Montreal's women had a keen interest in fashion, and in the latest clothes that might arrive each season from France. Even their best and most expensive dresses were soon discarded when something new was available. Sunday was their day for dressing up. They wore neat little jackets, "and a short skirt which hardly reaches halfway down the leg, and sometimes not that far ... The heels of their shoes are high and very narrow, and it is surprising how they can walk on them." On weekdays they dressed more plainly and worked hard at the household chores. Yet all week long, even when in the kitchen, their hair was "always curled, powdered and ornamented with glittering bodkins and aigrettes."

Between the girls of Montreal and those of Quebec was much rivalry and bad feeling. Montreal girls felt those in Quebec enjoyed unfair advantages. The Quebec girls saw more men, the men who came to Quebec from abroad. Ships from France put into that port. The journey farther up the river took too much time and trouble, through a tortuous channel, with the very real risk of running aground on the sand bars in Lac St. Pierre.

The girls in Montreal were "not often as happy" as those in Quebec. At 18 a Quebec girl was "reckoned very poorly off" if she could not "enumerate at least twenty lovers." A Montreal girl felt she was missing out on something by living too far upstream. Kalm wrote: "The girls at Montreal are very much displeased that those of Quebec get husbands sooner than they."

Weddings were followed by dancing — dancing that might go on for several days. Not only after weddings but at every other opportunity French-Canadian girls were ready for a dance, and they danced extremely well. In the 1840s praise came from George Warburton, a young officer of the British garrison in Canada: "I never saw one dance badly and some of them are the best waltzers and polkistes I have ever seen in a ballroom." Of one French-Canadian girl he remarked: "Her tiny feet spin round so fast they

can hardly be seen, she seems not a feather weight on them."

Even when not dancing, the tiny feet of the French-Canadian girl had attractions. Another garrison officer, Lieutenant-Colonel Burrows Sleigh, saw French-Canadian women, about 1846, in wintertime on the Champ de Mars. They were wearing Indian moccasins "tastefully worked in beads of various colors." "The (French)-Canadian women," he thought, "look very pretty ... and their feet, which are very small, look so saucy in those elegant little moccasins!"

In the countryside around Montreal the French-Canadian women were usually much better educated than their husbands. Nuns of the Congrégation de Notre Dame, founded in Montreal in the 17th century by Marguerite Bourgeoys, had gone out into the farming areas and set up convents near the parish churches. Rural schools for boys were far less frequent. The importance of the French-Canadian farm woman was observed by John McGregor, a Scottish-born writer. In a book published in 1832, McGregor noted that a French-Canadian farmer rarely concluded any business deal without first saying that he would consult his wife: "J'en parlerai à ma femme."

McGregor believed that the French-Canadian farm wife had two great advantages. She was not only better educated than her husband but also enjoyed (under the old law of "community of property") the legal right to half of all he owned. These advantages, McGregor thought, gave the wife "a great deal of consequence, and even an air of superiority to the husband."

The old narratives of visitors to Montreal have less to say about English-Canadian women than about French-Canadian. The explanation probably is that the French-Canadian women attracted more attention from the visitor because they were unfamiliar, whereas English-Canadian women were rather similar to those seen in England. As the 19th century reached its middle years, however, visitors began to notice that English-Canadian women were developing differences of their own — characteristics that made them something in their own right, as being no longer entirely like English women, or like Americans either.

Such was the impression of two English travellers who came in 1858 and 1861. On the title page of their book they were identified only as "two brothers." They wrote: "The (English)-Canadian girls are very attractive, and in many cases very fascinating in their manners. They are free and easy in their deportment when in company, and

Tourists found 19th-century Montreal women different.

exhibit very little of that reserve so often found in young ladies in England. "American girls," they said, "carry their freedom and easiness of manner to too great an extent, extreme boldness being the result, but this does not characterize the Canadians; they have the elegance of English girls, with more self-confidence." An American, writing in *Harper's Magazine* in 1889, had the same impression. English-speaking women in Canada were neither English nor American. He believed that "the original stock was good, the climate has been favorable, the athletic habits have given them vigor and courage...."

The Montreal women, the French and the English, were impressing visitors to the country with their two different ways of being distinctive, while both being Canadian.

The Telephone Seemed an Intrusion

When the telephone was introduced into Montreal in the 1870s and 1880s, many Montrealers wanted nothing to do with it. The telephone seemed an innovation that was also an intrusion. An agent tried to interest Sir William Macdonald, founder and owner of the Macdonald tobacco business, in having a phone installed in his office. "So you want everyone to have me by the ear, do you?" he asked. "Well, I'll not have it."

Some of Montreal's most prominent lawyers also disliked the idea. One of them was John Abbott, dean of McGill's Law Faculty, and later knighted and the Prime Minister of Canada. Abbott could not see how any scrupulous lawyer could preserve confidentiality in dealing with his clients if he spoke over a telephone. Someone on the wire might listen in to the conversation, or someone in the office might overhear what the lawyer was saying.

When Abbott at last consented to having a phone installed, he insisted on having it placed in the office vault. The vault's steel frame had to be bored to allow the passage of the wire. Whenever he wished to phone, Abbott would retire into the vault. There, he believed, he could be assured of the necessary privacy. This location of a phone in an office vault was not merely an eccentricity of Abbott's. Other eminent lawyers felt as he did. Among them was Strachan Bethune, Batonnier of the Montreal Bar. Bethune also had a phone installed in the vault of his law office, turning the vault into a sort of steelclad telephone booth.

Medical doctors were another category of professional men who looked upon the telephone with misgivings. It might subject them to intolerable exploitation. Patients might begin consulting their doctors over the phone. Doctors could not see how professional advice, given in this way, could be charged for.

Moreover, as doctors in that era were still making house calls, patients might begin ringing them up at all hours of the night, asking the doctors to come to see them. Before the telephone came, the only way of summoning a doctor was by sending a servant, or some member of the patient's family, or some kind family friend, to the doctor's house with a message. It was considerable effort, especially on winter nights when snow lay deep in the streets. This difficulty in summoning a doctor acted as a form of screening. A doctor was unlikely to be aroused at night except for good reason. But if telephones came into use, a doctor might be awakened by any fussy, demanding, unreasonable or hypochondriacal patient with trivial or exaggerated ailments. The doctor would become the telephone's victim.

Shopkeepers also had doubts about the value of having a phone. While a phone might enable customers to call and leave orders, it would also attract a stream of miscellaneous people from the street who would come in to ask if they could "use the phone." Montreal druggists, with their conspicuous corner stores, were particularly vulnerable. One druggist described what would happen. A woman would come into his store. "May I use your telephone, please?" she would ask. Her request had to be granted, for it would never do to refuse someone who might be a customer. Often the druggist would overhear one side of the conversation. It would go on, he said, something like this:

"Is John Jones there? May I speak to him please?" "Is that you Jack? Well, how are you feeling to-day? That's good. Oh, I'm all right, thanks. Hope you did not catch cold last night. I enjoyed it finely; the drive was just lovely. You won't forget to-night. You know where. Eight o'clock. I hope it won't rain. Well, good–bye, Jack. Mind, I shall expect you sharp on time."

After such a conversation on the druggist's phone, which might go on for any length of time, the woman would leave the store. On her way out she would smile and say "thank you." It was very unlikely that she would spend a cent. This druggist, in describing such incidents, would resort to a sort of pun. There was nothing he could do, he would say, except to "bottle up his wrath."

To Montrealers in those Victorian days the telephone seemed often as much an inconvenience as a convenience. There were other reasons why they might not want one. Reception on early phones was poor. Subscribers had difficulty hearing others or making themselves heard. Insulation was so bad that the voice of the person speaking might easily be lost among several other conversations going on over the same circuit. When long-distance service was first established between Montreal and Quebec, only one conversation could be carried on at a time. Customers had to line up and take their turn. After a while the telephone company began giving its regular customers preferential treatment. Such customers could use the wire to Quebec by appointment. Others, however, still had to line up.

From time to time telephone service might break down. Montreal, being an island, had its wires laid across the river in submarine cables. Cables were broken by anchors or carried away by ice. Early telephones were not only unreliable; they might be dangerous. Sparks flew alarmingly from then during thunderstorms. Telephone directories carried a warning in big bold type: "Do not use the telephone on the approach of or during a thunderstorm.''

Selling telephone services had still another difficulty. When the number of subscribers was small, many non-subscribers did not consider it worth while to have a phone. In 1879, Lewis B. McFarlane, who was the president of the Bell Telephone Company of Canada from 1915 to 1925, was sent from Montreal to Saint John, N.B., to introduce the telephone there. He and an assistant worked hard for two weeks, trying to sign up subscribers. Only one person was found willing to have a phone. His subscription had to be returned to him. He could hardly be charged for a phone when he would have nobody to talk to.

In Montreal, in the early 1880s, the company did not have enough subscribers to justify the printing of a directory. But it did its best to arouse interest in the telephone by publishing the names of subscribers in a series of advertisements in *The Gazette.* On January 15, 1881 the first of the series appeared. It comprised the names of the 20 ''Grain, Produce and Provision Merchants'' who were ''connected with the Exchange'' and would ''fill orders received by telephone.'' The series was continued for five days. The last advertisement included the undertakers who had phones.

Gradually the prejudices against the telephone were overcome. Its early faults and failings were corrected. By the beginning of the 20th century, the phone had become no longer a dubious intrusion into old habits but an essential way of life in an inevitably modernizing world.

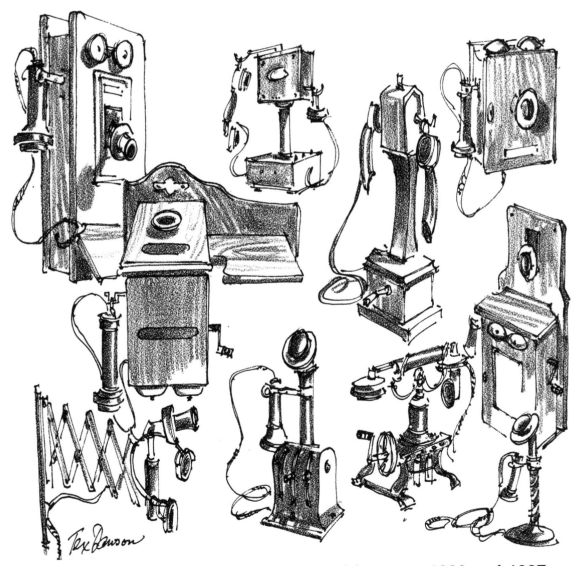

The many types of telephones used between 1900 and 1907.

Montreal in the 1911 "Free Trade" Election

"**I** am out to do all I can to bust the damn thing." One of Montreal's most eminent citizens was speaking. He was Sir William Van Horne, former president of the Canadian Pacific Railway, who came out of retirement to join the battle.

What had aroused Sir William Van Horne to this extremity of rage was the reciprocity proposal introduced by the Laurier government — the proposal that Canada and the United States should reach an agreement for partial free trade between the two countries. Van Horne saw such a proposal as the thin end of the wedge, as the beginning of

Laurier was booed at Place Viger Station in 1911

Canada's doom. "We shall trail at the tail of the commercial cart of the United States," he was convinced. "Canada must largely lose her independence." It might prove in the end the death of the nation. "We are making a bed to lie in — and die in." Van Horne was not alone in his rage. Fear and anger were spreading in Montreal.

When Laurier brought his reciprocity bill before the House of Commons, it was vigorously obstructed in every possible way by Robert Borden's Conservatives. In the end, Laurier, in frustration rather than in wisdom, did exactly what Borden hoped he would do — he went to the country in a general election. Laurier, aware of the crowds Borden was attracting, felt the tide might be turning against him, after his 15 years in office. He learned that even Liberals, of old Liberal families, were beginning to desert him and were supporting Borden.

Most spectacular, most damaging of all these defectors, was Clifford Sifton, later Sir Clifford. Sifton, in times past, had been one of the towering figures in the Liberal party and in Laurier's own cabinet. Laurier did not underestimate the immensity of the loss. "Mr. Sifton," he remarked, "was the mastermind in Parliament." The master mind was now being used for Borden's benefit. Even before the election had been called, while reciprocity was still being debated in Parliament, Sifton had parted from Laurier. He was going about the country, warning the people of the awful danger of Laurier's policy.

In March 1911, Sifton was coming to Montreal to address a Conservative meeting at Windsor Hall, alongside the Windsor Hotel. At McGill University those students opposed to reciprocity made arrangements to have him address them, earlier in the evening, in the ballroom of the McGill Union — the building on Sherbrooke Street, opposite the McGill campus, now the McCord Museum. The students had persuaded Professor Stephen Leacock to be the chairman of this meeting. Leacock did not need much persuasion. He had already come out as an active supporter of Borden on the free-trade issue. His wide popularity, and the fact he was professor of economics and political science, made him an effective ally.

Liberal students disrupted the meeting with a "hideous" uproar. Leacock appealed to them for free speech and fair play. It did little good. Sifton gave up and left for the bigger meeting at Windsor Hall. The Tories had organized a procession. Sifton would ride in an open cab, accompanied by a brass band and torch bearers. Liberal students burst through the procession. Bandsmen and torch bearers were scattered. The carriage was toppled.

Nothing, however, could stop the triumphal advance of the opponents of free trade. Everywhere prominent Liberals were abandoning Laurier to back Borden. Nowhere were the desertions more disturbing than in Montreal. The number of disillusioned Liberals grew. In one day, 14 prominent Liberals in Montreal announced they were supporting Borden. Cracks were beginning to appear even in Montreal's Jewish community, a traditional bastion of Liberalism.

Not for many years had politics in Montreal been so intense, so vehement, so loud. Even the sedate became noisy. Westmount, where elections were generally decorous, entered the storm. A political rally in Westmount was addressed by Laurier's minister of agriculture, Honorable Sydney Fisher. There, said a reporter, Fisher was confronted by "such a tumult of heckling and jeering as seldom falls to the lot of any speaker on a Canadian political platform." Reciprocity — the free-trade proposal — was the main issue. Fisher had trouble from the beginning. At times "it looked as though the meeting would break up in a row."

In the province of Quebec, the Liberals had alienated many French Canadians with another measure, unrelated to free trade. Laurier had earlier adopted the policy of establishing a Canadian navy. To French-Canadian nationalists, a Canadian navy meant eventual involvement in Britain's imperial wars. The nationalist leader, Henri Bourassa, separated from the Liberals. At least so far as this election was concerned, he would urge the province's nationalists to support the Conservatives.

On September 3, 1911 Montreal's Liberal organizers held a conference in the Windsor Hotel, in an attempt to retrieve their sinking fortunes. A group of them was seen standing in the hotel's rotunda. A reporter noted "the downcast look on the faces." They appeared like a group of "chief mourners at a funeral." On the evening of September 16, Sir Wilfrid Laurier, leaving Montreal for Quebec, went to the Place Viger Station, the old building on the south side of the square, now used as offices. A crowd of young French Canadians had gathered. As Laurier moved toward the station "they raised that ominous sound which is neither spoken nor yelled out." Laurier was being booed in his own province. He heard it, and raised his head a little more erect than usual. He hurried through the station to the platform at the rear, where he boarded his private car.

On September 19, Borden made his final appeal to the voters: "I make an earnest and sincere appeal to rise above all party ties, to take heed of the higher considerations...for the preservation of our heritage, for the maintenance of our commercial and political freedom, for the permanence of our commercial and political freedom, for the permanence of Canada."

On the evening of September 21, the results of the voting were announced. Borden was in on a landslide. The extent of the victory, he remarked, "was a matter of amazement throughout the country." Laurier's free-trade policy was dropped.

When Balbo Roared In

No one who was in Montreal on July 14, 1933 will ever forget that day. In the early afternoon, in hazy midsummer heat, General Italo Balbo arrived. Himself a dazzling personality, he came into Montreal in a stunning way. He roared in with a formation of 24 seaplanes of the Italian Air Force.

Balbo made aviation history. Until that July day, only single planes had ever succeeded in crossing the Atlantic by the treacherous east-west route. The first attempts were made in 1927, only six years before Balbo. All ended in tragedy. Planes flew out but were never seen again. In 1928, the German plane Bremen, starting from Ireland, reached Labrador. It barely made it. Fighting head winds had exhausted its gasoline supply. From 1928 to 1933, successful east-west flights remained few. All these pioneer aviators were regarded as heroes, tempters of fate. Every arrival was a miracle.

In July 1933, however, General Balbo arrived, not with one plane, but with two dozen. Had he failed, it might have become aviation's worst tragedy. As he had succeeded, it became one of aviation's greatest triumphs. No wonder the Montreal waterfront was jammed with spectators, waiting to see history in the making. They had squeezed into the entire space from below the Vickers shipyards to the pier in front of the Italian steamship line, Lloyd Mediterraneo. So aggressive was the pressure that those in front were in some danger of being shoved into the river. Yet the crowd remained cheerful, even in the pitiless heat. It was like a holiday crowd, gathered to see a regatta. In the river, ships fluttered with decorations.

Suddenly the sky roared. An eyewitness records: "The first group of six seemed to spring very quickly into view in less time than anybody had anticipated. The warning 'they are here' seemed hardly expressed when the planes were booming overhead on their harbor encircling flight...."

Balbo's fleet swept low over southern Montreal. Everyone could see its majestic precision. The formation arched widely, recrossed the river, passed inland, then dipped for the landing on the ship channel. The planes kept their triangular formation until the dive for water was signalled. Then they snapped into line. One after the other they reached the river. Huge plumes of spray leaped up, glistening in the sun. All the while a band played on shore; crowds cheered; ships' sirens screamed. General Balbo remained in his plane until the last of his fleet was in and moored. A motorboat brought him to the jetty. There a ladder had been set in place for his convenience. Ignoring it, he "leaped nimbly from boat to landing stage." The gesture was typical. He was all action, quick-moving, vital,

friendly in a completely confident way, a man distinguished by flashing eyes and a black Van Dyke beard (unexpected in the 1930s, when beards were seldom seen).

At the jetty were Montreal's Blackshirts, about 500 of them. Without authority, they had taken over, pressing aside the official guardians, the Quebec Provincial Police. Even invited guests and newspaper reporters were not allowed to come near without the Blackshirts' permission. Their methods "were a little beyond the laughing point." One reporter, holding pad and pencil, attempted to pass the Blackshirt' line. Fascist fists sent him staggering back, his hat flying. Only then was he asked to produce his pass and allowed through.

General Balbo was an eminent Fascist, one of the most popular. In 1922 he had led one of the four columns in "the March on Rome" — the coup alleged to have placed Mussolini in power as Italy's dictator. Balbo rose rapidly in the Fascist hierarchy. Eventually, as air minister, he reorganized the Italian air force, developing its extraordinary precision.

After the welcome on the Montreal waterfront, the general was taken uptown to the Mount Royal Hotel. Twenty motorcycle policemen accompanied the motorcade. At the door of the hotel, another phalanx of Montreal Blackshirts took over. They forced the crowd aside and made a clear passage. General Balbo stepped inside, between rows of arms, raised in the Fascist salute.

In the Mount Royal Hotel (then only some 10 years old), two whole floors had been reserved for the general and his men. Balbo went to his suite. There a barber stood waiting, ready to trim Balbo's beard and to shave his face to the line where the full beard began. Seated in a chair, swathed in the barber's white sheet, Balbo held his press conference. He was lively, good–humoured, bantering. He told the reporters he was a newspaperman himself, the owner of a paper in Italy. "How many papers are there in Montreal?" he wanted to know. When told, he remarked: "Bad! Too many. You ought to amalgamate."

The phone rang. Balbo was informed that Mussolini (Il Duce himself) wished to speak to him. Balbo leaped from the chair to the phone, with soap on his face and still in the barber's sheet. Reporters looked on and listened. They heard him saying in Italian, again and again, "a thousand thanks! a thousand thanks!" Mussolini was congratulating him on his success. At the close of the phone call, Balbo stood for a few moments in reverie, awed and silent. He made the Fascist salute — rather incongruously in his barber's sheet. Becoming once more aware of the presence

Mount Royal Hotel where Italian aviation hero General Italo Balbo stayed in 1933.

of the reporters, he said: "Ah, Messieurs! You do not know what he means to us... God and Mussolini are our religions." One reporter believed he had said, "Mussolini and God," in that order.

The next day, at 11.09 a.m., General Balbo left with his 24 seaplanes for Chicago. There he became a feature of the Century of Progress exhibition. On August 12, Balbo arrived back in Rome. He was accorded a triumph such as the emperors might have received. He and his men paraded afoot under the ancient Arch of Constantine. Cannon boomed. Thousands of Italian women tossed flowers and laurel leaves in his path.

Mussolini raised him to the rank of air marshal. But Balbo's success was his undoing. He was becoming too prominent, too popular for Mussolini's acceptance. Mussolini shifted him away from the centre of influence. He appointed him governor general of the Italian colony in Libya. Balbo never returned from Libya. During the Second World War his plane was shot down over Tobruk by Italian gunfire. An explanation was given. It was all a mistake. His plane had failed to give the correct recognition signals. Rumors spread that his death had been arranged. But such rumors were never confirmed.

Wartime Peril on the Sea

When John Molson set sail from the River Thames to settle in Montreal in the spring of 1782, he had an adventurous journey over the Atlantic. Those were dangerous days at sea. Great Britain was at war both with France and with its own American colonies, which became the United States. The sea lanes were menaced. It was perilous for merchant ships to sail the Atlantic alone. Most sailed in fleets, convoyed by one or more ships of the Royal Navy. The glimpse of any sails on the horizon was enough to put the merchant ships in a state of alarm and the ships of the navy into readiness for battle.

Young John Molson, later founder of the brewery, was then only 18 years of age. He was making the voyage under the care of an old family friend, James Pell. Journeying with them was Pell's son, James Pell Jr., probably about John Molson's age. The merchant fleet and its convoy set out in fine weather. They lost sight of Land's End on May 5. They were now at sea, with a seven weeks' journey ahead of them, not knowing what enemy ships they might encounter along the route. James Pell came to distrust the ship in which they were sailing. Twice she had lost touch, in stormy weather, with the convoy. Twice she had sprung a leak, and water, several feet deep, splashed about in her hold. The captain, moreover, "frequently got drunk." Pell managed to transfer himself, his son and Molson to the warship that was convoying them.

The journey was nearing its end when four sails were sighted. This seemed the moment they had feared all the way over the Atlantic. The commander had the guns readied for action. Orders were shouted for the crew to take up positions ready for defence. He ordered James Pell to the cockpit, to be on hand to help the surgeons to care for the wounded. He sent young Molson and Pell to the foretopsail braces.

The strange ships were closing in. Spyglasses were trained on them. One was sailing considerably ahead of the others. As she approached, her flags were seen to be British. Tension at once subsided. But John Molson was rather sorry that it had turned out to be only a scare. A fight at sea would have been a lively experience. "I was sorry," he wrote in his diary. He would have liked to have "seen something of the kind."

In time of war every nation encouraged attacks on enemy shipping. Officers and men of the Royal Navy were offered the lure of "prize money." Any enemy merchant ship they seized would be their "prize." The ship and its cargo would be sold and the proceeds divided, in varying amounts, among the officers and seamen. This was an attractive arrangement. Officers could grow rich. When peace returned, they could retire in comfort, even in luxury.

Not only naval officers were urged on by prize money. Private owners of ships of any kind were licensed as "privateers." If they seized merchant ships of the enemy, they would own them and any cargoes found in them. Privateering was risky. But it was the best get-rich-quick scheme of the time. Even the fishermen of Nova Scotia joined the game.

Montreal had its privateers. One of them was James Richardson, later a founder of the Bank of Montreal, the Montreal General Hospital and the Montreal Board of Trade. As a young man he joined a privateering expedition. They had initial success, capturing several prizes. Then they ran into misfortune. They met a British man-of-war, which opened fire on them, thinking they were enemies. Several of the crew were killed; the ship was crippled. The British commander realized his mistake. But he simply sailed off. The privateers were left to creep back to port as best they could.

The only security the sea offered was for those who sailed in convoy. Montreal had one ship in particular that regularly crossed the Atlantic, in the convoyed fleets of merchantmen. This ship was the *Eweretta*, commanded by a Scot, Captain Alexander Patterson. The *Eweretta* was often the first ship from overseas to reach Montreal in spring. All summer she lay in the river, near the foot of St. Sulpice Street. Then, at the season's end, she sailed for England, laden with the furs of the North West Company, and with such passengers as wished to spend the winter overseas. In those years the *Eweretta* would sail downstream to Bic in the Lower St. Lawrence. There she would take her place in the fleet of merchantmen and wait for the warships that would accompany them across the ocean.

There is a reminder of those convoys in Nelson's Monument, on Notre Dame Street, at Place Jacques Cartier. The original ornamental stone work on that monument was brought to Montreal aboard the *Eweretta*, sailing under convoy in 1808. The bill of lading for that shipment reads: "Shipped by the Grace of God, in good order and well-conditioned... upon the good ship called the Eweretta whereof is Master, under God, for the present Voyage, Alexander Patterson, and now riding at Anchor in the River Thames, and by God's Grace bound for Quebec & Montreal with Convoy: Seventeen Cases containing Ornamental Stone Work for a pillar to be erected at

Montreal to the Memory of the Immortal Nelson.''

The monument is also a reminder that Horatio Nelson himself, in his younger days, commanded the ship *Albermarle,* which convoyed fleets of merchant ships sailing from the Lower St. Lawrence to England. Captain Nelson did not like his service in Canada. The weather appalled him. On April 2, 1782 he wrote to a friend: ''I am now ordered to get the old ship Albermarle out of harbor ... to go with ... a convoy to Quebec, where, worse than all to tell, I understand I am to winter. I want much to get off this confounded voyage....'' In the following October he wrote to another friend that he had orders to convoy a fleet from Bic in the Lower St. Lawrence to England. ''A very pretty job at this late season of the year,'' he said, ''for our sails are at this moment frozen to the yards.''

Not all merchant ships sailed as fleets in convoy. Some ventured out alone. Yet any ship that sailed alone ran great risks. Such were the risks taken by the Holmes family from Scotland, when they sailed for Canada in 1797. Their ship was captured by a French frigate. They were brought

into the port of Cadiz in Spain, as Spain was then the ally of France.

Mrs. Holmes was pregnant. Her child was born in Cadiz. The parents wanted the child to be baptized. When no Protestant church could be found in Cadiz, they took him for baptism to the Roman Catholic Church of St. Jago. As a reminder of the unusual circumstances of his birth, he was given, as his middle name, the Spanish name of Fernando. Four years later the Holmes family reached Montreal. The boy born in Cadiz became in later years an eminent Montreal physician, one of the founders of the Montreal Medical Institution, which in 1829 was ''engrafted'' on to McGill, as its faculty of medicine. Dr. Holmes was dean of the faculty when he died in 1860.

He lies buried in Mount Royal Cemetery. On his stone may still be read his name — ''Andrew Fernando Holmes,'' that surprising middle name recalling the old adventurous days at sea. Dr. Holmes had the unusual distinction in Montreal of being able to say that he had been captured at sea before he was born.

Nelson's Monument

A ship in convoy brought Ornaments for Nelson's Monument.

Winter Carnivals: Good or Bad?

Should Canadians do all they can to conceal from the outside world knowledge of the ghastliness of their winters, as if they were hiding a national disgrace? Or should they invite the whole world in to share the exhilaration of sport in the ice and snow? The question was being seriously debated in Montreal in the 1880s. It was a time when Canada was doing its utmost to attract immigrants. The Canadian government had its agents abroad in the British Isles and on the European continent, trying to encourage people to settle in Canada. Posters pictured vast fields of wheat ripening under a benign sun.

Never was there a picture of icicles, snowdrifts, swirling storms.

Winter carnivals in the 1880s: "The night sky gleamed and trembled with colors."

Trouble had arisen. Montrealers had launched a campaign to celebrate and publicize winter. It would hold winter carnivals. Visitors would be attracted from other lands to enjoy the bracing cold, revel in the snow, and marvel at palaces built of ice. Montreal's publicity campaign to attract winter tourists, and the Canadian government's publicity campaign to attract immigrants, were working at cross-purposes. Montreal was promoting what Canada ought to be downplaying.

The idea of holding a winter carnival, and inviting the world to join in, orginated with a 24-year-old Montreal lawyer, Robert Davidson McGibbon. At the annual meeting of the "Tuques Bleues" of the Montreal Snow-Shoe Club in 1882, McGibbon replied to the toast, "Our winter sports." In his remarks that evening, McGibbon made his novel proposal. Was it enough, he asked, for Montrealers simply to enjoy the sports of their wonderful winters? Why should not the clubs of the city unite in one great winter carnival? "Why not call in the world to see us as we are in all the gaiety and fervor of our mid-winter sports?"

The idea seemed practical. The manager of the Windsor Hotel, George Iles, was ready to back it. If it attracted many visitors, it would fill the hotels. It would also benefit the retail merchants. The railways would be interested. They might even run "carnival specials" to bring winter tourists from the United States. *The Gazette* applauded: "It is scarcely necessary to point out how largely such a carnival would advertise Montreal. That it would attract a great number of visitors there can be no reason to doubt, and if successful, as there is every cause to believe it would be, it would go far in popularizing our city as a place of winter resort." Principal citizens came forward to support the proposal with their personal prestige. The list of names on the honorary committee was dazzling. There could be no doubt that the carnival had the most solid approval in the city, whatever might be thought of it by those trying to attract immigrants.

The first winter carnival opened in January 1883. Montreal was suddenly crowded by "large reinforcements of strangers." They filled the streets, bought blanket coats and moccasins, and learned how to snowshoe. They marvelled at Montreal's sleighs, with their "robes of sea otter, seal, bear, tiger, and even imperial sable itself." The silence of the streets astonished them, with all sounds muffled, except for the jingling bells. Tourists gathered at the top of Peel Street, for toboggan slides down to Sherbrooke. There was a great carnival ball at the Windsor, with dancing till 3 in the morning to the band of the 65th Regiment. But the highlight of this first carnival, as of all that followed, was the Ice Palace on Dominion Square.

The Ice Palace was incredibly massive — 90 feet square, with a central tower rising about 100 feet. Inside colored lights glowed in the night. Each time the color of the lights was changed, the palace was transformed. For the carnival's greatest event, 25,000 people crowded into Dominion Square. The palace was to be attacked by some of the snowshoe clubs, defended by others. Their weapons were fireworks discharged into the night sky. The attackers came down Mount Royal, each man carrying a flaming torch, making a snake of fire against the dark mountain. They marched into the square, singing. Then the onslaught on the palace began. Attackers and defenders showered the winter sky with rockets, until it gleamed, sparkled and fluttered in the cold night.

The first carnival's success astonished even its most enthusiastic planners. At the Windsor Hotel the health of Robert McGibbon was drunk with Highland honors. *The Gazette* remarked: "We hear no more of the terror of our Canadian winter. It is the Winter Carnival now that strangers talk and write about. It was surely Canada's good angel that whispered the idea to Mr. McGibbon." The first carnival was so successful that others were held, year after year. Every year the program was elaborated. Every year the ice palace in Dominion Square was built from new and always more ambitious designs.

Articles on the winter carnivals were appearing in magazines in many lands. In England, *Murray's Magazine* declared they were as exciting as Mardi Gras in Italy — "a carnival of careless life," and a "riot of fun and forgetfulness!" The enthusing reporter for the New York *World* likened the ice palace to "a great heap of jewels dropped upon a sheet of crystal."

The more successful the winter carnivals became, however, the more opposition to them grew. They were spreading far and wide in the world the image of Canada as the land of the ice and the snow. Russia was the only other country on earth that seemed to be building ice palaces. But who would want to emigrate to Russia? The carnival people of Montreal were making Canada appear in the eyes of the world as the Siberia of North America.

At first such criticism came from outside Montreal. Gradually it was being expressed also by the city's big businessmen. The idea of holding winter carnivals now seemed less like the good angel's whisper in the ear of Robert McGibbon. This celebration of the rigors of winter was chilling the prospects of the whole country. Mounting criticism, and also rising costs, brought the dazzling series of Montreal's winter carnivals to an end. The last in the series took place in 1889. The Montreal Board of Trade urged that such carnivals be discontinued.

In later years, as in 1893, attempts were made at revivals. New forms were adopted, as in the Fête de Nuit on Mount Royal. But the old spirit, and the old scale of festivity, could never quite be recaptured. Charles W. Stokes, in a Montreal guidebook in 1924, remarked: "Old timers will tell you that Montreal in winter is not what it used to be. They recall the carnivals and ice-palaces of the eighties."

The Tragedy of Frobisher's Daughter

A 19-year-old Montreal girl — daughter of an English father and a French-Canadian mother — is commemorated by an elaborate memorial, complete with sculptured figure, in Exeter Cathedral. This venerable building, dating from the 14th and 15th centuries, is one of the glories of Devonshire and one of the grandest cathedrals of England.

The white marble memorial records this Montreal girl's self-sacrifice and her tragic death. The inscription reads: ''Sacred to the Memory of RACHEL CHARLOTTE O'BRIEN, wife of Capt. E.J. O'Brien of His Majesty's 24th Reg.Mt. and daughter of JOS. FROBISHER *Esa.,* of *MONTREAL, CANADA.* Her death was occasioned by her Clothes catching Fire; seeing the Flames communicating to her Infant, all Regard to her own Safety was lost in the more powerful Consideration of saving her Child, and rushing out of the Room, she preserved its Life at the Sacrifice of her own. She expired on the 13th day of Dec., A.D. 1800, in the nineteenth year of her Age.''

No further details are given, whether her clothing took fire from a candle or sparks from the grate. She saw flames spreading from her own clothes to those of her child. Desperate to save her child, she rushed from the room for aid. Helpers were in time to snatch the infant from her and save it. But before they could turn to her, she had been burned beyond recovery.

Joseph Frobisher, her father, was one of the foremost fur traders in Montreal, a founder and a leader in the North West Company, the Montreal rival of the Hudson's Bay Company. Beaver Hall, his mansion (built of logs), stood on the slope north, near to where the Bell Telephone building is today. He named it Beaver Hall — a name given later to the street, Beaver Hall Hill. His daughter's middle name, Charlotte, was the first name of her mother, Charlotte Joubert, who married Joseph Frobisher in 1779. Many of the English and Scottish fur traders in Montreal married French-Canadian women. Frobisher had earned his fortune in a hard, adventurous way. He had lived the life of the trader in the wilderness of the far Northwest. He knew what it was to face starvation. Once he kept himself alive by gnawing on fur pelts.

After so strenuous a life, Frobisher, having made himself rich, thought it was time to retire and enjoy himself. He gave up business in 1789, when about 58 years of age. His idea of leisure, however, seemed as strenuous, in its own way, as his idea of work had been. Life for him became a round of dinners — dinners he gave to his friends, dinners his friends gave to him, and dinners at the uproarious Beaver Club. Dining became so much of his life that he kept a diary just to keep a record of them — the ''Diary of my dinners.'' Entertainment was almost incessant. He listed his guests — sometimes 11, sometimes 23. Often he included among his guests officers of the British garrison stationed at Montreal. Frobisher's daughter had many opportunities of meeting them. One of the entries in her father's diary reads: ''... in the evening, Ladies and young officers.''

Among the young officers in the garrison was Captain Edward J. O'Brien of the 24th Regiment. No doubt he was among the guests at Frobisher's dinners, and they were fellow-guests at stag dinners at other places in town. At these stag gatherings the entertainment was rigorous. At times it was too rigorous even for Frobisher. He would take advantage of the customary privilege accorded the married men among the those present — the privilege of retiring before the exacting end.

An account of such a gathering was written by a lieutenant in the Montreal garrison in the 1790s — Lieutenant George Landmann of the Royal Engineers: ''In those days we dined at four o'clock, and after taking a satisfactory quantity of wine, perhaps a bottle each, the married men...and some others retired, leaving about a dozen to drink to their health.'' Among those who retired were Frobisher and Captain O'Brien. After they were gone, the remaining guests tried to dance on the table. They finished by breaking ''all the plates, glasses, bottles, etc., and the table also.''

The statement that Captain O'Brien left with the married men, before the dinner's frenzied end, seems to suggest that he and Frobisher's daughter had been married while the captain was still stationed in Montreal. When his tour of duty in Montreal was over, he returned with his wife to England. There the tragedy of her death soon followed. The need, then, was to provide for the future of the child she had saved. A young army officer on active service would be quite unable to care for an infant son. The little boy, named Edward after his father, was committed to the care of his grandfather in Montreal.

As soon as Edward was old enough to go to school, Frobisher placed him in one of high reputation. This was the boy's school in Cornwall, run by Rev. John Strachan, later to be the first Anglican bishop of Toronto. Boys were sent to his school by prominent families, both east and west. When the school term was over, Frobisher went to Cornwall to bring the boy back to Montreal. ''Set off for Cornwall,'' he wrote, ''to bring down my grandson Edward; came down all the rapids.'' Often he brought down with him the sons of other Montreal families as well:

A ship in convoy brought ornaments for Nelson's Monument.

"Brought down 14 boys. About as many as last time." Frobisher did not live to see his grandson grow up. He died in 1810, when Edward was only about 10 years old. Edward followed his father and became an officer in the British Army. His was not to be a long life. He died in 1833, at the age of 33.

When Captain O'Brien planned to erect a memorial to his wife in Exeter cathedral, he employed the sculptor J. Kendall. Many other memorials were also Kendall's work,

and he made Exeter cathedral's altarpiece. Kendall's memorial to Rachel Charlotte O'Brien consists of a female figure, symbolizing grief, sitting, with head bowed, beside a tombstone. The inscription on the tombstone gives the details of her death. Below, on stone drapery, is carved a poem. It calls to anyone who sees the memorial to give a tear and "one tender, sympathizing sigh" in tribute to the very young woman who was —
"... summon'd to an early tomb,
"Cloth'd in the pride of youth, and beauty's bloom."

When the River Flowed Uphill

On the Friday morning of April 22, 1887, guests at the Albion Hotel, looking from the windows, saw themselves beside a river. When they went to bed the night before, no river had been there. The Albion Hotel stood on McGill Street. It was a street busy with the rattling of wheels, the pounding of horses' hooves. On that morning, traffic still flowed up and down. But now it moved in silence. Instead of carriages and wagons were boats and rafts.

Shortly before 5 o'clock that morning, ice floating down the St. Lawrence jammed near Ile Ste. Hélène, at the foot of St. Mary's Current. Water backed up behind the barrier. Unable to flow forward, the St. Lawrence spread sideways. It streamed over the low-lying banks of the South Shore. Northward, it swept against the stone revetment wall along the Montreal waterfront — the wall built to keep floods out of the city.

Water rose to the height of the wall. Then it began spilling over. Two pumping engines were kept working, forcing water back to the river. By 6 o'clock further defence was impossible. Water was rushing over the wall. In the end, the river topped the wall by four feet seven inches. It was rising more slowly as the land grew steeper. But it crept up into St. James and on over Craig. The Grand Trunk Railway's Bonaventure Station (On St. James, near the foot of Windsor) "looked like a huge swimming bath." When the flood entered Victoria Square it had reached its highest limits. Thousands, living in the lower levels of the city, found the water almost at the top of their doors. They retreated upstairs. Soon "every window was filled with anxious faces gazing despondently at the rushing water below." In a glove shop on St. Paul Street clerks were standing on a table.

Attempts were made to drive wagons through the flood. Risks were high. At the corner of McGill and College a horse was drowned. Another driver tried to take a team and wagon across Chaboillez Square. One horse fell and drowned. The other, unhitched with difficulty, was led to safety. The wagon was left in the flood. Horses and wagons were not meant for flooded streets. Boats or rafts provided the only way of getting about. Boats were expensive. Charges rose to $10 an hour — a heavy price in 1887. Cheaper transportation was possible on rafts. Wooden sidewalks rose with the rising water. Often they broke loose and floated free. If caught, they made serviceable rafts. They could be propelled by poles.

Even in boats or on rafts, flooded streets were hazardous. Debris was afloat everywhere — barrels, planks, hay, heavy pieces of river ice. Where ice accumulated below the surface, boats might be grounded. They often could be freed only when the boatmen towed them to safety by stepping over the side and wading through the filthy water. Here and there rapids formed. At the corner of Atwater and Murray, the water was dammed by stranded ice, pieces of sidewalk, other wreckage. Over this dam the flood rushed like a millrace. One rowboat ventured too near. It was drawn into the vortex and swamped.

The fire brigade and the police both took to boats. So did City Council's Relief Committee, headed by Alderman A. A. ("Sandy") Stevenson, commander of the Montreal Field Battery. Bread, cheese, tea and sugar were ordered in huge quantities. Bakers and grocers delivered them to McGill Street, just above the flood. Firemen loaded them into boats. Members of the Relief Committee were the distributors. From boats they tossed bread into upper storey windows. Some stranded householders let down ropes. Provisions were hauled up. At one window "an anxious looking female of matronly appearance" was shouting down to Alderman Malone: "Mr. Malone, we want some bread; my bairns are starving." Irish were looking after their own. Officials of St. Patrick's Society were out in relief boats. So were their counterparts of the Irish Protestant Benevolent Society. Scots were being looked after by the Charitable Committee of the St. Andrew's Society. Priests of St. Ann's in Griffintown were also out in boats.

On Sunday, April 24, flood-bound churches were closed. No bells rang over the flood. But family worship could be heard. From the upper window of one flooded house came Scottish voices. They were singing: "The Lord's my shepherd, I'll not want...." Sick had to be cared for. A relief worker found "a poor woman sick." He rowed off for medicine and brought it back for her. The dead had to be buried. At a house near the Haymarket, preparations had been made for a funeral. The coffin was lowered by ropes from a window into a boat below.

Not all seemed anxious or depressed. Young people thought the flood great fun. One young man had made oarlocks on either side of his raft. Seated in a "cushion chair," he rowed slowly down his street. Here and there he stopped for conversation with friends at windows or on balconies. On Notre Dame some young men were sailing about as an amateur orchestra. Their music was "both vocal and instrumental." What "it lacked in quality it made up in quantity." Two other young men managed to lay hold of a section of wooden sidewalk about 20 feet long. By building benches on it they "provided accommodation for quite a number of their lady friends."

Ludicrous happenings brought lighter moments to the flood districts. At one street corner a drunk, waist high in water, had "anchored himself to a lamp post." There he was "frantically entreating" to be taken away. He was "only advised to taste a drop of the strong liquor, with which he was surrounded."

On April 24 the flood was beginning to recede a little, as the ice jam eased. It sank slowly. Not until April 28 was it really gone. Water-soaked streets took long to dry. At Bonaventure Station, water still lay between the tracks like so many canals. Railway platforms had shifted. Here and there they had broken up. Teams, splashing through water, were removing freight from sheds. The whole flood area of

Montreal had been left with an appearance of general dilapidation. Planks from sidewalks had drifted into piles in some places; elsewere they were gone altogether, probably carried out into the river by the retreating flood. Deposits from muddy water lay everywhere. In many houses tables, chairs and other furniture had been floating about downstairs. When the flood left, they lay scattered about in odd positions. Chilling dampness clung to every flooded building.

The flood of 1887, following upon an even worse one the year before, led to determined action. Flood control won the priority it had long deserved. Never again would 27 miles of Montreal streets be under water.

How Place Royale appeared during floods of the 1880s.

Sarah Maxwell: "One of the Bravest"

Sarah Maxwell has a memorial tablet in Christ Church Cathedral on St. Catherine Street. Its inscription reads: "In Memory of Sarah Maxwell, Principal of Hochelaga School, who gave her life in a noble attempt to save the pupils, at the destruction of the building by fire on Feb. 26th, 1907. Erected by the Congregation of Christ Church Cathedral."

When Church Maxwell's funeral was held in the cathedral, the streets were jammed — "a living, eddying sea." The funeral procession left from St. Urbain, near Prince Arthur, where she had lived with her mother. Her coffin, heaped with flowers, was followed by 12 firemen and a contingent of mounted policemen. After her immediate relatives came members of the school board,

Plaque on wall of Christ Church Cathedral honors heroine teacher Sarah Maxwell.

representatives from city hall, school children, then a mass of citizens who had come to do her honor. When the head of the procession reached the cathedral door, the long line behind stretched far away, up Union, and along Sherbrooke. The cathedral became so crowded that people had to be seated in the chancel. Sarah Maxwell was buried in Mount Royal Cemetery, in a lot donated by the trustees as a last tribute.

At the time of her death, Sarah Maxwell was a young woman, only 31. At the Hochelaga School she was both principal and a class teacher. It was only a little school, in the east end of Montreal, on Préfontaine Street, not far from St. Catherine. It was rather flimsy in construction, wood covered with a brick casing, two storeys high, with "a sort of garret" where the caretaker, Mrs. Hands, had living quarters. In the basement was a hot-air furnace. Wood was the fuel, stacked in a nearby room. In this wood-pile the fire began. The school had no fire escape. Dr. W.O. Opzoomer, the medical school inspector, had recently filed a report. Under the heading "Fire Protection" he had written: "Nothing of any kind."

In the early afternoon of that February day in 1907, Sarah Maxwell was teaching in her classroom on the ground floor. What happened was told by a girl in her class, Mary Haysay: "Miss Maxwell had a pointer and as soon as she saw the smoke ... she ran right toward us. She didn't tell us to form in line, but just called out for everybody to hurry outside.... I knew ... that we didn't have time to get our things. Miss Maxwell had some of us by the arms, and she just would do anything to get us out toward the front door."

Once her own class was safely out, she ran up the "narrow twisted staircase" and burst into the kindergarten. She found the children already in panic. Some were hiding beneath desks, others huddled in corners. All were trying to cover their faces. She lifted one child in her arm, gripped another by the hand. Groping downstairs through smoke, she got them to the front door. Mrs. Hands, the caretaker, saw her going back up the stairs to the kindergarten. "I called out to Miss Maxwell to escape while there was yet time," she said, "but she rushed upstairs exclaiming, 'I must get to the children.' That was the last I saw of her."

People outside had seen smoke coming from the school. They called No. 12 station. As it was wintertime, the fire reels moved on runners. In turning a corner, the ladder wagon caught on a curbstone. Time was lost while firemen pulled it free. Greater misfortune accompanied the pump wagon. When it arrived at the school, it was found the water pressure was low. About half an hour was lost before an adequate stream could be turned on the upper storey of the burning building. By this time the fire had gained its advantage. Hochelaga School seemed a "whirling mass of flame and flying splinters," concealed at times by a curtain of heavy smoke.

Sarah Maxwell had three teachers to help her on the second floor. By this time the smoke on the staircase was overwhelming. There was no hope of getting through to the front door. They shattered the glass in the kindergarten windows. Two of the teachers, blinded and suffocating, had to climb through the windows to the ladder firemen had set up. The third teacher fainted and had to be lifted out. Miss Maxwell was the only teacher left in the building. She had not only to hand the children to the firemen on the ladder; she had first to find where they had hidden. One after another she passed children to the firemen, who carried them down the ladder to the safety of the street. By then flames had followed smoke into the kindergarten.

She made no cry till the end. "Oh! I am burning!" she screamed. It was a frantic scream, heard even in the street below. At the top of the ladder were Fireman Benoit and Captain Carson. They shouted to her to come out at once; if she stayed any longer she wouldn't have a chance. "There are more to save," she told them, and turned back. Smoke was choking her. She staggered and began to fall. Captain Carson climbed beyond the ladder to the window sill. Reaching in, he caught hold of her dress. With one hand, he was dragging her toward the window. The piece of her dress in his grip tore loose. She sank into the smoke.

From somewhere in the school came an explosion. Flames shot into the firemen's faces. Benoit's hair was singed. He and Carson had to scramble down to the street. When they pulled the ladder away, its upper rungs had burned. Toward the end of the afternoon firemen entered the school. The chimney, gaunt and ice-glazed, rose through the shattered roof. Long icicles hung from eaves and window sills. Water gushed through the main doorway. The only sounds were the splashing footsteps of the firemen.

Bodies of children were found, one after another. The final toll was 16. As the bodies were carried out, parents waiting in the street pushed forward through the crowd to look at each child's face. Firemen set up a ladder to the kindergarten window. They climbed up and in. On the floor, near the window, lay the body of Sarah Maxwell. They lifted it down the ladder "reverently, as became her heroic death."

Sergeant Bélanger of No. 4 police station, on duty at the fire, spoke of the way she had died: "It was one of the bravest things I ever saw.... She ... could have made her escape easily, but she remained in the building to help the children out."

And Mrs. Hands, the school's caretaker, said: "A kinder girl never stepped in shoes. She was kind to her scholars, but why talk about it; she was kind to everyone, kind beyond describing."

Stagecoach Days in Montreal

Montreal ranked very high in the era of the stagecoaches. Its coaches, drivers, horses — all won praise, even from much-travelled visitors from abroad. In 1832 an Irishwoman, Mrs. William Radcliff, was writing about Montreal's stagecoaches to a relative in Dublin. "The coachman," she said, "drove the six in hand and turned into lanes but little wider than the carriage, with wonderful dexterity. The horses are particularly well trained, and answer to their names. At the end ... it was agreed by all that they had never seen so good horses, or coachmanship, before."

Montreal's service to travellers was known as "the Upper Canada Stages." Actually these coaches never went to Upper Canada. They travelled no farther than the nine miles to Lachine. The name "Upper Canada Stages" was applied to them because this nine-mile route was the first stretch on the way from Montreal to Upper Canada (as the province of Ontario was then known). In those days, when the Lachine Rapids blocked navigation on the St. Lawrence, Montreal had two ports. Travellers reaching Montreal, but intending to go farther west, had to re-embark at Lachine.

The two ports had different outlooks. The port of Montreal looked downstream toward the Old World beyond the Atlantic. The view from the waterfront at Lachine was in the opposite direction. It looked away from the Old World toward the New. The importance of the Montreal stagecoaches was that they connected the two ports. By carrying passengers the nine miles along the road to Lachine they were taking them to the gateway to the west.

For many years the starting-point for Montreal's "Upper Canada Coaches" was the courtyard of the Exchange Coffee House. This coffee house (actually an inn) stood near the northeast corner of St. Paul and St. Pierre Streets. Its courtyard could be reached by a narrow passageway from either street. That courtyard had all the picturesque character of a coaching inn, such as Charles Dickens was to describe in the 1830s in his *Pickwick Papers*. Even the proprietor of the Exchange Coffee House had a Dickensian name: he was a Mr. Goodenough. Puns on his name were inevitable. People used to say of his inn: "...and good enough it was for the best." Goodenough was a big man who lived on a farm in what is now the Rosemount Avenue area of Westmount. He rode on a big grey horse. They made an imposing pair, "galloping into town in the morning."

The courtyard of Goodenough's Exchange Coffee House was filled with an excited crowd when the coach was about to set out for Lachine. The expert drivers knew how to arrive with a flourish, as the coach dashed in through the narrow passage from the street and abruptly drew up. Everyone in the Coffee House seemed to come out to see the departure. One of the preparations for a journey was piling the passengers' luggage on the roof of the coach. Stacking so much in a space so small was itself an art. An observer remarked: "How the number of parcels, travelling bags and trunks were to be disposed of was a mystery, but the driver, usually good humored, had a dextrous way of placing them."

The courtyard would also be crowded by outsiders — people not going anywhere but hoping to induce somebody to take letters for them. The Royal Mail was costly and not always reliable. Many Montrealers preferred to have their letters carried for them by passengers and delivered by them. It was an imposition on stagecoach travellers, especially as this service was supposed to be performed for nothing. But it had become a custom.

Travellers might resent it, but felt obliged, as a courtesy, to give in. Charles Kadwell, an employee of the Montreal firm of Gillespie and Moffatt, grumbled: "I might fairly consider myself a mailbag on legs. My pockets as well as my portmanteau being crammed with letters handed to me by sundry merchants and others (for delivery en route) many of whom I knew merely by name, others not even at all. But such being the habitual custom of infringing on other people's good nature, I had to submit."

The coaches that came and went at the courtyard of the Exchange Coffee House were not built the same as the English coaches. They were of the American, or "Yankee" type. Charles Kadwell, in all his travels in Canada, had only once seen a coach of English build and that was on the Ottawa route. Yankee coaches were more heavily built to endure the rough Canadian roads. The body of a Yankee coach was very large. It had three long seats, accommodating, in all, nine or ten passengers. The middle seat, opposite the doors, was movable, to allow passengers to get in out. It was equipped with a broad leather strap to support the backs of passengers sitting there.

The Upper Canada Coaches were drawn by four or six horses. The horses were harnessed in pairs, one pair in front of another. These pairs of horses needed skilful handling. Among other things, a driver had to learn how to handle a whip long enough to reach the pair in front — not an easy art when there were six horses. But it was a skill drivers liked to display.

Much of the pleasure of the nine-mile drive to Lachine was the lovely, mellow scenery. Farmlands along the route had long ago lost their pioneering rawness. They were lush,

Montreal's stagecoach drivers had "wonderful dexterity."

mature. An English traveller said they resembled old English farms more than any others he had seen in Canada; and Mrs. Radcliff seemed to think they were as good as the best farms of Ireland. "The country was most beautiful all the way," she wrote; "not a single point of view that did not afford rich and varied scenery to the admirer of the picturesque."

Montreal's stagecoach era came to an end, at least so far as the trip to Lachine was concerned, in the 1840s. The first railway line was then built on the Island of Montreal. Naturally it was built where the passenger traffic would be greatest — on the route to Lachine. This Montreal & Lachine Railway was opened in November 1847.

Against railways, the stagecoaches could not compete. But the passing of the stagecoaches was regretted by many of the travellers who had known them. A Montrealer, Mrs. John Lovell, in her old age, looked back on the stagecoach days and recalled the friendliness that soon developed among the nine or ten people travelling slowly together. "There was an interest and sympathy," she said, "among the passengers, which one does not meet with in our days of quick travel."

In the Days of the Wooden Sidewalks

Those walking at night on Sherbrooke Street in the 1860s, especially in the stretch betwen Bleury and St. Laurent, were advised to imitate King Nebuchadnezzar, who resigned as king of Babylonia some six centuries before Christ. Nebuchadnezzar, as described in the Bible, crawled about for years on all fours. The ancient king acted in this strange way because he was out of his mind. Those walking on Sherbrooke in the 1860s were told to imitate him if they wanted to be sensible. The reason was to save themselves from stumbling and falling on the dilapidated wooden sidewalks.

At that time on Sherbrooke Street, as in most of the city, plank sidewalks had been laid either end to end or sideways, from the curb inwards. The wood decayed by exposure to the weather, and by the wear and tear of people walking over the sidewalks. Unless replacements were made promptly (and they were seldom replaced promptly enough) their condition became alarmingly dangerous, especially after sundown. On Sherbrooke some of the planks were broken, some had big holes in them while in others half the length were missing. *The Gazette* warned of the risks of walking there at night. "The only safe way of getting home in the dark," it suggested, "is either to walk on all fours, after the manner of Nebuchadnezzar... or take the middle of the road." And it added: "It has been proposed to ask the road committee to a party in this locality on some dark night, only it is thought they would be wary enough to come in carriages."

Newspapers were ceaselessly complaining about the condition of the wooden sidewalks. In 1867 *The Montreal Herald* reported on those in front of Victoria Square. Several planks were loose and very dangerous, for want of a few nails. Also on St. Antoine, just east of Mountain, was "a very dilapidated piece of sidewalk." It had, strange to say, been overlooked when all the rest of the street had been repaired. Montreal's civic administrators favored wooden side walks because they were cheap, not in the long run, but cheap at the start. Hemlock was sometimes used. It was the cheapest of all, but decayed the fastest. Most sidewalks were laid with three-inch pine planks. Their life was about four years on busy streets, about eight years on streets where few people walked.

Though wooden sidewalks served well enough until they began to decay, they surprised visitors to Montreal who were not accustomed to them. In their eyes they appeared unsightly and countryfied, more suitable for a rural village than in a large modern city. It seemed definitely odd to find such primitive footpaths in front of massive and stately buildings that would not have been out of place in New York or London.

The impression they gave of civic backwardness was seen in the comment of English journalist Samuel Phillips Day, who came to Montreal in 1862. He found that the boards in the "plankway" were "either rotten with age or partially devoured by rats — a species of animal that flourishes wonderfully in a Canadian climate." Even worse was the scorn of English novelist Anthony Trollope in 1861: "I should say that the planks are first used in Toronto, then sent down...to Montreal, and when all but rotted out there, are floated off by the St. Lawrence to be used in the thoroughfares of the old French Capital."

By the 1870s, the city surveyor, Percival St. George, was urging Montreal's aldermen to give up, gradually at least, the practice of laying wooden sidewalks. They should adopt a type of material that would "give the city that handsome and metropolitan appearance that Montreal, as the chief city of the Dominion, should have." He recommended the use of flagstones, good in appearance and long-lasting. They would cost more to begin with — $2.25 a square yard, as against 52 cents for pine planks. But instead of rotting in four to eight years, they would last indefinitely. And the cost of maintenance would be only 26 cents per yard.

His plea was heeded. In 1875-76, flagstone sidewalks were laid on some of the principal streets. They replaced the wooden planks on St. Catherine from Guy to Bleury, on Dorchester from Beaver Hall Square to the city's western limits, on Sherbrooke from Guy to St. Denis. A number of other streets were given flagstone sidewalks, including Union from St. Catherine to Sherbrooke, and upper Peel between Sherbrooke and Pine.

These flagstone sidewalks were financed on a new basis. Previously the city paid the full cost of all sidewalks. Now it was billing the property owners for one half. These new sidewalks were generally the blue stone from quarries in Canada or New York. They certainly gave a fine, dignified appearance. But they were not without problems. They tended to become uneven. The stones would sink or tip up, each at its own angle. Water gathered in the hollows.

The best hope of providing smooth walking surfaces lay in cement. The civic surveyor made his first experiment with cement in 1874. One of the two samples was laid on la Gauchetière, at the head of Côté. For whatever reasons, cement was only slowly adopted. For years it was not used at all. As late as 1909, only 3,245 yards of cement sidewalks were laid down as against a total of 70,326 yards of flagstone or asphalt. In the next two years, cement made rapid gains. By 1911, it had become the principal material for permanent sidewalks. Wooden sidewalks were still being laid here and there, in the less frequented parts of town, but they were on the way out. Montreal had outgrown them.

The flagstone sidewalks had so long a life that they survived on some parts of Sherbrooke as late as the 1920s,

even, in a few places, as late as the 1930s. They may have become rather uneven, but they certainly did have a fine appearance, not least because of the coloring they added to the street. There was even something to be said for the old wooden sidewalks. A writer of the 1860s admitted, despite all their disadvantages, the "springy boards," before they had begun to decay, were "by no means unpleasant to walk upon." They gave an agreeable spring to the walker's step.

Montreal's St. Paul Street featured sidewalks made of wooden planks laid crossways.

A Whale That Came to Montreal

In 1823 a whale came upstream, all the way to Montreal. It found a way of getting through the treacherous shallows of Lac St. Pierre. It simply followed a steamboat and came up by the ship channel. This steamboat was the *Lady Sherbrooke,* which plied regularly between Quebec and Montreal. The whale had only to follow the boat to be safely piloted along the intricate channel.

The captain of the *Lady Sherbrooke* did not like to have a whale following so closely. He feared it might ram the boat off course, or in some other way interfere with the

Capt. George Brush plunges harpoon into whale near Ile Ronde.

navigation. Several musket balls were fired from the deck. The whale seemed to turn away, but soon it was back, still following the boat's course. The *Lady Sherbrooke* reached Montreal. Only a little while later the whale appeared also. In those autumn weeks in 1823 Montrealers had the novel spectacle of a whale sporting itself in front of the city. It was not only a curiosity; it seemed a menace, as many of the boats on the river were small.

The very presence of the whale was a challenge to the hunting instinct. But Montreal, a city far inland, never had a whaling industry. Some whaling equipment, however, was procured. "Several enterprising inhabitants" went out in boats in an attempt to hunt the whale down. Nothing came of these forays. Whale hunting was not for amateurs. It demanded exact experience and involved high risk. A whale, fearful and aroused, was an intimidating opponent. Back in 1806, Hugh Gray, a British traveller in Canada, had seen the strength of a whale attacked in the Lower St. Lawrence: "... he flounces about, blowing and making a tremendous noise; dashing the water to a tremendous height, and occasioning a sort of local storm." It reminded him of the description of the Leviathan in the Bible: "... he maketh the deep to boil like a pot."

The danger in whale hunting lay particularly in the need to come close. A harpoon, thrown by hand, could not penetrate a whale if hurled from a distance of more than eight or ten yards. Getting so close was not only a danger; it was a problem. A whale quickly became aware that something was coming near. It was warned by the approach of a boat and the splashing of the oars. It took off at once and was soon beyond reach.

No expert in whaling was at hand in Montreal to give instruction, or to undertake the hunt himself. But Montreal had an unusually determined and ingenious man in Captain George Brush. He devised a plan of his own. Brush was a 30-year-old American steamboat captain from Vermont. He had come to Montreal to join another Vermonter, John D. Ward, in the management of the Eagle Foundry. This foundry near the Montreal waterfront was making engines for steamboats on Lake Champlain and the St. Lawrence.

Brush went out to hunt the whale but found he could not get near it. He observed, however, that it often passed through a stretch of deep water near Ile Ronde — the little island that was to be joined to St. Helen's Island (Ile Ste-Hélène) 144 years later in preparation for Expo '67. His plan was to lie still in a boat at that spot, waiting to harpoon the whale when it came by. But the water near Ile Ronde was rough with the St. Mary's Current. Anyone trying to lie still in a boat in that current would soon be swept down the river.

Captain Brush solved the problem. He used a rope to attach his boat to St. Helen's Island. He allowed his boat to be carried downstream in the current until it reached the desired spot near Ile Ronde. He then held it by the rope from going any further. In this way he could keep his boat floating at the right spot without movement and without the use of oars. The whale, swimming by, would see nothing moving, mothing to scare it off. Meanwhile the captain would be ready with his harpoon.

The harpoon was made of iron, about three feet long. It terminated in an arrow-shaped head. Inside this arrowhead were barbs, resembling fishhooks. Once plunged into a whale, the harpoon clung and could not be torn out. At the other end of the harpoon was a rope. This rope was attached to the boat. A whale, feeling the harpoon, would try to escape. But it could not get away from its pursuers, because the rope from the harpoon dragged the boat after it wherever it went. Captain Brush had two other men in the boat with him: Baxter Bowman and a shipbuilder named Young. The moment he threw the harpoon they were to cast off the mooring rope that held the boat to St. Helen's Island. It would then be free to be pulled away by the harpooned whale.

They had to wait to see whether the captain's plan would work. Eventually the whale could be seen approaching, as the captain had believed it would. Suspecting nothing, it swam close by. Captain Brush hurled the harpoon. It struck. The other men in the boat at once cast off the mooring rope. The boat went dashing away, yanked to and fro by the rope from the harpoon embedded in the whale's back. This wild and terrifying rush about the river, as the boat splashed behind in the whale's wake, went on for several hours. Toward nightfall the whale gave up. It got into shallow water near Boucherville Island. Weakened by loss of blood, exhausted by frenzied exertion, it rolled over on its side and died.

Next day the grotesquely huge body was towed across the river to Windmill Point on the Montreal waterfront. The whale could now be examined. It was of the type known as pike-headed. The measurements were 42 feet, 8 inches in length, 6 feet across the back, 7 feet deep. On the beach it was "exhibited in a booth fitted up for the purpose, for the gratification of the inhabitants." Thousands came to view it, all paying seven-pence halfpenny for the privilege. The dead whale was then loaded on to a Durham boat (a sort of barge) and towed downstream. It was exhibited at Three Rivers, then at Quebec. In the end it yielded 14 to 15 barrels of oil.

A relic of this whale lingered long in Montreal. Its jawbones were acquired for Gilbault's Garden — a combination of a botanical garden, a zoo and an amusement park. There the jawbones were set up as an arch over the entrance on Sherbrooke Street. As for Captain George Brush, he long survived his own daring exploit. In 1847 he became the proprietor of the Eagle Foundry. He was still the proprietor when he died in 1883, in his 91st year.

Why Cathedral-Basilica Is Where It Is

In the early 1950s Cardinal Léger, as archbishop of Montreal, faced a hard decision. The cathedral-basilica on Dorchester Boulevard was in serious need of renovation. Structural repairs and redecoration would be extensive and costly. Two choices were before him. He could make the heavy outlays needed to restore the 19th-century building. Or the site (one of the largest and most valuable properties in all downtown Montreal) could be sold and the proceeds used toward building a new cathedral-basilica somewhere else. Cardinal Léger conducted a thorough investigation. He announced his decision in 1955: "... we have decided to leave the cathedral in its present location, and to restore it." And, he added, the site was so strategic, "that today we would have to build on the same spot, were it not already found there." That strategic site had been chosen a century earlier — back in 1854. It had been chosen by an early bishop, Mgr. Ignace Bourget. This bishop had the foresight to see exactly where the centre of the city would be a century beyond his own time.

The cathedral of the Roman Catholic diocese had stood on St. Denis Street near St. Catherine. It was well-placed in the heart of east-end Montreal, where French-Canadian Roman Catholics were concentrated. The fire of 1852 had destroyed the cathedral. Catholics were expecting it to be rebuilt on the same spot, or no farther away than St. Denis and Sherbrooke.

In August, 1854, Bishop Bourget announced his decision. The people were dismayed. The new cathedral would be built on neither of the sites proposed. It would not be built in the east end at all. The bishop, instead, had selected a site at the western fringe of the city, far away from the French Catholics, in the area where the Protestants had gathered. Astonishment quickly turned to anger. Bishop Bourget seemed to be turning his back on his own people; he was deserting them.

Some laymen went so far as to threaten the bishop. They told him they would not give so much as one cent when he held out his hand for aid to build the cathedral on a site so outlandish, so absurd. The site chosen by the bishop was on Mont Saint-Joseph. This was the land running south from Dorchester to la Gauchetière, between Mansfield and Cathedral.

The bishop had his reasons. He was not building for the convenience of the present but for the needs of the future. The centre of town was shifting westward. The new cathedral should not be left to one side as the years went by; it should anticipate the coming core.

He was aware, however, of one serious weakness in his position. His credibility was still at stake. People might still expect that, sooner or later, he would have to change his mind, especially if the protests were steady enough, loud enough. Bishop Bourget had to prove his decision was irrevocable. For this reason he moved quickly. Though he would have to wait until funds could be raised to build the new cathedral, he would, in the meantime, build his residence — his "palace" — on part of the new west-end property. This is the plain red-brick building still standing on la Gauchetière, at the corner of Cathedral.

The reason why it is so plain is that it was put up so speedily, using whatever funds were available, and not lingering for elaboration or ornament. To prove again that he was not to be pressured into changing his mind, Bishop Bourget built a temporary cathedral just back of his palace and connected with it. It stood alongside Cathedral Street (then known as Cemetery Street). Today the brick presbytery and offices of the cathedral-basilica occupy the site. This temporary cathedral, like the bishop's palace, was a plain red-brick building, little more than a chapel. It was a poor, mean structure. As one commentator remarked, it was "more than modest, certainly."

Bishop Bourget had a double aim in building this "more than modest" temporary cathedral. Not only did he intend it to be evidence that the west-end site had been unalterably chosen; he hoped its wretched appearance might embarrass and shame the Catholics of the diocese to build the new, far grander cathedral he had in mind.

Raising funds was hard. One day he remarked to Thomas Jean-Jacques Loranger, a prominent and friendly layman: "They are heaving stones at me from all sides, but... I will build my cathedral."

To this remark Loranger replied: "May I make a suggestion, Monseigneur. Gather together these stones they are throwing at you and you'll have enough to build your cathedral."

Many years were to pass before funds enough could be raised even to make a beginning of the great cathedral. Not until 1870, 16 years after he had announced his decision to move to the city's outskirts, was the cornerstone laid. Work was started, but before the end of the 1870s it was halted by the long economic depression. Walls and columns, supporting no roof, stood like premature ruins.

In the end the very forcefulness of Bishop Bourget brought him into trouble. He could handle the controversies; these did not deter him. But he encountered increasing

Cathedral's site seen as best back in the 1850s.

difficulties in handling the diocese's debts. He had forged forward in so many directions that his reach exceeded his grasp. The accumulating debts expanded into a financial crisis. Battered by diocesan debt and the country's economic depression, the bishop was besieged by yet another adversary. Old age was encroaching. His nervous vitality was being overtaken by the uncertainties of ebbing strength. He arranged his resignation. He retired into an invalid's seclusion at Sault-au-Récollet, on Rivière des Prairies.

Something, however, of his old restlessness of will remained. He had one last plan. He would make a tour, from parish to parish, pleading for money to revive the diocese from the financial dangers in which he had left it.

Such a tour had to be approved by his successor, the new bishop of Montreal, Mgr. Edouard Charles Fabre. The new bishop hesitated. The spectacle of a sick old man in his eighties, struggling from parish to parish begging donations, would be pitiable. Mgr. Bourget remained eager to make this final gesture. Bishop Fabre yielded. The strong-willed invalid set out from Sault-au-Récollet. He travelled rough roads, by wagon and sleigh, to

150 parishes. Pneumonia dragged him down en route. He recovered and went on. This last gesture won. Mgr. Bourget raised $100,000. This sum, added to the advantageous sale of several properties by Bishop Fabre, reduced the debt of the Montreal diocese to manageable proportions. Financial crisis had been averted.

Mgr. Bourget withdrew into ultimate seclusion to prepare himself for death. The end came on June 8, 1885. Later in the same year his successor felt the work of construction on the cathedral could be resumed. Nine years later, in 1894, this building, modelled after St. Peters in Rome, was opened for worship in Montreal. Forty years had passed since Mgr. Bourget had chosen the site. In 1931 a chapel, lined with exotic marble, was completed off the cathedral's eastern aisle. It was to be a mortuary chapel, the burial place of all the bishops and all the coadjutor (associate) bishops of the diocese. At the centre of this chapel, in a magnificent sarcophagus, the bones of Mgr. Bourget were reinterred. Across the top of the sarcophagus lies his effigy in bronze. "He was a man of vision," said Cardinal Léger in 1955, "and it was this that inspired him to erect his cathedral in the very centre of the future metropolis of Canada."

The Leaning Spire of Montreal

It was a Sunday evening in the autumn of 1871. Montreal was buffeted by a storm, the worst in years. At Christ Church Cathedral on St. Catherine Street the congregation shuddered. The wind shook the cathedral. The officiating clergy remained calm; the churchwardens gave assurances. Most of the people in the congregation could stand the tension no longer. In the midst of the service many left. Others lingered. They hoped the storm would abate. But even some among them began to slip away. The service came to its close. The benediction was pronounced. By that time the cathedral was almost empty. That night the worshippers in the cathedral had reason to be alarmed. They feared the tall stone spire might topple. Tons of stone might come crashing through the roof, crushing the people in their pews below.

The spire stood on uncertain foundations. Even before the cathedral was completed in 1859, the southern piers of the square tower (on which the spire rested) had already sunk to a depth of five inches. The cathedral had been built on dubious ground. The whole area had once been a swamp. The cathedral's spire soared 127 feet from the tower, or 224 feet from the ground. Its very height, and the immense weight of its stones, gave rise to anxiety. Foundations of the tower were shallow — only a few feet below the level of the neighboring sidewalks. Moreover, they rested on a mixture of sand, gravel, and hard clay. About 15 feet lower down this clay turned soft, no stiffer than putty.

The rector and wardens of the 1850s realized someone had erred. They refused to make the final payment to the builder. The builder sued for his money. He claimed he had only followed the instructions of the architect. The case was carried in appeal to the Privy Council. The builder lost. "Truly he built on another man's plans," said the Privy Council's judgment, "but his duty was to see what he was about." The tower was repaired sufficiently for the time being. But worshippers in the cathedral continued to wonder what might happen if that spire were to come down upon them.

On the Sunday evening of September 17, 1899, another wave of terror swept through the congregation. It was about 7:45. Suddenly heavy stones crashed and thudded. By the sound, they were falling just outside the cathedral's walls. Dean Norton felt the shock. The cathedral shook, he said, as in an earthquake. Panic might have gripped the congregation, as in 1871. But the sound and tremor came and went in a few minutes. Some people could not get over their uneasiness; they got up and left. Most remained, preoccupied and wondering. When they came out into the September night they peered around. The spire was not lying in ruins on the cathedral's green lawn. But looking across University Street, they saw what had happened.

Three floors of the Queen's Theatre Block — the floors occupied by the department store of Scroggie Brothers — had collapsed. Stones weighing half a ton had bounced on the sidewalks and the pavement of University and St. Catherine, only a few feet from the cathedral. A Mr. Carroll, of John Lewis' Pharmacy at the south corner of St. Catherine and University, had heard "a scrunch-noise" from time to time during the afternoon. He paid no attention. About 7:40 he heard it again. This time he went out into the street. The plate glass in Scroggie's windows began to split. Minutes later the walls spilled out in an avalanche of stones.

The people coming out of Christ Church Cathedral were relieved to see that it had not been their spire that had fallen. As it was a Sunday evening and the streets were empty, no one had been killed or injured, except a distant passerby, struck in a finger by a sliver of flying stone. But the cathedral's congregation realized, more vividly than ever, what could happen if stones, even heavier, smashed through the roof at service time. Yet the old spire of the cathedral stood for nearly three decades more, though the south piers continued to sink. By the 1920s they were down as much as two feet. The spire, in consequence, was leaning two feet toward St. Catherine Street. The cathedral's rector and wardens called in experts for an opinion. These experts found the tower and spire "literally floating about" in the yielding soil. The spire, they estimated, weighed 3,250,000 pounds. The situation "might easily develop into a catastrophe."

The rector and wardens acted at once. The great spire, chief glory of the cathedral, was taken down. For 13 years the cathedral stood deformed. No spire seemed ever likely to replace it. The cathedral could not afford it; the soil could not support it. In 1940 came a proposal. It was as ingenious as it was mysterious. A trust company informed the church authorities that a client was prepared to reconstruct the spire. The cathedral would be put to no expense, nor need stone be used. A new spire could be built of aluminum, on a light steel frame. There was only one condition: the benefactor's name would not be disclosed.

An offer so generous, so genuine, so surprising and so desirable was accepted at once. From spring to autumn in 1940 the work went forward. Problems had to be solved. Gleaming aluminum had to be made to match the old grey stones of the cathedral, darkened through some 80 years. A perfect imitation was achieved. Aluminum plates were molded on specimens of the old stone. They were stained with acid until they had become the right tone. The spire, when erected, was a replica so remarkable that it seemed as if the spire of the 1850s had never been removed. Only one last unexpected problem remained to be solved. Light could be seen shining through the spire, at places where the aluminum plates could not be fitted precisely enough together. This embarrassing difficulty was overcome by hanging sheets of material inside the spire.

The name of the mysterious benefactor was unknown for nine years. It was disclosed in 1949, when James Stuart Douglas died. Douglas was a Canadian mining engineer.

He had gone to the United States, become an American citizen, and made a fortune. In old age he decided to return to Canada and resume his Canadian citizenship. He lived quietly in an old house on Crescent Street.

The family was notable for generations. His grandfather, Dr. Douglas, was founder of the asylum at Beauport and a pioneer in the humane and enlightened treatment of mental patients. His father, like himself, was a highly successful mining engineer in Canada and the United States. The son of James Stuart Douglas was Dr. Lewis Douglas, principal and vice-chancellor of McGill University, and later ambassador of the United States to the Court of St. James's.

Christ Church Cathedral's spire once leaned two feet.

Shooting Woodcock
on Phillips Square

"**F**ishing is very good there... as is also game of all kinds; and hunting is good, stags, hinds, does, caribous, rabbits, lynxes, bears, beavers and other... animals which so abound... we were never without them."

This is a description of the wildlife to be found on the Island of Montreal. It is a record made before the first permanent European settlement was established on the island 31 years later. This picture of Montreal in its natural state was written by the French explorer Samuel de Champlain. He came in 1611.

One of those in Champlain's exploring party, a man named Louis, lost his life because the hunting in the region was so good, and so easy. An Indian had told him of an island,

Montreal fox hunters at times gathered in Dorval at the Forest and Stream Club.

just above the Lachine Rapids, where the herons were so many that the air was filled with them. Louis, a great lover of hunting, at once wanted to go to this "island of the herons." Several Indians took him there. Hunting was as fabulous as they had said it would be, and "they took as many herons as they wished." As it turned out, they took too many. On the return down the rapids the canoe was weighted low with the dead game. The "swiftness of the water overmastered them." Louis and one of the Indians with him were drowned. The island above the rapids, where they hunted, has continued to be known as Heron Island.

The settlement of Montreal from 1642 onward gradually obliterated the habitat for the prolific wildlife Champlain had described. But at first the growth was slow. Most of the island long remained suitable for birds and animals. For about two centuries after the foundation of the city, its expansion was east and west near the waterfront, rather than northward toward the mountain. Wildlife could still be found not far from the city's streets. Until after the 1830s, little construction took place above Craig Street (now part of St. Antoine Street).

Craig Street itself, in fact, was the bed of a small river. Though generally called "the creek," it had the official name of the Rivière St. Martin. Those early days were still a living memory for some very old Montrealers as late as the 1890s. One of them was John Stafford, a merchant tailor, then believed to be the oldest tailor in town. His father had brought the family to Montreal in 1828. "There were only a few shanties on Great St. James Street when we came to Montreal," he would recall, "and boys were in the habit of shooting and trapping muskrats on Craig Street." The creek also attracted sportsmen in search of snipe — a word used for any of the various long-billed marsh birds, allied to woodcock and much sought as a game bird. Major George Horne, the Montreal stationer, recalled in his old age: "I have many times shot 10 or 12 brace of snipe in this creek of a morning before breakfast."

Other hunting grounds had much to offer sportsmen. Though farther away than Craig Street, they were still conveniently close to town. Wherever there was marsh or swamp, wildlife was plentiful and the sport good. Marshlands covered the site where Phillips Square and Christ Church Cathedral are today. In the 1830s, this was a favorite hunting site. Woodcock were there in flocks. George Horne used to say it "was no uncommon thing... to bag from 25 to 30 couple of cock in a day's hunt." Other swamplands made for good hunting. One of the largest lay near the waterfront. It began about the foot of what is now Peel Street and extended westward beyond the area where the Turcotte railway yards later stood.

Still other good hunting grounds were to the north and the northwest: the head of the Papineau Road (now Papineau Avenue); the rear of Longue Pointe village; or between the two mountains.

Duck shooting in those days attracted little interest. Snipe and cock were considered "most worthy of the attention of sportsmen." No game laws then existed. Sportsmen hunted whenever and wherever they wished. They shot as many birds as they pleased. The greatest distinction, however, was "to have the honor of killing the first cock of the season." For weeks before the birds arrived, sportsmen were out in the early morning, ready with guns and dogs. The first cock each season was displayed in the window of Dolly's Chophouse, the headquarters of the sporting men. The event was reported in the papers, as interesting and important news.

One of the clearest and widest evidences of the extent of wildlife on the Island of Montreal, and of its gradual decline, is in the records of the Montreal Hunt Club. Generally, the hounds had little difficulty in finding a fox and the pursuit would begin. Some of the earliest hunts, in the 1820s and 1830s, took place near Côte des Neiges Road, or on the Priests' Farm, or near the Papineau Road. As late as 1881 the Montreal Hunt built its clubhouse on Delorimier Avenue. Foxes were found and pursued over the vast Domaine to the east, the property of the Seminary of St. Sulpice. William Drysdale, the club's huntsman, later could remember those days when "of a morning we'd see half a dozen brace of foxes there."

Other areas where foxes could be roused and pursued were Pointe aux Trembles, the Crawford acres in Verdun, the fields in Outremont, or near the Back River. Even Westmount could be hunting country. Pupils at the old Westmount Academy at times were distracted from their lessons in the mid 1890s, when riders went by, as the hounds followed a scent to Westmount mountain.

No hunting area on the island lasted so long as fox country as the lakeshore, or West Island, from Dorval. It was known to the Montreal Hunt Club as "the old happy ground." Sometimes the Forest and Stream Club, on its point in Dorval, served as the gathering place, where the hunt breakfast was held. A GTR train left Bonaventure Station in Montreal for Dorval, with a coach for the members and several cars for horses and hounds. The cost was about $50, paid for by a subscription among the members, or by one member alone. *The Gazette* gave an account of the members, after the breakfast, mounting their horses and riding off for the chase.

The whole island of Montreal was changing. Early in the 20th century, the Montreal Hunt Club moved from Delorimier Avenue to Côte St. Catherine Road. Then, in 1920, it moved off the island and set up its kennels at La Grande Fresnière, below the foothills of the Laurentians. Far away were the days when Samuel de Champlain could say that "game of all kinds" abounded on the Island of Montreal.

The Bells of Notre Dame

The churchwardens of Notre Dame Church in Place d'Armes decided to order 11 bells. The church, at the time it was built, was the largest in North America. Notre Dame had to have bells in keeping with its pre-eminence. In the eastern tower they would have a carillon of 10 bells. In the western tower would be one gigantic bell, hanging alone.

The churchwardens consulted bell manufacturers in Paris, Lyons, Tours and London. They chose the Whitechapel Foundry of Messrs. Mears in London and awarded it one of the largest contracts for bell-making ever known. The carillon of 10 bells was completed first. Before they were sent to Montreal, the Roman Catholic organist and composer in London, Vincent Novello, was engaged to test their tone. He reported that the tone of some of the bells was not quite right. He had them improved by filling them on the inside. In the end he was satisfied. They had been exquisitely adjusted — a perfect octave. These 10 bells reached Montreal on May 24, 1843. They were baptized with elaborate ceremony. Each was given a name. As with the christening of children, they had sponsors and godparents — eminent Montrealers. For the ceremony, the bells were draped in velvet and flowered gold cloths, with lace.

The sound of this carillon brought a new pleasure to the ears of all Montrealers. Visitors, too, heard the bells and were moved. One of these visitors was Rev. William Drew, a Unitarian minister from Augusta, Maine, who came in 1851. He wrote: "When we arrived at the wharf, about 9 o'clock Sunday morning, we did so under the chimes of Notre Dame Church, which is the most splendid church in America... There are bells enough... to fill all the notes of the octave, and the music that floated over the city was solemn and inspiring, calculated to subdue and chasten the public mind, and prepare it for the solemn devotions of the day."

The problem of Notre Dame's bells has always been their weight. Hanging silent, their weight is easily supported. In motion, however, they tug violently at the beams as they swing. Accidents have happened. One came at high mass on Sunday, July 21, 1952. Belgium Independence Day was being celebrated in Montreal. A parade was entering the church from Place d'Armes. The bells in the eastern tower were ringing far above. The second heaviest of these bells, weighing about 3,633 pounds, snapped the supporting axle. It crushed a heavy beam, plunged through the floor directly under it, and bent another beam.

As it fell, it punctured the sprinkler system. The break signalled the fire brigade. Firemen arrived. They smelled no smoke. A search of the tower led to the bell. It was tipped sideways, at an awkward angle in the tower, supported only by the half-shattered beam beneath it. "It's a lucky thing the bell didn't go through the last beam or it would have gone all the way down", said Captain Georges Rocher, officer in charge of No. 1 Station. Had it gone the whole way down, it might have tumbled on people using the two flights of stairs in the tower to reach the choir benches.

The western tower had been reserved for one great bell, so great that the tower could have held no other. This gigantic bell, known as Le Gros Bourdon, was said to weigh 16,325 pounds. It was bigger than any bell in the British Isles, bigger than any bell in North America. The arrival of the Gros Bourdon in Montreal in October 1843 was a sensation. A crowd jammed the dock.

The bell was put ashore from the sailing ship, *Lady Seaton*. Creaking pulleys slowly raised it to view. The watching crowd gasped. The higher the bell went, the more astonishing its dimensions appeared. A crane swung it around. It was lowered to a wagon with six wheels. Flags were draped over it. Volunteers tugged at the long ropes. They dragged it from the waterfront to Place d'Armes. Its entry into the square was a triumph. All 10 bells in the eastern tower of Notre Dame clamored in welcome. For several days the Gros Bourdon stood in Place d'Armes, at the foot of the western tower. Police guarded it every night.

Baptism came next. Le Gros Bourdon was hauled into the church. It was placed on a platform near the altar. On the afternoon of October 29, the baptismal ceremony took place, with sponsors and godparents. The bell was christened Jean Baptiste. Te Deum, the hymn of thanksgiving, was intoned by the choir. Then the officiating priest struck the bell three times. Its deep vibrations echoed under the balconies or slowly faded in the vaulted roof. Installed in the western tower, Le Gros Bourdon was kept silent on purpose for nearly two months. Its voice, as planned, was to be heard for the first time at midnight on Christmas Eve. On that night, 20 men pulled on the ropes. Gradually the huge bell began to swing. Its voice rang out, marvellously deep. Its echoes rolled away into the night. Some said they could be heard as far away as Mont St. Hilaire.

All went well until June 23, 1844. To celebrate the eve of St. Jean Baptiste Day, the great bell was rung. All at once its rich voice turned hoarse and harsh. The ringers immediately released their grip on the ropes. The bell muttered into silence. Examination disclosed fractures in

Notre Dame's towers have 11 bells — including one of world's biggest.

several places. The churchwardens accused Messrs. Mears of providing a defective bell. The manufacturers accused the churchwardens of abusing the bell, by inserting a new and heavier tongue, to magnify its sound. The churchwardens denied the charge; they said it was scandalous. Further examination in Montreal proved the bell weighed less than it ought and had been made from inferior metal. Confronted with these embarrassing facts, the foundry agreed to make a new bell. Metal of the first bell was broken into 177 pieces and shipped back to London.

The new bell was even bigger than the first. Raising it into the western tower was a feat of engineering. The Montreal & Lachine Railroad Company lent equipment — ropes, pulleys, cranes. On June 22, 1848 all Montreal seemed to have crowded into Place d'Armes to watch. The bell went up, inch by inch. The ascension took almost the whole day. By 7:30, this second Gros Bourdon was in its place.

There in the western tower of Notre Dame it has hung ever since. In 1939 the wooden beams from which it was suspended were replaced by steel. No longer do bellringers tug at ropes; the great bell is rung electrically. The deep bass voice of Le Gros Bourdon, like its weight, is tremendous. It has a range of some 18 miles. The Montreal poet, Leo Cox, has written of its "iron seas of sound," drenching the air.

Old Wooden Street Signs

In the days when a British garrison was in Montreal, young officers "were always at some prank to kill time." One evening several of them were strolling about the streets. They came to the spot where St. Lawrence Street (later to be known as the Main) led to Lambert Hill. There they gathered under a druggist's sign. This sign (a big wooden, mortar and pestle) projected several feet above the sidewalk. It hung from a strong iron bar. The officers had some prank in mind. Perhaps they intended to steal the sign and make off with it as a sort of trophy. One of the officers was hoisted on the shoulders of the others. He grasped the iron bar and swung himself astride it.

No sooner was he in this position than someone shouted "Police!" His brother officers scattered and vanished. Police came running to the spot. The young officer astride the bar was out of reach — several feet over their heads. The situation became ridiculous. The police stood staring up at him. He sat staring down at them. Somehow, in the end, the police got him down. The puzzle then was what charge to bring against him. Nothing had been stolen, nothing damaged. All he had actually done was to sit astride the iron pole of a druggist's sign. He was judged more mischievous than criminal, and dismissed with a reprimand.

An incident such as this gives a glimpse of the appearance of Montreal's streets more than a century ago. This druggist's big wooden mortar and pestle would have been one of hundreds of signs projecting on iron bars over the sidewalks. These signs were symbols. The aim was to do without words. Words could not be read easily, if at all, from a distance; and in those days illiteracy was not uncommon. A simple sign, signalling at a glance the nature of a business or profession, would guide customers clearly to the door.

The 19th century was the great age of the street sign in Montreal. On the city's business streets the pedestrian had signs over his head all the way. The form of most signs was traditional rather than original. Identification was more certain when the symbols had become fixed and agreed upon. A big wooden boot was the sign of the shoemaker. A huge wooden knife indicated a cutler; a pair of shears, a tailor; a big hand, a glover; a barrel, a brewer; a huge gold molar, a dentist; a pair of eyes peering through spectacles, an optician. Hardware merchants displayed enormous hammers. Sellers of music and musical instruments put up a wooden lyre or harp. Furniture dealers, in later Victorian days, had signs more complete

than others. They hung oversized rocking chairs above the sidewalk.

Tradition had at times stabilized these images, even after flashions changed. A big wooden hat, of the distinctive "stovepipe" type, always symbolized a hatter's shop. Such a hat was known as "a beaver." It dated back to the days when beaver skins were used in making the tall hats. In later years, felt was replacing beaver. Hats took new shapes. Yet the old beaver type of stove-pipe hat remained as the sign of the hat shop. In the same way, a bonnet remained the symbol of the milliner, long after bonnets had gone out of fashion. An example of far longer fashion was seen in the three wooden balls of the pawnbroker. These were derived, it was believed, from the coat-of-arms of the Dukes of Medici. From their estates in Florence and Tuscany had come many of the early bankers. These bankers advanced money on valuable goods, as did the pawnbrokers of later times.

Though wood was not used exclusively, it prevailed in sign-making. It lasted long. It could be shaped in any form. It could be painted in vividly attractive colors. Orders for shop signs of any designs could be filled without difficulty. Montreal's Victorian years were the age of the woodcarver. The demand was wide; the number of craftsmen was high. Furniture was being elaborately carved. Figureheads were needed for sailing ships. Builders required woodcarving for cornices, balconies, window frames, newel posts, capitals for wooden columns.

As the Victoria age advanced, some shop-keepers were demanding more ambitious street symbols — not for signs only but life-size figures. The biggest demand came from tobacconists. They wanted the so-called "Cigar Store Indians." Some of them were real works of art, the products of such eminent French-Canadian wood sculptors as Louis Jobin. A life-size Indian chief, or Indian "princess," arrested the attention of passersby. These carved figures were almost startling, as they stared into the street with their impassive faces, while holding a bunch of wooden cigars in one hand. A man named Chichester was credited with introducing the cigar store Indian. It happened in New York in 1850. The idea was natural enough, as the Indian had taught Europeans the practice of tobacco smoking. By the end of the century these wooden Indians had become almost the standard tobacconists' symbol throughout North America.

Carved life-size figures were not for tobacconists only. Other figures were made for other businesses. From 1870 till 1900, a wooden admiral in uniform was displayed on Notre Dame Street, at the shop of Hearn & Harrison, dealers in nautical instruments. A life-size wooden sailor, in white uniform with round hat, was long at a sailors' inn on Commissioners Street.

By the late 1890s, the wooden street signs of Montreal were rapidly disappearing. Some accidents had happened. Heavy signs had broken away from their supporting poles. They had crashed on the heads of pedestrians beneath. A civic bylaw discouraged their use in future. The disappearance of the signs did not go unregretted. They

had lent an undoubted picturesqueness to trade and commerce. Rev. J. Douglas Borthwick, long the rector of St. Mary's Anglican Church in Montreal, was writing in 1897: "No doubt when all the signs and signboards disappear, the streets will look bleak and barren for some time. How silent it will feel at midnight, especially when the wind blows, and there are no signs to shake and creak on their hinges? What a difficulty in finding out the shops one wants to go to, and how, above all, mostly everybody, and especially the old people, will grumble...."

Montreal streets in the 19th century were made picturesque by merchants' signs.

Men Who Had Two Wives

Many Montrealers, in the days of the fur trade, had two wives. It was not that they believed in polygamy. Their two wives belonged to two different worlds. In their younger years these Montreal fur traders served at posts in the far wilderness. In later life they returned to Montreal or its neighborhood. Such traders often had a wife belonging to their days in the wilderness, and a later wife belonging to their days in town. While this custom of having two wives could not really be approved, it was generally accepted. Any Montreal woman who married a man who had been a fur trader could scarcely claim to have been deceived. She had good reason to suppose another wife (an Indian wife) had preceded her.

One fur trader who left Montreal in 1800 to serve at distant posts described the wilderness custom in a neat, matter-of-fact way: "... it is customary for all gentlemen

An 1867 decision in the old Court House on Notre Dame Street shook many families.

who remain, for any length of time, in this part of the world to have a female companion, with whom they can pass their time more socially and agreeably than to live a lonely life, as they must do if single.''

When a trader's days in the Northwest were over, and he was returning to Montreal to live, he was confronted with a hard decision. He had somehow to dispose of his Indian wife and his children. Several options were open. One option was simply to abandon the Indian wife and the children. It was a cruel but not infrequent decision. Other traders, though leaving their Indian wives behind, brought at least some of the children (generally the sons only) back with them to Montreal. They sent the boys to school, hoping to train them for city jobs. But such efforts to bring these children of the wilderness into city life were rarely successful.

In the 1830s a number of these traders' sons were boarders at Alexander Workman's school on Hospital Street (rue de Hôpital). Many years later Julius Scriver, the MP for Huntingdon, recalled them. ''Mr. Workman's school,'' he wrote, ''was one for both boarding and day pupils. The former in my time numbered 12 to 15. All of these but three... were sons of chief traders or chief factors in the Hudson's Bay Company by Indian mothers, the fathers, with but one exception, being of Scotch nationality. These half-breed lads and young men (two or three of them were 18 or 20 years of age) were of fair average mental capacity, and apparently of sound physical constitution; and yet, so far as I know, none of them were successful in the business or professional careers which most of them engaged in, and all of them, I believe, died comparatively young — most of them of disease of the lungs....''

Some wilderness marriages, often beginning harshly and casually, developed into happy and satisfying unions. One such trader was John Rowand, son of an assistant surgeon at the Montreal General Hospital. He left for the Northwest in 1802. While out hunting alone, he was thrown from his horse. The riderless horse galloped back to the trading post. An Indian girl, knowing something had happened to him, jumped on her own pony and rode out by the route the horse had come. She found Rowand lying on the ground, unable to walk, his leg broken. She set his leg and nursed him.

When Rowand recovered, he married her. His later career as a trader was outstandingly successful. Sir George Simpson, Governor of the Hudson's Bay Company, regarded Rowand as perhaps the best chief factor in the company's service. A career so successful would naturally have ended in a return to Montreal, with an ample income for living well among the amenities of a prosperous town. But Rowand's love for his Indian wife led him to settle permanently beside the Saskatchewan River, on what is now the site of Edmonton.

Another fur trader who could not bring himself to give up his Indian wife was Daniel Williams Harmon. In 1800 he had set out for the Northwest to serve as an agent of the Montreal fur trading partnership, McTavish, Frobisher and Company. As a young man of principle and scruples, he resisted for five years the temptation to take an Indian wife. In October 1805, he succumbed. He began living with a half-breed squaw, a girl of 14, daughter of a woman of the Crees, living west of the Rocky Mountains.

After 20 wilderness years, the time came when Harmon could return to Montreal. But he could not bring himself to come back alone, or with the children only. He wrote: ''Having lived with this woman as my wife, though we never formally contracted to each other... and having children by her, I consider that I am under a moral obligation not to dissolve the connection if she is willing to continue it.'' As for the children, he wrote: ''How could I tear them from a mother's love, and leave her to mourn over their absence to the day of her death?'' Harmon brought his wife and children with him from the wilderness. He eventually settled at Sault-au-Récollet, on the north shore of the Island of Montreal. He died at Sault-au-Récollet in 1843; his wife of Cree descent died in 1862. Her grave is in Mount Royal Cemetery.

Fur traders who left their Indian wives behind, and were married to white women when they returned to Montreal, never thought they were bigamists. Their Indian marriages they regarded as no marriages at all, even though sometimes they went through the Indian marriage rites. In 1867 a legal bombshell was dropped in Montreal. Mr. Justice Samuel Cornwallis Monk gave judgment in the Court House on Notre Dame Street (rue Notre-Dame) — the ''Old Court House'' still standing, a little west of the City Hall. In this building, Judge Monk ruled that a certain fur trader's marriage to an Indian woman in the Northwest was the legal marriage, and his subsequent marriage to another woman in Montreal was invalid. The children of the first marriage were legitimate, those of the second marriage (which was legally no marriage) were illegitimate.

This decision of the court brought consternation to a number of Montreal families, whose circumstances were similar to the case judged. Later, however, another case went to law. Here an opposite judgment was given, repudiating the validity of an Indian marriage. These conflicting judgments seemed to leave the whole question up in the air. The point of validity could be decisively settled only if a case were taken to the Privy Council in England, then the court of last resort for Canadians. But no such case was ever taken to final appeal.

On the whole, the traders' Indian wives were good wives, deserving better than they got. One of the principal historians of the fur trade, Dr. W. Stewart Wallace, gave his judgment: ''These dark-skinned consorts of the fur-traders were... wonderful wives. In the whole of the literature of the fur trade I have come across only a single case of infidelity among them; and this is... a glaring exception.''

The Duels That Never Came Off

Many duels were fought in Montreal. But some duels never came off. Challenges were issued. Pistols, however, were never discharged. Such abortive duels were few. Once a man was challenged, a duel was almost inevitable. The rules of duelling were the rules of society. They were affairs of honor among gentlemen. Cowardly evasion was everlasting shame. Yet there were duels initiated but not completed. No challenge was withdrawn unless the person challenged could explain that no insult had been intended, that a misunderstanding had arisen. Or the person challenged might admit his fault and offer his apologies. In all such cases, however, only the challenger could call off the duel. He had to be convinced that the explanations were real, or that the apologies were ample and not hedged about with evasions.

Such an explanation was made in Montreal in 1844 by Lewis T. Drummond, lawyer and politician. He had spoken harshly about Sydney Bellingham, another Montreal lawyer and politician. Bellingham claimed his personal character had been publicly defamed. Drummond explained. He had only been attacking Bellingham's political views. He had "in no way" meant to cast reflections on him "as an individual." This explanation was accepted by Bellingham. No duel was fought. But as the attack on Bellingham had been reported in the press, Bellingham published Drummond's apology in a Montreal newspaper of the day, *The Times*.

About 12 years earlier Sydney Bellingham had come close to being involved in a duel, in the role of a second. Bellingham had been asked to act as a second by Dr. William Robertson, the first dean of the McGill Medical Faculty. The doctor felt he had been publicly insulted by Louis Joseph Papineau, whose radical and reformist views were to be among the causes of the Rebellion of 1837.

Dr. Robertson, as a magistrate, had called for the assistance of the garrison troops in Montreal to control rioting in a rough election in 1832. The troops had fired on the rioters. Three deaths resulted. Papineau denounced Dr. Robertson. He even called him "an ugly likeness of the Devil." The doctor, believing such language intolerable, asked Bellingham to go to Papineau's house on Bonsecours Street. He was to ask Papineau name his second, in order that a duel might be arranged.

Papineau received Bellingham courteously. He took him to his study. Bellingham was impressed: "... his room bespoke the house of an accomplished and elegant scholar; many volumes, handsomely bound, graced the shelves." Papineau seated Bellingham on a sofa and sat down beside him. He listened while Bellingham issued Dr. Robertson's challenge to a duel.

At once Papineau ridiculed the idea. As a political leader, he felt he had to be free to deal frankly with the issues of the day. He was entitled to speak out, to use harsh words when he thought them justified. It would be impossible, it would be absurd, for a political leader to engage in duels with all who might be displeased with what he said. He then changed the subject, and went on to a pleasant discussion of politics in general. Bellingham went back to the waiting Dr. Robertson. He "reported on the barren result of the mission."

The Papineau house, where Bellingham went that day, still stands on Bonsecours Street, on the west side, a little below Notre Dame. It was rescued from dilapidation in 1961 by Eric McLean. He restored it as his residence, and stimulated interest in the preservation of Old Montreal.

One of the worst kinds of disgrace was to violate the rules of duelling, such as firing before the signal was given. Another unforgivable violation of the rules was to arrive on the duelling ground alone and without a second. Under such circumstances, a duel could not proceed. In any duel there was always the possibility that one of the contestants might be killed. Such a killing might appear as murder, unless the seconds were present. They were the representatives, the friends, of the duellists. They conducted the formalities. They saw that all was done fairly and in order.

One of the most eminent duellists was disgraced in 1839 by arriving ready to fight a duel, but unaccompanied by his second. The ensuing disgrace rankled within him till the day he died. This duellist was Major John Richardson. He was a veteran of the War of 1812. He had also seen service in Spain from 1834 till 1837, with the British Legion sent to support Queen Isabella against insurgents who sought to drive her from her throne. Major Richardson was also a writer. His book *Wacousta* was one of the first novels written in Canada.

Major Richardson was a highly experienced duellist. But he fell into a trap of his own unintentional making. He met an enemy of his while walking along what is now known as "the Main (St. Laurent Blvd). They exchanged furious words. Richardson was known to be "touchy," quick-tempered, given to sudden rages. That day his passion blinded his judgment. "Now you scoundrel," he shouted, "I will meet you in half an hour!"

Richardson had no sooner spoken than he realized his

The Louis Joseph Papineau house on Bonsecours Street still is in use.

mistake. He had left himself with little time to find a second and get to the duelling ground on the outskirts of the city. Frantically he ran about the streets. The few persons he knew who might act as his second were either out or declined to get involved. Time was passing. With only minutes left he hurried to the duelling ground. His opponent was there waiting, with his second. Richardson, arriving alone, explained his inability to find a second. He begged for a postponement. His opponent had him in his power. He was determined to make the most of it.

That evening the worst thing happened to Richardson that could ever happen to any man of honor. He was "posted." The custom of "posting" consisted of putting up placards in public places, naming and denouncing a man who

had defaulted on a challenge. Richardson knew he was technically in default. He could do nothing about it. Walking in Place d'Armes, a few days later, he came upon a group of officers of the Guards. All knew him. Yet, as he passed, all acted as though they had never seen him before in their lives.

There was one other way a duel might be prevented from coming off. But anyone who resorted to this means was held in contempt. A person challenged might call upon the police to protect him and arrest his challenger. In general, however, the law stayed out of duelling. A duel was regarded by the police and the courts as a private matter, of little public concern. The police, it was thought, had no place on the duelling grounds of the country.

Drama in the Pulpit

On the Sunday morning of February 19, 1911, Dr. Andrew J. Mowatt had been the minister of Erskine Church for a little over 20 years. He knew that his active ministry was close to its end. He had been ill for two months. The time had come when he must resign. But he wanted to get back to his pulpit for a few last sermons. He knew it would be a big effort to preach again. His strength had not come back and probably never would. He had asked Rev. Dr. Ephriam Scott to conduct the service, leaving him only with the sermon.

The service under Dr. Scott had proceeded. The time for the sermon was drawing near. The hymn before the sermon was being sung. Dr. Mowatt at first joined in it. Then he stepped back. He seated himself in one of the three chairs behind the pulpit. An anxious pause came when the hymn ended and Dr. Mowatt did not get up to speak. He had slumped over in his chair. He was carried to the vestry. Dr. Scott returned to the pulpit. He announced that the man who had been minister of Erskine for 20 years had died. He had been about to preach from the text in Revelation 1.17: "And when I saw Him, I fell at his feet as one dead."

Another dramatic text was that chosen in April 1827 by Rev. Alexander Mathieson, minister of St. Andrew's Church (Church of Scotland). As the minister who had to conduct the funeral service, Rev. Mathieson found himself in a unique position. He was not only to officiate at the funeral of a member of his church, and a friend; he was to speak of a murder he himself had witnessed. It happened on the evening of March 30, 1827, about 10 o'clock. The victim was Robert Watson, whose house was on the main street of the Récollet Suburbs. He was Montreal's Inspector of Flour, an important post in those days. On that evening he was sitting in his parlor talking to his minister. Unknown to the two friends sitting there in conversation, the unknown murderer was taking aim through an opening in the shutter. Suddenly the glass of the window was shattered, the room filled with smoke. Robert Watson rose convulsively from his chair and sank back. The gun, loaded with duck shot, had been well aimed. When Watson's shirt was opened, his right side was seen torn into a great wound. At first the surgeon was not without hope, even though he had to remove more than 150 pieces of buckshot from Watson's side; but Watson, after showing signs of recovery, grew worse. He suffered agonies. Hope ebbed away. He died in his house a few days later.

Robert Watson, from his prominence in the city, would have been given a large funeral in any case. But the horrible drama of his death brought 1,500 people to the old St. Andrew's Church on St. Peter Street (rue Saint-Pierre). Mr. Mathieson Rose to the occasion. He gave the text of his funeral sermon. It was from Jeremiah, the IX chapter, the 21st verse: "For death has come up into our windows."

Fortunately drama in the pulpit did not always take the form of tragedy. There was also the drama of eloquence. Few preachers in Montreal had so much pulpit eloquence as Rev. James Carmichael. He was rector of St. George's Anglican Church from 1882 to 1906, and bishop of Montreal 1906 to 1908.

In the pulpit James Carmichael risked theatrical effects. They would have been ludicrous if they had failed; but he knew how to carry them off. The impression made on his congregation was awesome. One Sunday he was speaking about the angels in heaven veiling their faces in the presence of God. The statement itself, even with his eloquence, was only moderately effective. What made the statement unforgettable was his accompanying gesture. He drew his sleeve over his face. For a few moments he stood veiled in the presence of his congregation.

A gesticulation so startling had to take its chance of being a failure. James Carmichael took a chance even greater when he was preaching about Baalam. He was describing how the spirit of God came upon Baalam and "transfixed" him. The idea of anyone being transfixed by the spirit of God was rather vague. Carmichael made it vivid. As he uttered the word "transfixed," he shrank back in the pulpit. He threw up both arms, and gazed at the ceiling. In this pose he stood motionless before the congregation, looking as if he had entered into another state of consciousness and was no longer aware of what was about him.

Rev. James Carmichael's dramatic advantages were many and valuable. An Irishman from Dublin, he had a rich Irish brogue. No actor could have been blessed with a profile more superbly cut. Advancing years did nothing to diminish his dramatic advantages. His head of wavy hair grew all the more becoming after it had turned white.

The pulpits of Montreal saw other types of drama. Sometimes it was the drama of humility. This was seen in the pulpit of St. Patrick's Church in 1887. On that day the Golden Jubilee of Father Patrick Dowd's ordination as a priest was being celebrated. It was a tremendous celebration, for Father Dowd had earned the love and honor of the whole Irish community. He had been brought from Ireland, as a young priest, in 1848. The Irish of the city, mostly recent immigrants, were sheep needing a shepherd. And a firm shepherd he was to be, a man of stern warning as well as thoughtful compassion. He had guided his Irish people, who had often arrived desperate from hunger, disease and political unsettlement. He led them into a way of hopeful life in their new country.

At the anniversary gathering in St. Patrick's Church old Father Dowd was lavished with tributes, lauded for all his many virtues. The moment came for him to enter his pulpit at St. Patrick's, to make his reply. It was a time when he might have been pardoned for basking in the adulation. But Father Dowd spoke in a way no one had expected. He preached against the delusions of human vanity. "Fifty years ago such kindness would likely have been dangerous to me," he said. "The 'old boy' would no doubt whisper into my ear something like this: 'If you were not somebody; if, in fact, you were not a great man, these friends, so serious and so enlightened, would not say such things of you.''

"Fifty years ago this would have been a real danger; today, if I know myself, it is not so. Behind, and not far behind, the opinion which your affection and kindness form of my actions, I see the judgment of another tribunal. Before long, I cannot say how soon, I shall have to stand before that tribunal and answer to an all-seeing, and all-knowing God, for the thoughts, words and deeds of my fifty years of priesthood. You, my dear friends, will not be there to excuse me. I shall be there alone with my works, by which I must stand or fall for all eternity. Poor silly vanity has not much standing room there.''

Those who heard those words say that a palpable stillness came over the huge congregation in St. Patrick's Church. Father Dowd had taken the opportunity of a lifetime to preach his most dramatic sermon. That reminder of the higher tribunal, coming after a tide of heedless human praise, made him, above all, the priest, on the Golden Jubilee of his priesthood.

Pulpit in St. Patrick's Church where Father Dowd spoke.

Chief Crowfoot in Town — the Government's Guest

One hundred years ago — in the autumn of 1886 — Crowfoot came to Montreal. He came on an escorted tour, the guest of the government of Canada. Everything possible was done to entertain and honor him. This visit was arranged as a reward. Crowfoot's influence had been critical during the Northwest Rebellion, only the year before. Crowfoot was one of the most powerful Indian chiefs on the Canadian prairies — a chief of the Blackfoot Indians. When Louis Riel planned his rebellion among the Métis of the Northwest in 1885, he also began at once to negotiate with Crowfoot. If Crowfoot's Indians joined the Métis, the

Chief Crowfoot toured the east as reward for staying out of Northwest Rebellion.

rebellion would gain in scope and resources. Riel made a strong appeal to the Indians. They, like the Métis, were alarmed by the coming of the white settlers, by the surveyors of the land and the builders of the railroad. They saw the disappearance of the buffalo herds that had provided their means of survival. They feared the loss of their ancient homelands to the white intruders.

Had Crowfoot given the word, the Indians he controlled would have joined Riel, as did the Crees under Poundmaker and Big Bear. The basis was there for a common cause. After a period of silence, Crowfoot spoke. To join Riel's rebellion would be folly. It could have no end but defeat and disaster. The prime minister, Sir John A. Macdonald, telegraphed a message: "The good words of Crowfoot are appreciated by the big chiefs at Ottawa... Crowfoot's words shall he sent to the Queen."

When the rebellion was over, Sir John A. expressed his appreciation by bringing Crowfoot to see the cities of eastern Canada. This Indian chief had never seen a big city in his life. As Crowfoot spoke no English, he took with him his favorite interpreter, Jean L'Heureux, and his old friend, the missionary priest, Father Albert Lacombe. A few Indians also went with him, including his half-brother, Three Bulls. Rooms in Montreal were reserved for Crowfoot and his travelling companions at the Richelieu Hotel. The hotel stood on St. Vincent Street, the little street below Place Jacques Cartier. Crowfoot was well pleased with the accommodation. The Richelieu Hotel, he said, "was fitted out well, and had good rooms and good beds, and was in every way much more desirable for a permanent abode than his family wigwam, and better than all, everything was free."

On the morning of his first day in Montreal he was driven around Mount Royal and given an impressive view of the size of the city lying below. Luncheon was provided by Mayor Honoré Beaugrand at the Windsor Hotel. In the evening, Crowfoot was taken to the grand bazaar being held to raise funds for the new Roman Catholic cathedral. Three thousand people were there, many having come to catch a glimpse of him. This they could do, because the dinner table for Crowfoot had been placed on a specially erected dais, where the mayor sat also. It was said to be a breach of Indian etiquette for a guest to refuse to eat what was set before him. The "hospitable ladies" serving the tables of the bazaar were not aware of this rule of Indian decorum. They were eager to see that their guest was kept amply supplied. Crowfoot had much to consume but seemed to relish it.

After dinner the crowd waited to hear Crowfoot speak. Through his interpreter he said he felt very tired. He had been given "a royal welcome" wherever he had gone; but these things, to which he was not accustomed, had worn him out. Father Lacombe would have to do the talking for him. He would, however, say that he had learned that we must forgive each other. He asked his hearers to pray for him, as he had heard that white people were good at praying. He was sorry for many things he had done in his younger years (during his early love of the warpath). He now knew it was wrong to make war.

Crowfoot resumed his busy schedule next day. After a trip down the Lachine Rapids, he was taken to Mont St. Mary Convent, the Bank of Montreal and the offices of the Canadian Pacific Railway. At the CPR, the president, Sir George Stephen (later Lord Mount Stephen), and all his principal officers were waiting to greet him. On their behalf the general manager, William (later Sir William) Van Horne, said how grateful they all were for his loyalty during the rebellion and for protecting the company's property from Indian raids. He then presented the chief with a perpetual pass on all the CPR lines. Through his interpreter Crowfoot replied: "My heart has always been loyal... I would not let my young men go on the warpath... When I return my young men will protect the railway and the fire-wagons" (by which he meant the locomotives).

That evening he was again at the grand bazaar. This time Indians from Caughnawaga presented him with an address: "We salute you, great chief of the north." Then they laid many gifts before him — boxes of cigars, pipes, blankets, two handsome rifles. Crowfoot gratefully accepted everything, except the rifles. He knew too much now, he said, to desire any implements of war.

Montrealers had many opportunities to see Crowfoot during his visit. They found him an impressive presence, composed and dignified, and statesmanlike in utterance. He was described as of medium height, copper-colored, about 56 years of age. His small black restless eyes were "shrewd and farseeing." His nose was aquiline, "like an eagle's." The corners of his rather large mouth were turned down, the lips thin, indicating firmness, his chin rather pointed. Long, black, coarse hair fell over his shoulders and down his back.

Sir John A. Macdonald generally had more than one motive for everything he did. Not only did he want to reward Crowfoot for his help in the Northwest Rebellion, he hoped that Crowfoot would be suitably astonished and would take back to other chiefs his deep impression of the power that lay eastward, beyond the prairies.

Crowfoot, however, was not a man to be deeply impressed by big, crowded cities. He was a man who lived with nature, and uncluttered prairie horizons. When he lay dying, less than four years after his Montreal visit, he spoke of life itself in prairie images: "What is life? It is the flash of the firefly in the night. It is the breath of the buffalo in the winter time. It is the little shadow that runs across the grass and loses itself in the sunset."

Presbyterian Father
of Bohemian Artist

In the 1880s, a perplexing problem faced David Morrice. He was one of Montreal's richest Presbyterian businessmen. One of his sons, James Wilson, had an old idea. He wanted to become an artist.

The artist's father had nothing against art. In fact, he was an art collector, a strong supporter ot the Montreal Art Association (as the Montreal Museum of Fine Arts was then known). But while he appreciated art, he had never thought one of his sons would want to be an artist. David Morrice felt he could provide a sounder future for his sons in his own business. A Scot from Perthshire, he had started his business in Montreal in 1863. This agency, selling cotton goods wholesale, had grown bigger and bigger. By the 1880s, he was handling more cotton than anyone else in Canada. He wanted to pass on the business to his sons. Two of them had entered the firm. With pride he had changed its name to D. Morrice, Sons & Co. No longer was it his alone. It was a Morrice family business.

But he had this other son who wanted no part of it. David Morrice felt responsible not only for his son's material welfare; he also had reponsibility for his soul. If he consented to his son's wish, he would be committing him to study art abroad. The studios and cafés of Paris might tempt him into degrading vices, such as might bring him to a sad and early death. If his son did not wish to enter the family business, there were still other reputable professions he could follow. The father favored the law. He sent his son to the University of Toronto, then on to law studies at Toronto's Osgoode Hall. James Wilson Morrice was called to the bar of Ontario. But James was bored with the law. He was spending his time painting. The old problem returned. David Morrice again had to decide what he should do.

It seemed so strange, for at first James had been such an obedient boy, willing to respect the values of life in the Morrice home. In that home on Redpath Street, every Sunday was a day set apart from all the other days of the week. It was the Day of Rest, a pause for devotion, meditation, quietude, a time to ponder the meaning and duty of the religious commitment. In the Morrice home on Sunday, no one was permitted to read secular matter, such as the weekly newspapers. Even guests were discouraged; they might disturb the Sabbath calm.

For David Morrice, the Presbyterian faith, with its deep doctrine of the absolute sovereignty of God, was the bedrock of his existence. He was a pillar of the Crescent St. Presbyterian Church. He was particularly concerned with an adequate supply of young men for the Presbyterian ministry. In 1882 he built a magnificent hall for the Montreal Presbyterian College — the David Morrice Hall. In the one building were a hall for convocations or other large gatherings, a dining room, a dormitory and a library. Morrice had the building designed by John James Browne, the same architect who designed his home on Redpath Street and some of the cotton mills. Most of the old Montreal Presbyterian College has been since demolished and the college has moved to University Street. But the David Morrice Hall still stands, now serving other uses. It is massively Gothic, a sombre building for serious purposes. It stands on the east side of McTavish Street, just above the McGill Library, where a road leads from McTavish Street into the McGill campus. In making his presentation to the college, David Morrice had said:''The outlay will cause me considerable personal sacrifice, but I make it with pleasure, believing it of God.''

It was asking much of David Morrice, with his Presbyterian background, to consent to having his son adopt the irregular life of a Bohemian artist. But his son remained determined. He was supported by David Morrice's friend and neighbor Sir William Van Horne. Van Horne, president of the Canadian Pacific Railway, was not only an art collector but an artist. He had a studio in a high room of his Sherbrooke Street mansion. There he would paint far into the night. Van Horne was confident that James Morrice had fine artistic talent. Already he was painting well. Training would make him superb. In the end, David Morrice gave in. His son set out to study art abroad. David Morrice financed him.

After three years had gone by the father thought he ought to see what sort of work his son was doing. He asked him to send some examples. James sent a series of paintings to the Montreal art dealer William Scott & Sons. David Morrice could make nothing of them. His son had been influenced by French impressionism (even if he remained a rather independent impressionist). His father could not adjust himself to a style so strange. Sir William Van Horne arrived again to give his opinion. He pronounced the paintings splendid — so good, in fact, that he bought the whole lot for his own collection.

Gradually David Morrice was assured that his son really was developing into a great artist. Many of the principal art galleries in the world were acquiring his works. David Morrice came to understand his son's style as a painter. He felt a father's pride. This pride reached a point in 1907 when he wanted his business friends in Montreal to realize the achievements of his artist son. He presented to the Mount Royal Club one of his son's finest paintings — ''La

Presbyterian College erected by father of artist J.W. Morrice.

Place Chateaubriand, St. Malo.''

The bond between father and son remained unbroken. Strains, however, must have been severe. James had wandered far from his father's lifestyle. Nevertheless, he returned regularly to stay at the Morrice family home on Redpath Street. He was now making no attempt to accommodate himself to his father's standards of thought or conduct. On these Montreal visits he remained the Parisian Bohemian. He scorned social invitations and went his own way. When pressed, against his will, to visit a Montreal mansion to give his opinion of the owner's collection of paintings, he pronounced them all horrible beyond description. Yet these visits to his father's home continued until his parents died, both of them in the year 1914. He lost interest in ever coming back.

The sad end the father had feared for his son came to pass. James succumbed to a regrettable ''slavery to stimulants,''

as the Montrealer painter Edmond Dyonnet put it. He died among strangers at Tunis, in Northern Africa, in 1924. A French hospital doctor, the English consul and the clergyman of the English church buried him in a Tunis cemetery. It was far from the Morrice family lot in Mount Royal Cemetery, where his parents had been buried 10 years before.

By agreeing to allow his son to follow an artist's career, David Morrice had made a contribution to Canadian art, even to the art of the world. He had provided his son with the regular income to work as he wished, to travel wherever he wanted. No financial stringency ever hindered his artistic progress. And those Presbyterian Sundays in the Montreal home on Redpath Street may had lent a certain tone to his life's work. The French art critic Ary LeBlond detected ''a feeling of gentle melancholy.'' He commented: ''... one always feels he does his paintings on a Sunday afternoon.''

Montreal's Downtown Cemeteries

On the east side of Victoria Square, about midway between St. James and St. Antoine (rue Saint-Jacques and rue Saint-Antoine), is Fortification Lane (ruelle des Fortifications). The origin of the name is explained by a tablet. The lane marks the approximate line of the northern wall of the old fortifications that once enclosed Montreal. These walls were built in the 18th century, under the French regime, by Chaussegros de Léry, a military engineer in the reign of King Louis XV. The western wall stood at about the present line of McGill Street and the roadway that marks the eastern end of Victoria Square. The eastern wall was about Berri Street; the southern wall about Commissioners Street. In fact, Commissioners Street received its name, not from the Harbour Commissioners, but from those appointed in the early years of the 19th century to supervise the demolition of the walls, which had become a hindrance to the town's expansion. Beyond the walls were straggling suburbs. But the centre of Montreal's military, administrative, ecclesiastical, business and social life was within the walls. As part of this compact organization, the cemeteries were within the walls also.

The principal cemeteries were just inside the northern wall marked by Fortification Lane today. They occupied the area beginning close to the wall and extending down to about the middle of what is now St. James Street. And they ran from about St. François-Xavier Street (rue Saint-François-Xavier) to the present beginnings of Victoria Square. This means that the buildings on the north side of St. James Street today are standing in these old cemeteries. When the custom of burying "within the walls" was abandoned, most of the old bones were left lying where they had been interred.

Later, when foundations and cellars for the buildings on St. James Street's upper side were being dug the bones were unearthed. Even then, in some cellars, the bones were not all removed. They were left lying above ground. A story of a cellar full of bones is told about a building at or near the corner of St. James Street and Victoria Square. A writer in *The Gazette* in 1872 said: "The writer has frequently been told by a gentleman who in his boyhood resided in St. James Street... that a wine cellar of more than ordinary depth was almost paved with bones and skulls, and that for this reason none of the servants could be induced to go into the place alone, save an old butler who had the cellar in charge, and who cared so much for his wines that all the ghosts in a dozen grave yards would not have frightened him from them."

Back in the French regime the Roman Catholics began burying their dead south of the wall. When Protestants started to settle in Montreal, after the coming of British rule in 1760, they needed a burial place also. They, too, opened a cemetery just south of that northern wall. Most of the interments in the Protestant cemetery "within the walls" were performed by Rev. David Chabrand deLisle. He was a Protestant clergyman from France, "un Français de France," who was appointed to be the "Protestant episcopal minister" (Anglican).

The government had selected deLisle, hoping he might be able to convert French Canadians to Protestantism. He proved doubly unsuccessful. He made no progress in French Canadian conversions; and he spoke English so badly that his Protestant parishioners could scarcely understand what he was saying. Nevertheless, David Chabrand deLisle was the Protestant minister in Montreal for nearly 30 years. For much of the time he was the only one. This meant that he read the graveside services for most of the Protestants in the town. When he died in 1794, he himself was buried in the same cemetery.

These cemeteries "within the walls" were extremely convenient, particularly for the Roman Catholics. The Catholic funerals were held in Notre Dame Church in Place d'Armes (not the present building, but an earlier church, standing just in front of today's Notre Dame). When the body was carried from the church, it had to be taken only a few feet away for burial. By the end of the 18th century, however, continued burials "within the walls" were causing increasing concern. Public health might be endangered. The closing of an old cemetery required the permission of the Attorney General of Lower Canada. The churchwardens of Notre Dame submitted their petition. The reply of the Attorney General went beyond approval. He demanded the closure of the cemeteries. Burials "within the walls" would have to cease.

Catholics and Protestants both established new cemeteries beyond the walls. Neither foresaw how rapidly the city would grow. Much of the new Catholic cemetery acquired in 1799 is now Dominion Square and Place du Canada. Much of the new Protestant cemetery is now the Complexe Guy Favreau. Meanwhile the erection of buildings, where the old cemeteries "within the walls" had been, unearthed the remains that had been left. As the demand for real estate on St. James Street increased, many of the first buildings erected were torn down and replaced by bigger ones.

This rebuilding resulted in repeated and deeper excavations. Bones missed by the earlier builders were turned up by those who followed. In 1860, M.E. David, making excavations for shops on the north side of St. James Street (on the site later occupied by the Canada Life Building), discovered several skeletons. One was the skeleton of a woman. It still had its "beautiful long flaxen hair." In July 1907, laborers were digging foundations for the Canadian Bank of Commerce, near St. Peter (on the site previously occupied by the St. James Street Methodist Church, forerunner of the St. James United Church on St. Catherine Street). Their picks uncovered two skeletons near the street line of Fortification Lane. Earlier excavators on the spot had just missed these bones. Had they gone down three inches deeper they would have found them.

Such a discovery had an air of unreality. A reporter of the time remarked; "The remains were gathered up and a small box built for them. Now they rest in a corner awaiting the arrival of some official to remove them. Meanwhile the little box lies unnoticed, and, of itself, without attraction." The bones were those of men. Their identification would never be known. The place where the skeletons had been uncovered was already swarming with construction workers. Even the dead and the buried had to give place to the future.

Fortification Lane from Victoria Square shows historical plaque on building.

For Sale: A Haunted House

❝ … the Celebrated Haunted House… will be Sold…'' This announcement appeared in an auctioneer's advertisement in Montreal on November 8, 1853. It might seem that anyone trying to sell such a house would do his best to conceal its reputation for being haunted. But the auctioneer, John Leeming, was making the most of it. In this case, concealment would have been impossible. The haunted house was one of Montreal's most conspicuous landmarks. It stood far up on the slope of Mount Royal. In those days, no clutter of high-rises intercepted the view of the mountain. From any point in town this big stone building could be seen, sombrely looming.

For nearly half a century it had been known as ''the Haunted House'' — a massive ruin, a mansion never finished, never occupied. It stood in fields where no streets ran. Today its location may be defined at just below Pine Avenue (Avenue des Pins), between Peel and McTavish (rather nearer to Peel). Its haunted reputation was supported by more than legend. Montrealers testified to strange things heard, strange things seen. Out of the ruin came moans and screams, or a gurgling, as of someone dying by strangulation. White figures leaped in and out of vacant cellar windows. On clear nights, in a particular phase of the moon, a ghostly figure appeared on the high tin roof.

Parts of a "haunted house" are in Duggan House on McTavish Street.

All these spectral allegations seemed confirmed by the house's history. The tragedy of the house invited hauntings. Simon McTavish had ordered the house to be built in 1804. For the times, it was a mansion, the symbol of pretentious wealth. Possibly Simon McTavish was the richest man in Montreal in 1804. He had come from the Highlands of Scotland as a penniless lad. Fur trading made his fortune. He was a leader of the traders of Montreal who formed the partnership — the North West Company. Their aggressive vitality challenged the old Hudson's Bay Company itself in the productive wilderness.

McTavish's mountainside property was immense. From Mount Royal it spread southwards, down to the borders of the town. Its western boundary would today be about Stanley, its eastern boundary the middle of Mansfield. By building his mansion near the uppermost limit of his property, McTavish not only assured himself magnificent views. He also made sure that his mansion would have maximum visibility. His prosperity could be seen by all.

McTavish died in the summer of 1804 while in the midst of building his mansion, long to be known as "McTavish's Castle." On his deathbed his request was that he not be buried in a crowded cemetery but on his own spacious land. He is said even to have chosen the very spot. It was high on the mountain, above his house. There he had sat on summer days, reading. At that favored spot McTavish still lies in a mausoleum. It is above Pine Avenue, just west of the stone wall marking the limits of Sir Hugh Allan's old property (now the Allan Memorial Institute of Psychiatry). Though the mausoleum is there, no longer can it be seen. Many years ago it was covered with earth. It had to be protected against vandals.

Documents on the history of the McTavish house were collected by Montreal notary Dakers Cameron. Included are many affidavits, signed and attested, in which those who had known the McTavish house had set down their memories of it. In these documents the ghostly stories are explained. That gurgling sound, as of someone dying by strangulation, came from a rill flowing under the house and exposed during its demolition. The tradition had been that McTavish had hanged himself from a beam in his unfinished house. Actually, he died of natural causes — of pneumonia. Moans and screams heard in the haunted house had been real. But they came from vagrants seeking shelter in it and trying to scare away intruders. Other ghost stories, though based on things seen, had similar ordinary causes. White figures leaping in and out of cellar windows were only sheep from the fields round about. As for the ghost on the tin roof, it was a phenomenon created by a dazzling gleam of moonlight on a certain angle of the roof, at a certain hour.

John Leeming's auction sale in 1853 disposed of a huge portion of the McTavish estate, from the "Base of the Montreal Mountain" down to Sherbrooke Street. The auctioneer declared: "It is about the last of the opportunities which will be offered at public sale of securing lots on this favored position. This side of the Mountain is now well nigh taken up, and we think that the next generation will envy the present owners." The auctioneer pictured the elegant developments certain to come to that area: "In addition to the enchanting scenery which will for ever be uninterrupted from this renowned locality, its immediate neighborhood will ere long be vastly improved and embellished."

For purposes of the auction, the McTavish land had been divided into five large sections. Each was sold separately. Section five was bought by Hugh Allan (later Sir Hugh), the shipping magnate. This was the section northeast of the McTavish house; it ran nearly 700 feet on to the mountain. At that time Hugh Allan was living on St. Catherine Street (rue Sainte-Catherine), where the St. James United Church now stands. Later, from 1861 to 1863, he was to build his new mansion, Ravenscrag, on the McTavish land, above Pine Avenue. Section 4 in the sale was described as "A MAGNIFICENT EMPLACEMENT, about 3000 feet Square — including the Celebrated Haunted House." It was bought by Augustus Heward, listed as a "general broker."

Prices seemed high. Hugh Allan paid $2,250 for his section. Heward paid $2,650 for the Haunted House and the surrounding 3,000 square feet of land. John Frothingham, of the hardware firm, was present, but did not bid. He wrote in his journal: "enormous prices I think, but people feel rich."

McTavish's Haunted House, though never finished, had survived rather well since built in 1804. It had been so well built that the work begun by McTavish could still be brought to completion. Among the papers in the Dakers Cameron file is a handsome plan, drawn up to show how the work could be done. It was a plan by one of the leading architectural firms in Montreal — Hopkins, Lawford & Nelson. Though undated, it belongs to the late 1850s, after the auction sale. Such plans, though considered, were abandoned. In 1861 "the Celebrated Haunted House" was demolished. Yet even then it did not altogether disappear. Its high-quality materials were incorporated in a new house, built a little northeast of it by O.S. Wood, of the Montreal Telegraph Company. In an affidavit in the Cameron file, Wood says: "The house was removed in 1861 by the mason who built the new house. All of the material of value in the old house was used in the new house, coach house, driveway and walks... The joice (first quality pine) from the old house was cut up by my carpenter, Mr. Robert Weir and used for doors, window frames and finishing in the new."

The house built by O.S. Wood was later owned by Mathew Hamilton Gault, who founded Sun Life in 1871. Eventually it passed into the possession of George Herick Duggan, noted civil engineer and yachtsman, one of the founders of the Royal St. Lawrence Yacht Club. From him it went to McGill University. In this way the Duggan House, as it is known at McGill, stands at the head of McTavish Street as a tangible link with "the Celebrated Haunted House" of Simon McTavish.

When the Troops Fired
on Beaver Hall Hill

Father Alessandro Gavazzi was coming to town. And the coming of Father Gavazzi meant trouble. Before he would leave Montreal a riot seemed inevitable. He was due to reach Montreal on the steamboat from Quebec about five o'clock in the morning of June 9, 1853. He would arrive with a scarred face. On the evening of June 6 he had been the centre of a riot in Quebec. He was lecturing from the pulpit of the Free Presbyterian Church on St. Ursule Street (now Chalmers United Church). In the midst of his discourse someone shouted from the audience: "It's a lie!" Other shouts followed: "Turn out Gavazzi! It's a lie!"

Sticks and bludgeons appeared. The rioters beat about them "without respect to persons." Then they surged toward the pulpit. In the pulpit Father Gavazzi folded his arms. He calmly "surveyed the tumult." Bibles, hymn books flew at him. Some hit him, but he did not change his attitude. When the mob scrambled onto the platform, Father Gavazzi seized a chair. He cracked down on his attackers. In his hands the chair burst into splinters. He snatched up a stool and bore down on others. Numbers counted against him in the end. They grabbed him, tossed him over the pulpit. He fell 15 feet to the floor below. His supporters had been fighting their way towards the platform to help him. They hurried him away down a staircase to the schoolroom in the basement.

As Father Gavazzi was to lecture in Montreal, more riots were feared. They would probably be even worse. This Italian, expelled from the order of Barnabite monks, was heading a campaign against the Papacy. His claim was that he was a Catholic still; he wished to restore the church to its primitive simplicity, as it had been before the idea of the Papacy had been engrafted on it. His lecture topic was provocative: "The Popish System — Its Blindness, Intolerance and Slavery." Wherever he lectured, Father Gavazzi appeared dressed in the black cassock of a Barnabite monk. He did not wear this costume habitually. It was carried by him in a bag to the lecture hall. He would put it on before appearing on the platform.

The French Canadian Catholics paid little attention to Father Gavazzi. As far as they were concerned, he might have come and gone without open disturbance. The fact that he was speaking in English may have limited their interest. Vehement opposition, however, came from the Irish Catholics. Many of them were recent immigrants from an unhappy and tormented land, where riots had become an accepted expression (even the only available expression) of religious, political or other protests. Some Protestants hailed Father Gavazzi as a valuable ally. Others disapproved of the man and his methods, but upheld the principle of free speech.

Arrangements had been made to have him give his lecture in Zion Congregational Church. This church stood on the west side of Beaver Hall Hill (Côte du Beaver Hall), a short distance below la Gauchetière. Rioting broke out. An invading mob was thrown out of the church and pursued, in a running flight. Police had been marshalled in strength. But they were unarmed (except for batons). They could not cope with rioters firing revolvers. Soon the police were beaten back. Anticipating serious trouble, the mayor had earlier appealed to the British garrison for help. Two divisions of the Scottish 26th Regiment, the Cameronians, a little more than 100 men, were assigned to support him. In the Engine House on the Haymarket (now Victoria Square) they had been concealed, ready to be called into action.

The sight of policemen running away unnerved Mayor Wilson. He hurried to the Engine House, flustered and confused. He requested the officers to have the soldiers load their muskets with ball cartridge. "There is no time to be lost!" he said, as he hurried them up near to the church. Onlookers thought he was almost beyond himself — so frantic as scarcely to know what he was doing. He asked the officers to draw up the troops in two lines, one facing south toward the Haymarket, the other facing north up the hill.

By this time the trouble seemed to have passed. Rioters had moved below to the Haymarket. Some movement among them could be seen down there but nothing menacing. Father Gavazzi had concluded his lecture. The people were coming out of Zion Church and were walking slowly northward up the steep slope of Beaver Hall Hill. From somewhere in the Haymarket a few revolver shots were fired. Their report was weak; probably the shots came from small pocket pistols. They were aimless; no one was hit. In fact, nobody seemed to pay much attention. There was no rush for cover. Groups stood about talking quite unconcerned.

To Mayor Wilson these shots were the final exasperation. His nerves, already strained near the breaking-point, gave way. "The people are murdering each other," he said. Then and there he read the Riot Act. Little was accomplished. In the Haymarket the crowd was too far away to hear what he was reading, or even to know what it was about.

Then came the terrible volleys. The division of the Cameronians facing south fired into the Haymarket. The men aimed high. Most of the shots went into the air. But

Beaver Hall Hill where troops fired up and down the street.

some of them struck. About a minute after this volley, the division of the regiment facing north fired also. The northern volley rained on the people from the church as they walked up Beaver Hall Hill. They swayed, staggered, tumbled to the pavement.

The Montreal notary John Helder Isaacson wrote in his diary: "I heard someone shout aloud, 'Fire' — the next moment the soldiers below sent a volley into the Haymarket... and then after the interval of but a few seconds the troops near me took up the firing and shot down the people coming out of Zion church. I never saw such a massacre... my escape from being riddled was most wonderful having been immediately in front of the soldiers and within a few feet of their muskets. As soon as I heard them commence firing I threw myself flat on my face and remained on the ground until it ceased... within six feet of me a little lad of about it was shot down, the poor little fellow only said 'I'm shot — I'm shot.' "

Next day all Montreal was aghast and outraged. City Council met. Mayor Wilson endeavored to defend himself. "I... read the Riot Act, but I never gave the word to fire," he insisted. "When the other division fired I ran up to them and cried, 'For God's sake what have you been doing? What cause had you to fire?' This I vouch for before my Maker." Isaacson wrote in his diary about going to see the mayor on Sunday morning, June 12 (three days

after the massacre). "McIver called on me this morning sent by the mayor who wished to see me. I saw His Honor, who is, as well as he may be in a very troubled state of mind, a fearful charge is brought against him, and until it is removed he must naturally be very uneasy — Poor Mrs. Wilson too is very unhappy — well indeed it would have been for Mr. W. had not his ambition prompted him to be mayor for the third year."

A long, patient investigation failed to find out what had actually happened or why. All seemed a mystery. The Cameronians were professional soldiers, well-trained and disciplined. Their officers knew well that any attempt to quell a civil disturbance should be done with the utmost prudence and restraint. The investigation could not find out who had ordered the troops to fire as furiously as on a battlefield. The colonel of the Cameronians, and the other officers, absolutely denied having given any such order. The mayor continued to insist he had never given the order himself, or asked any officer to give it.

The Cameronians could never live down their volleys on the hill. No regiment in Montreal had ever been so unpopular. Isolated soldiers, walking on dark or lonely streets, were waylaid and beaten up. There was only one thing for the government to do: send the Cameronians off to duty somewhere far away. It was done. Soon they were despatched to Bermuda.

Terror Amid Floating Ice

There was a time when anyone wishing to go between Montreal and the South Shore had to risk his life. It was the dangerous in-between season — the season when the river was full of floating ice, before it had frozen hard from shore to shore. In that season ice was charging downstream with the speed of the turbulent current, ready to smash anything that got in its way. The last of the steamboats to linger on the river were the paddle-wheelers that ferried passengers to the South Shore. Even they had at last to scurry for shelter. Running into an ice-floe might be as bad as running into a rock.

In most years the river did not freeze entirely until the middle of January. Once it had frozen solidly from shore to shore, it could be crossed on the ice road — a good road, smoothed and marked out with fir boughs. But for these two months — from the middle of November till the middle of January — anyone needing to go from Montreal to the South Shore had to take his chances among the ice-floes, hoping for the best, but often almost scared out of his wits by the experience.

The only way of getting across during that in-between period was by canoe — not the birch bark canoe, but canoes made of heavy wood. The heavy canoes could withstand a good deal of battering from the ice. But they could go down if caught among contending ice-floes and overwhelmed.

The crews of these big winter canoes were the "canotiers." They were hardy French Canadians of the voyageur type, men who made a livelihood by exertion in danger. Canotiers with their canoes would gather along the Montreal waterfront. They waited for passengers. These passengers, as they arrived, would be seated on the bottom of the canoes, wrapped in buffalo robes. When enough passengers were in a canoe to justify a trip, the canotiers said a prayer, crossed themselves, seized the gunwales of the canoe and jumped in as they launched it on the river. One canotier, the skipper, sat on a raised platform at the stern, steering with a specially shaped paddle. Another canotier was at the prow, peering ahead for lanes of open water, his hand shading his eyes. In his forward position he met the spray. Hoarfrost soon whitened his clothes; icicles dangled from hair and beard. At both sides of the canoe other canotiers paddled.

Some oncoming ice might be thrust aside with paddles. Some of it might be dodged. But floes might be drifting downstream as big as rafts. Where these floes came together the way ahead would be blocked. Canotiers then leaped from canoe to ice, pulling the canoe after them. Suddenly the canoe became a sleigh. Canotiers dragged it over the ice till clear water was reached on the far side. With a splash the canoe was launched again. Meanwhile passengers, still seated on the bottom, were jolted and tumbled about. Passengers, from their position at the bottom of the canoe, saw everything at its most intimidating angle. For them a crossing was more than excitement. It was a ceaseless alternation between anxiety and panic.

No journey to the South Shore at that season was ever for pleasure. A crossing was made only when it could not be avoided — only on urgent business that could not wait. In 1797, Lieut. George Landmann had been ordered to leave England at once to report for garrison duty in Canada. It was December when he reached the South Shore of the St. Lawrence. Being a newcomer, he was appalled to learn that he could reach Montreal only by crossing the river "amidst the most alarming confusion of floating ice rushing along at a frightful speed."

The crossing was even more difficult than usual. For six hours they were on the river, battling the ice. He wrote of "numerous escapes from being crushed between large moving islands driving upon each other while we were betwixt them." Always there was the risk of being carried downstream far below Montreal. When at last Lieut. Landmann reached the Montreal waterfront, he found "some hundreds of persons... gathered on the shore." They had been fascinated by watching the struggle, not knowing how it would end. He was now congratulated on his safe arrival.

In December 1856, Montreal accountant Philip S. Ross had a compelling reason for crossing to the South Shore. His fiancée was arriving from Scotland. The harbor of Montreal being closed for the season, she would be landing at Portland, Maine. He had to get there, to meet and greet her. Ross made his crossing of the St. Lawrence on December 5. He and some other passengers went along the waterfront to find a canoe. They caught one just setting out. All jumped in. Ross wrote: "... we labored away and what with the jabbering and disputing and screaming of the crew and the yells of a dispirited passenger... and the blessing of the company of one priest and two nuns, we arrived without damage on the other side." Ross, however, had a soaking. Near the South Shore the ice seemed thick and strong. The canotiers had drawn the canoe on to it and were dragging it along. "Being benumbed," wrote Ross, "I got out to heat myself by exercise and was busy lending a helping hand pulling along the vessel when down goes the ice — the canoe is floating and I hang on by the side... my legs laved as high as the knees in the cool waters...."

Ross reached Portland in time to meet his fiancée on her arrival. They journeyed toward Montreal. When they reached the South Shore it began to rain; then came snow, followed by a hailstorm. Unpleasant as such weather was, it at least was comparatively mild. Ross learned that one of the paddle-wheel steamboats had come out of its winter quarters. It might venture a few more trips across the river. If the weather cleared sufficiently it would be leaving St. Lambert. At once Ross hired a sleigh. With his bride he headed for St. Lambert. He found, however, there was now some doubt whether the ferry would be running after all. For about three hours he and his bride huddled together on the quay, sheltering themselves as best they could.

The ending was happy: "The storm, however, almost cleared off and we got across safe..." Philip S. Ross had been fortunate. Though he himself had to cross the river in a canoe when setting out to meet his fiancée, he had been able to take her over the river on the steamboat. It was bad enough to have to introduce her to the Canadian winter by spending three hours waiting on the St. Lambert quay. But to terrify her in a canoe, crossing amongst scurrying ice, would have been too much.

Sturdy wooden canoes were used to cross St. Lawrence River during the winter.

Montreal's "Crusaders' Chapel"

Montreal has a crusaders' chapel. It might seem such chapels would be found only in ancient churches in the British Isles or in Europe — memorials of the great crusades of the Middle Ages. But Montreal has one, too. The crusade it commemorates came much later, in the 1860s and 1870s. But it was in the spirit of the ancient crusades. Those who took part were leaving their native land to go far away to defend a holy place. This Montreal chapel may be seen on the east side of the Cathedral-Basilica of Mary Queen of the

World. On four large marble tablets, the names of the 507 crusaders are cut in gold letters. In glass cases along the north and south walls are documents, medals, military caps, pieces of accoutrement, old photographs. A silver model of a steamship hangs from the ceiling, a votive offering in gratitude for deliverance from storms at sea.

At the time of this crusade the Popes ruled not only the Vatican but all of Rome and large states in other parts of Italy. The Papal States, as they were called, were said to

The Cathedral/Basilica Mary Queen of the World houses a "crusaders' chapel."

be necessary if the Pope was to remain independent of all earthly powers. If the Pope lost these states (above all Rome, the ''Eternal City'') he might no longer be free to act as the independent head of an international church. In the 1860s the movement for the unification of Italy, in which Garibaldi was the commanding figure, was attacking the Papal States and threatening even Rome. The Pope called on the Roman Catholics of the world to come to his defence.

In Montreal, the Roman Catholic bishop, Mgr. Ignace Bourget, called for recruits from every parish in his diocese. As this was a holy crusade, no recruits were enrolled unless they had from their parish priests certificates of sound moral character. The bishop called upon every one of the 400,000 Catholics in his diocese to contribute 30 cents a year — a total of $100,000. Larger subscriptions came also from those both wealthy and devout. He also called upon the women in the religious orders to make the uniforms. These uniforms were modelled on those of the Zouaves, a celebrated regiment in the French army. The Canadian recruits were known as ''Les Zouaves Pontificaux'' — the Papal Zouaves.

It is doubtful if even the great crusades of the Middle Ages could have evoked more mystical, more fervent feeling than this crusade of 1867-70. This feeling surged in the ceremonies at Notre Dame Church in Place d'Armes on the evening of February 18, 1868 — the evening before the first detachment of Zouaves (six other detachments were to follow) were to depart for Rome. As early as three o'clock in the afternoon some of the congregation had taken their places in the pews. By seven o'clock the crush was ''tremendous.'' Even the tiered balconies were jammed. The vast church was brilliantly lighted, everywhere decorated.

Ceremonies began at eight. The Zouaves, headed by a band, marched in. After a musical program, Mgr. Louis François Laflèche, coadjutor bishop of Trois Rivières, who enjoyed ''a high reputation as an orator,'' spoke. ''The Christian,'' he said, ''is, above all men, a soldier, and belongs to a combatting society... the normal state of the church is a state of war. A terrible struggle is going on. The Church is a military society. We in Canada have a special mission to fulfill.'' Bishop Bourget then presented the Zouaves with their colors. The flag was white silk, with the papal mitre and keys embroidered in gold, and with the Zouaves' motto: ''Aime Dieu et va ton chemin.'' (''Love God and go on your way.'')

This first (and the largest) detachment of the Papal Zouaves from Quebec entered Rome, wildly welcomed. Quarters were assigned them in the monastery of St. Francis. There they hung up an oil painting of St. Jean Baptiste they had brought with them — the patron saint of French Canada.

One day that summer Pope Pius IX invited the Canadian Zouaves to the Vatican. He received them and himself conducted them on a tour of its great art galleries. The Pope stepped lightly, setting a quick pace. He then led them into the Vatican gardens. Under a marble pavilion he thanked them for their devotion to the church, and gave each gifts, including a silver medal bearing his effigy.

Not all was solemn. He livened the gathering with a practical joke. He pointed to a gap in the hedge. There, he said, was an incomparable view of Rome. ''Take a look,'' he urged them. Some of the Zouaves went to the spot. Suddenly a spurt of water from concealed pipes drenched them. They turned and ran. The Pope was laughing, tears running down his face. How would they withstand the enemy's fire, he asked, when they retreated in disorder from a mere shower of water? The reception ended in general merriment.

No attack had been made on Rome by Garibaldi's army. The Pope's garrison had been strengthened by troops sent by Napoleon III of France. A change came in 1870. War broke out between France and Prussia. French troops were recalled from Rome. Garibaldi soon took advantage of the Pope's weakened defences. On September 20, 1870, at five o'clock in the morning, the first cannon was fired. It was the signal for a general bombardment of Rome.

The Canadian Zouaves fought with spirit. But the Pope knew the capture of the city was inevitable. To continue resistance would only waste lives and risk the destruction of Rome's ancient churches and art treasures. He sent word to surrender. But the Zouaves still kept up the fight. Only when a second, severe command came from the Vatican did the firing cease. On the following day the Canadian Papal Zouaves marched out of Rome. They passed the Vatican. ''Let us see the Holy Father once more!'' they shouted. The Pope, though exhausted, heard their voices and the tramp of their feat. He hurried to a window. As the Zouaves marched away they saw the Pope stretching out his arms in a last blessing.

The Zouaves were welcomed home with every honor. They had been crusaders, even though the crusade had failed. Some 50,000 people crowded Place d'Armes and spread into the neighboring streets. As the Zouaves marched to Notre Dame Church the bells in the towers rang in welcome. At a ceremony in the church, Bishop Bourget praised them for the example of devotion they had set, by their unhesitating response to the appeal of the Pope for defenders.

To honor these 19th century crusaders, the chapel was dedicated to their memory. Visitors to the Cathedral-Basilica today, peering through the grill of the chapel's gates, may see the little painting of St. Jean Baptiste that once hung in the Zouaves' headquarters in Rome.

Smoking and No Smoking in Victorian Days

The movement to protect the non-smoker by isolating the smoker is actually a revival of Victorian methods. In Montreal's Victorian days, smokers were often required, at least by custom, to smoke by themselves or among themselves.

Women, of course, did not smoke; that is, respectable women did not. Etiquette dictated that no gentleman should ever smoke in the presence of a lady. It was not a question of asking the lady's consent. If she were a lady, such consent would never be given. Even before the Victorian era had begun, a smoker who allowed the fumes of tobacco to drift towards a lady was regarded as unspeakable. An indignant entry about such smoking appears in the diary of Lady Aylmer.

In 1831, Lady Aylmer, wife of the governor-general, was travelling from Montreal to Quebec on the elegant steamboat, the *British America*. She thought the steamboat "very fine," and "fitted up with every convenience." Only one thing spoiled her trip. Some of the passengers chose to smoke on that sultry day under the awning on deck. They smoked in such a position that puffs of warm smoke were wafted across her face. When Lady Aylmer eyed the smokers she was not surprised. They had stretched themselves out on "two or three chairs, to support various parts." Not much in the way of good manners could be excepted of those who would loll about a deck with such vulgarity of posture.

Even the rough voyageurs on lakes and rivers had better manners. Anna Jameson, wife of a judge in Upper Canada, noted their courtesy, while she was travelling in a bateau from Sault St. Marie to Manitoulin Island in 1838. On this journey the voyageurs had been issued a fixed amount of tobacco. But with a courteous awareness that the smoke might distress her, they always contrived to smoke to leeward, so that the odor would be carried away over the water.

Many Victorian houses were planned so as to have a "Smoking Room." There the men of the family might indulge their "love of the weed" without in any way annoying the rest of the household. An architect writing in 1865 conceded that a billiard room (a room normally out of bounds for ladies) might be "allowed to be more or less under the dominion of the smokers, if contrived accordingly." Better still, said the architect, the plans should include a smoking room. Such a room should be detached from the house, or at least "shut off."

Victorian young men, however, might find themselves with no place to smoke when they visited houses where no men lived, such as the houses of their maiden aunts, or widowed grandmothers. Such ladies must never suspect that their guests were smoking. Unable to overcome their smoking habits, even on such visits, these young men had to resort to "pitiable resources." One method was to sit very close to a fire-place and puff the tobacco smoke up the chimney. Another way was to lean far out of a window and smoke into the outer air.

Victorian ladies expected to be protected not only from tobacco smoke itself. Gentlemen must not meet ladies if they were smelling of tobacco. Smokers were urged, after smoking, to remove the disagreeable smell as far as possible. One rule was that "the mouth should be freely washed with cold water." Washing the mouth with cold water would not be enough to decontaminate the smoker before he entered the society of ladies. His hair and clothes might still be reeking of smoke. To prevent this sort of offensiveness, the smoker should not light up, even in his smoker's room, until he had put on a special smoker's costume. He needed to wear a smoking cap and a smoking jacket.

Victorian ladies, being proficient in needlework, often made such caps and jackets as presents for gentlemen. They often made them as Christmas or birthday gifts. Smoking caps were round velvet pillboxes, often with long tassels. Smoking jackets were made of velvet, plush, cashmere or flannel, lined with bright–colored silk. Button holes took the form of military frogging. Caps and jackets were handsomely embroidered, in leaf patterns or decorative scrolls.

To Victorians, the idea that women themselves might take up smoking was a shocker. Occasionally a rumor went about that some daring young women were doing it. In 1872, the Montreal weekly magazine *The Canadian Illustrated News* had an article denouncing them: "... they use violet powder and various cosmetiques... and manipulate false hair with marvellous dexterity. A cigarette — may we whisper, a cigar — is no stranger to their ruby lips. Defend us, then, from these 'fast' young ladies and may their numbers become less!" Certainly their numbers throughout the Victorian era remained small. In November 1897, Fanny Davenport, the actress, was seen smoking a cigarette in the lobby of the Windsor Hotel. She was on her last visit to Montreal to perform in *The Saint and the Fool* at the Academy of Music. The spectacle of a woman smoking, and in a public place, startled many who saw her. It seemed an example of the seamy side of the theatrical life.

During Victorian era the safest place for gentlemen to smoke was on verandah.

Montreal, however, had a place where men could smoke to their heart's content. It was Morris' Smoking Parlor, on the south side of St. James Street (rue Saint-Jacques), near St. Peter (rue Saint-Pierre), on a site now covered by the Royal Bank. The Smoking Parlor was in the rear of Morris' tobacco shop. It was a large, comfortable room, like the reading room of a club. Lamps were green-shaded.

On long tables lay the best magazines of the day. Big chairs, big sofas, all upholstered in black leather, offered comfort. In that Smoking Parlor, only a few feet from the roar of St. James Street, an easy, contented hour could be spent by the smoker, in unoffending seclusion, enjoying "the pestiferous comfort of a good cigar."

The Prince of Wales at the Ritz

On all his many visits to Montreal, the Prince of Wales (who was to be king for some 11 months) stayed at the Ritz-Carlton. In this preference he broke with tradition. The old Windsor Hotel had long been favored by visiting members of the royal family — a tradition re-established by Princess Elizabeth, and confirmed by her when she became queen. For Edward, however, the Ritz-Carlton was far more his natural hotel. It was newer, smarter, more "uptown," closer to his mood. It was free of the ponderous Victorian atmosphere the Windsor embodied, an atmosphere he heartily disliked.

Though the Prince of Wales preferred informality on his visits, at times the panoply of royalty made the Ritz-Carlton the background of splendid drama. It was so in 1927. One morning a squadron of the Royal Canadian Hussars was drawn up in line on Sherbrooke Street, in front of the hotel. In the glitter of the summer morning, the hussars, "mounted on browns and blacks... looked very smart in their scarlet and blue uniforms and black-plumed helmets." The prince appeared in the doorway and entered the waiting automobile. The hussars turned, and rode into place before the car, and behind, with an officer riding on either side. The car and its escort moved off, on the way to the civic reception at City Hall. It was a touch of glamour and color, of dignity and discipline not often seen in the streets of Montreal, and "the Ritz" at such times was the royal headquarters.

The Prince of Wales was always well satisfied with his hotel. On the last day of every visit he called the manager, and presented him with a gift — an expression of appreciation for service to himself and his suite. Managers made every effort to satisfy his tastes. His rooms in 1923 were specially equipped with "a radio apparatus said to be absolutely the last word in that science, a handsome phonograph and two pianos of Canadian manufacture."

Such equipment recognized the Prince of Wales' passion for jazz — jazz itself being the rage of the time. In 1919 he visited the United States before coming to Canada. As an interlude of recreation he was taken by William Fox to movies at the Academy of Music in New York. An orchestra played the latest jazz. An American reporter wrote: "... the young prince just couldn't sit still. He moved first his hands and his head, and finally his whole body in time to the 'Jazz.' "

On his visits to Montreal he went to many private dances at Montreal homes. Yet not all his dancing was at private parties. One evening, on his visit in 1923, he invited a few friends to come with him to an informal supper dance at the Ritz-Carlton. "It was quite casual," said a reporter,

"and the entry of the royal visitor was in the manner most desired by himself, absolutely informal, although it cannot be said that it was unnoticed." He and his friends were ushered to a table at the centre of the hotel's famous Adam Room. Colored lamps cast "a pleasant rose-colored hue upon the assemblage." Table decorations were red roses alternating with white chrysanthemums. The orchestra, specially reinforced with "the traps necessary to augment percussion," was on the stage.

The Prince of Wales' preference for informality was seen in many ways. He not only went to the hotel's supper dance but sometimes lunched at a table in its dining room. One day he was seen walking back to the hotel after lunching at the University Club with Lieut.-Col. A.A. Magee and Major A.R. Chipman. On another occasion he arrived in a taxi for dinner and a dance at the home of A. Forbes Angus. He had come out of the Ritz-Carlton to find the official car parked on the other side of Sherbrooke Street. It was being dusted off, after a late afternoon's trip on country roads. He did not wait for it to be brought around. A taxi stood near the entrance to the hotel. He hopped into it. The Angus family, waiting for their royal guest, were astonished to see him drive up to the door in a taxi.

In the brief spaces between engagements he would invite some of his Montreal friends to visit him at his hotel suite. Sir Arthur Currie, whom he had first met in France in wartime, was often asked. It was his custom always to invite the mayor of Montreal. For nearly all his visits that mayor was Médéric Martin, who seemed to be perennial. Médéric Martin would arrive with his usual "cheerful and debonair" bustle. He was a member of the cigar twisters' union, and presented the prince with a special box of cigars made by his own hands.

When the Prince of Wales came on his visit in 1924, he learned that Martin had been defeated. He invited the new mayor, Charles Duquette. But Médéric was not forgotten. A phone call was put through to his house at Laval des Rapides, asking him to come and visit the Prince of Wales as usual. Emerging from the visit Médéric Martin declared: "The prince is even more charming than ever."

The abdication of 1936 changed much in the life of the man who was so briefly king. But it did not change his memories of former days — memories that brought him back to the Ritz-Carlton in Montreal in the 1950s. He reoccupied his old suite. But the glamour belonged now only to the past. His return to Montreal caused little stir. Few seemed to care whether he came or went.

On his first visit as Prince of Wales in 1919 he was 25 and at the height of a promise never to be fulfilled. Vast crowds, "mighty cheers," greeted the people's idol. When he came as the Duke of Windsor nobody cheered. He was no longer the man of promise. Many now viewed him as a tragic figure, without even the majesty of true tragedy.

He tried to follow some of his old customs. He would still invite some of his old Montreal friends to visit him at the hotel. One of those he invited was John Bassett, by that time the president of the *Gazette*. The prince had come to know Bassett as far back as 1919, when he visited Ottawa and Bassett was there as The *Gazette's* parliamentary correspondent. On his 1924 Montreal visit, he had invited Bassett to come down from Ottawa to see him.

John Bassett used to say how sad was the final visit, how much it contrasted with times past. The pathos of it all came in the Duke of Windsor's words, in the course of conversation, when he happened to say, "When I was king...."

The Ritz was the royal headquarters for the Prince of Wales's many visits.

"The Fifth Avenue of Canada"

"Sherbrooke Street is scarcely surpassed by the Fifth Avenue of New York in the magnificence of its buildings," said a writer in the 1880s. And in the 1890s another commentator remarked: "Sherbrooke Street has always been the aristocratic street of Montreal... it is such a 'tony' street." The great men who lived there had made their fortunes in commerce, but they wanted only the fruits of their wealth (not its roots) to be seen on the elegant street where they lived. Factories, warehouses, shops, offices and wharves were far away, down the slope, nearer the waterfront. When they returned from work they went up the hill. Once on Sherbrooke Street they drove, in summer, under an arcade of elms, which arched their branches overhead. In winter, in their sleighs, with splendid robes, they glided over the snow, creating a spectacle, with well-bred horses, such as only St. Petersburg was said to rival.

On Sherbrooke most houses had proportions that made them mansions. Some stood in large grounds, behind iron railings set in stone foundations, and with wrought iron

Lord Atholstan's Sherbrooke Street mansion has been preserved in Alcan project.

gates. Others were at the height of tall stone steps, or in tall, limestone terraces. As late as the early 1920s, Sherbrooke Street was still clinging to its status as a street of aristocratic residences. Once ranked as almost the equal to New York's Fifth Avenue, it now liked to claim a certain superiority. Fifth Avenue had allowed commercialization to creep in; downtown Sherbrooke Street as yet had not. In 1924 a guidebook writer commented: "For Sherbrooke has kept itself sacred from the incursions of trade. Broad, well-paved, shaded with old trees, it remains the stamping ground of rich citizens."

Yet toward the end of the 1920s the street was changing more than many were prepared to admit. At first such changes were subtle. It was becoming the street of the aged, those who belonged to an era now becoming fragile. This aging mood on Sherbrooke Street was felt by a McGill student of the 1920s — Leon Edel, who was to become renowned in the world as a literary critic and biographer. "Sherbrooke Street," he recalled in 1975, "was a parade of low Victorian buildings, constructed with a sense of dignity, soft grey, a bit on the shabby side. They were pleasing to the eye — they are even today, what's left of them. No chrome, no plastic, no neon; a bit of carving, an occasional niche with statuary, signs that human hands made them." On Sherbrooke in those days one might see "on cold winter days... wrapped up characters out of the 19th century... walrus moustaches, clipped beards, narrow lapels, long jackets... The older figures talked in the language of the 1880s...."

This aging world could not be kept indefinitely alive. A more contemporary type of elegance was being offered elsewhere. People were moving from Montreal's downtown area, out to the suburbs. During this period modern mansions were being constructed on Westmount Mountain, away from the increasing congestion of downtown and with more splendid views. The war had changed the way of looking at things. Victoriana was in artistic disrepute. It seemed far too ponderous, too solemn in its limestone heaviness, too oppressive in the interior atmosphere. Often those who inherited these mansions did not want to live in them, and new buyers were hard to find. Elegance was taking brighter forms. The modern rediscovery of the Victorian age, and the renewed appreciation of its attractions, was still about half a century in the future. In the 1920s and 1930s, and even later, the Victorian age seemed simply passé.

The great mansions, in many cases, were no longer kept up as they once had been. Shabbiness was creeping in. Despite a bylaw, commercialism appeared here and there. Some mansions had become boarding houses, or small apartments. Some cheap signs could be seen, generally at basement level: "Laundry," "Shoe Repairs," "$1 Cleaning." Some advertising billboards were even being set up.

Early in the 1930s W.S. Weldon had a plan to save Sherbrooke Street. He could save the street, he believed, only by changing it. Sherbrooke Street was not going to stay the way it was. If left alone, it would soon go downhill. It had long been known as "the Fifth Avenue of Canada." But it was now in danger of deteriorating into Canada's 42nd Street. From being stately, it could become razzle-dazzle. Alderman Weldon was in a position to do something about it. He was not only a member of city council, he was a member of the executive committee. He was also very well known in Montreal for another reason. For years he had been manager of the Windsor Hotel. He knew the downtown area; and the Windsor, like Sherbrooke Street, had been part of the city's Victorian graciousness and grandeur.

In the autumn of 1930 he came out strongly in favor of saving Sherbrooke Street from further decline and giving it a new future. As a street, it could be made as superior in its type of commercialism as it had been superior as a street of mansions. Sherbrooke Street could still be the Fifth Avenue of Canada, but only if it did what Fifth Avenue in New York itself was doing — combine commerce with elegance.

Backed by the City Council, Alderman Weldon sponsored a new bylaw for Sherbrooke Street. It listed the type of buildings that could be erected there in future: dwellings, exclusively residential; apartment buildings; clubs, banks, office buildings, telephone exchanges; hotels with a minimum of 100 rooms; churches parsonages, colleges, convents, university buildings, museums, and art galleries. The same bylaw also listed the prohibited buildings. It was a long list of 38. Included among the prohibited were factories, grocery stores, butchers' stalls, undertakers or funeral parlors, places for the display or sale of automobiles, gas stations, bowling alleys, dance halls, and taverns. The area covered by the bylaw comprised the north side of Sherbrooke between Shuter Street (later to be part of Aylmer) and the eastern limits of Westmount; and the south side from Westmount to City Councillors. Apartment houses and commercial buildings would have to be at least five storeys high. All other buildings must be at least 38 feet. No billboards of any kind could be erected.

Weldon wanted to find out how the residents of Sherbrooke Street would feel about such a change. He canvassed opinion up and down the street. His proposal met with decisive support. Even Sir Arthur Currie, principal of McGill University, concerned as he was about the university's environs, sent him a letter of approval. So did Sir Thomas Tait, one of the street's last titled residents. In the end Weldon found only one or two property–owners who objected. *The Gazette* supported the bylaw as providing the best possible solution to the future of Sherbrooke Street: "The citizens generally may be expected to uphold the decision to preserve the appearance of this historic old street, so that it may now continue to impress visitors in its new dress as in its old, while meeting the requirements of a great and growing city."

Marriage Customs and Incidents

In Montreal it was a French-Canadian custom for the bride and bridegroom, followed by their friends, to drive about the streets after the wedding. They waved as they went by and were pleased to be cheered. Always they made a point of driving through the old marketplace, where Place Royale is today. There they were sure of getting a roaring greeting. An English visitor to Montreal in 1816, John Palmer, saw these tours of the town by couples newly married: "I saw several French-Canadian marriages, which, I believe, from some superstition, are always on Monday... The bride rides first, and far from appearing reserved on the occasion, she calls out to her acquaintance on the street, or waves her handkerchief in passing them; the market people, who they take care to pass, greet them with shouts, which the party seems to court and enjoy."

When it came to dancing nothing could rival a French-Canadian wedding. By the end of the 19th century, wedding dances had been curtailed from about a fortnight to about four or five days. But they still lacked little in vigor. A wedding of the 1890s was described by William Parker Greenough, an American who spent much of his time in the province of Quebec.

Greenough was invited to a wedding where dancing began on the day before the ceremony, in the house of the bride's father. Two fiddlers were brought in from another parish. Dancing started in the afternoon; it was kept up till 11. Next morning the wedding took place at seven o'clock. Immediately after the breakfast, dancing was resumed. On it went till noon. A little after two, it began again. Dances were quadrilles and cotillions, with an occasional jig. A break came for supper at six. Afterwards they danced till five the next morning.

At two o'clock in the afternoon, the young couple set out for their new home. It was 30 miles away. They arrived to find fresh fiddlers on hand. Fifty or more neighbors had assembled. Dancing began again. It did not really end till noon the following day.

In all the marriage lore of Montreal, perhaps the strangest case was that of a widow in 1672. She married again before her first husband's funeral and burial. So far from being condemned, she was commended. New France needed new inhabitants. France did not wish to denude itself by sending too many settlers to this overseas colony.

It was up to the colony to provide its own growth. This widow was performing a public duty by returning as quickly as she could to reproduction.

Weddings not only had old customs, but difficulties as well. The marriage ceremony was not always free from unexpected happenings. At Hemmingford, 70 kilometres south of Montreal, a wedding ceremony was in trouble in the 1820s. The clergyman who was to officiate was a Presbyterian — Rev. John Merlin. He was a good, devoted man, serving a large area. His only fault was his absent-mindedness. At this wedding in the 1820s he failed to appear at the time appointed. Everyone waited. Hours went by. To pass the time, dancing was kept up until midnight. Still he had not arrived.

Some of the guests set out in the bright moonlight to look for him. They met him on the road. He was returning from a visit to a distant settlement, but seemed in no hurry. He had forgotten the wedding. They got him there as quickly as they could. He performed the ceremony in the early hours of the morning. Merrymaking was resumed. It went on till daylight.

Failure of an officiating clergyman to appear at a wedding at the appointed time was serious enough. Far worse was when the bridegroom was missing. It happened at Christ Church Cathedral in 1884. The wedding had been arranged to take place at three o'clock in the afternoon. Many guests were already there, others were coming in. An announcement was made. The wedding could not take place. The bridegroom had fallen suddenly ill — too ill to be present. Details began to emerge. The bridegroom had not taken ill. He had left town on the morning of the wedding day. Not even the family learned of it until shortly before the hour set for the ceremony.

It was a startling surprise. The bride's parents had no previous reason to doubt the character of the young man engaged to marry their daughter. He was Scottish, as was the girl's family. His father, who lived in Scotland, was rich. The son was reported "to be well off and in receipt of a handsome income." Nor was he a stranger. His brother had previously married the younger sister of his fiancée. His father in Scotland had expected the wedding to take place. That morning he sent a cablegram to his son, congratulating him on his marriage.

All details of the ceremony had been concluded. More than 500 wedding gifts had been received. Marriage contracts had been signed. Flowers decorated the cathedral. The bride was getting dressed for her wedding. The Anglican bishop of Montreal, Rt. Rev. William Bennett Bond, who was to perform the ceremony, was about to put on his robes. The groomsman (the "best man") was leaving the Saint James's Club for the cathedral before word reached him that there would be no bridegroom.

Old Market (now La Place Royale) where farmers cheered the brides.

Yet the bridegroom's decision to get out of Montreal had been premeditated. He had bought a ticket the day before the wedding – a ticket on the night train to New York. He had changed his mind, and spent that evening with his fiancée and her family. Next morning, the morning of his wedding day, he took the train for New York at 8 a.m. From a station along the route he sent a telegram to his housekeeper. He said he had left a letter in the house, and told her where she would find it. This letter was to be sent on to his brother. The letter said he felt he would be doing less injury to his fiancée and to himself if he left town, than if he went through with the ceremony. He did not have the nerve to face her and tell her himself. By the time the brother received the letter, and got to the house of her

parents, the time for the wedding had almost arrived.

The history of marriages in Montreal records other strange happenings. Some of them were only minor and amusing. At a wedding in Montreal in the 1840s, arrangements were being made by a Methodist "of the old school" — a Mr. Wadsworth. At Methodist weddings in those days a hymn was sung. The hymn he had chosen "struck some people as a little funny but brother Wadsworth did not see the fun of it." The wedding hymn of his choice began with the lines:

Come on my partners in distress,
Companions in the wilderness,
Who now your sorrows feel.

College as the Ruination of Girls

In its Saturday edition of October 23, 1897, the *Montreal Daily Witness* published a warning from Pauline G. Wiggin, an American college professor in Boston. She was advising parents not to think of a college education for their daughters. She had seen the effects such an education had on young women. They were wrecked by it. The chances were 10 to one, said Prof. Wiggin, that a girl graduate would be "ruined physically... a thing of threads and patches." Such a girl would have nothing to look forward to but "disappointment and nervous prostration."

Such apprehensions were not uncommon years ago when McGill University first admitted women. Sir Donald A. Smith (later to be Lord Strathcona) had put up the funds for the experiment. The new college girls came to be known as "Donaldas," after their benefactor. It was an anxious experiment. Some of the girls shared the forebodings. Perhaps they were submitting themselves to strains and tensions such as nature never intended them to endure. Unless they were very careful, the outcome might be sorrow and tragedy.

Helen R.Y. Reid, a graduate in the class of 1889, did not altogether share the fears of Prof. Wiggin. But she admitted, from her own experience, that higher education was far harder on young women than on young men. "The want of knowing how to rest," she said, "of economizing efforts in the general haste of rush and worry; of keeping cool during examination time; all these are strikingly seen in the Donalda department... to a much greater extent than in colleges for men." It was not that brains of women students were less capable than those of men, "but that their nervous system" had less "power of endurance." To conserve her strength, said Helen Reid, a college girl at McGill rarely went out to social events in the evening: "She has little time for evening dissipation and cannot stand the drain of late hours."

Sir William Dawson, McGill's principal, felt the need to provide girl students with a type of education specially adapted to their delicate nature. He believed they should be educated, as far as possible, separately from the men. The ideal arrangement would be to have lectures given to women students by women professors. The principal hoped, as more women graduated with higher degrees, that professors could be found among them. In the meantime, the university would have to do the best it could by having the male professors give their lecture twice — once for the men students, and again for the women. The girl students should be Donaldas, but they should not be co-eds.

When the principal first proposed this system to the male professors, they grumbled and protested. But he insisted and they gave in. Classes were held separately, and these professors were supposed, while lecturing to the girls, to adopt the "higher, more refining" tone. Some exceptions had to be made. In honor courses the women and the men would be in the same classroom together. One girl student, eager to take honors, still could not bring herself to endure the coarseness of co-educational classes. She had to content herself with taking the ordinary course instead.

Helen Reid was among those who took the risks of attending with the men. It was by no means as bad as might have been expected. She reported: "This can be said... that so far as is known... no evil whatsoever has resulted from the students working together." The men had "always behaved themselves like gentlemen, with an occasional ebullition of boyishness from the younger ones."

Though a certain degree of co-education was cautiously introduced at McGill, many classes continued to be given separately for women. In 1899, Lord Strathcona provided women at McGill with a realm of their own when he established the Royal Victoria College. There they had their residence, their dining hall, their library, and their classrooms. It might seem that this sheltering and segregation, and the provision of a special type of refined education, would not prepare young women to face, after graduation, the harsher world beyond the campus. But the educational system of those years had no intention of training women for the same "battle of life" men would have to face.

The higher education that Principal Dawson had in mind would fit young women to be better wives and mothers in homes of their own. It was conceivable that some of the graduates might become teachers or librarians, or pursue other genteel professions suitable to their natures. But the idea that women should be trained to force their way into the workplaces of men, and compete with them there, was considered "against all the healthier instincts of our humanity." It would be "simply impracticable."

Especially unthinkable was the idea that women should be permitted to enter McGill's Medical Faculty. The very idea of young girl students studying human anatomy in the same classes as men, and then attending male, as well as female patients in hospitals, was rejected as revolting. In the late Victorian years, Dr. G.E. Fenwick, an eminent medical teacher at McGill, threatened to resign if women were admitted. It "would be nothing short of a calamity," said Dr. Francis J. Shepherd, the professor of anatomy. Similar was the reaction of Dr. Thomas G. Roddick, secretary of the Medical Board of the Montreal General, a McGill teaching hospital. He reported that women students "would be detrimental to the best interests of the patients, of students themselves and of the hospital as a whole." Not until 1922 were women granted medical degrees by McGill. And these first students had been admitted to the dissecting room by a private side door and assigned a table of their own in a far corner.

There was an overshadowing anxiety when women were first admitted to higher education at McGill, that they might cease to be ladies. Lord Strathcona, who was providing the funds, admonished the girls not to become highly educated women only, but "ladies in the higher sense." But not everyone was sure it could be accomplished. If young women were to achieve higher education at the cost of their ladylike qualities, the injury to them might be even worse than that "nervous prostration" Prof. Wiggin foresaw as the ultimate fate of the girl graduate.

Today's Pollock Hall was once McGill's Royal Victoria College for women.

Householders Had to Shovel the City's Sidewalks

There was once a time when anyone walking along any of Montreal's streets in winter could not see who was walking along the sidewalk on the other side. Between the two sidewalks lay two immense piles of snow, sometimes as high as 10 feet. In Victorian Montreal the city refused to assume any direct responsibility for removing snow from sidewalks. That obligation it placed upon the owner, or tenant, of every building. And on the owner of every vacant lot. These citizens were compelled by law to do the job themselves, or to make private arrangements to have someone do it for them at their expense.

When the law made you shovel snow.

When the sidewalks were cleared in this manner, the snow was never carted away. It was simply thrown into the road alongside. As one snowfall followed another, the piles grew higher and higher. At the same time, the snow-shovellers' work grew harder and harder. Snow had to be tossed to a greater and greater height. Those walking along Montreal's streets had a curiously enclosed feeling, as if they were walking through a mountain pass. On the one side were the towering snowbanks, on the other the tall three-storey Victorian houses.

The civic bylaws enforcing snow removal on the citizens were complex — so complex, in fact, as to be confusing. Snow had to be shovelled from the sidewalk within one hour "after the ceasing to fall of any snow, whether by snowstorm or from the roofs." If the snow had accumulated overnight, it had to be removed by nine o'clock the next morning. Snow did not have to be shovelled right down to the sidewalk. It had, however, to be made "uniform level" with the snow on the adjoining sidewalks. In no case was snow to be left to a depth of more than six inches.

Though the City of Montreal had assumed no direct responsibility for removing snow, it still had a responsibility to see that the work was done. This responsibility it placed upon the police. The constable on his beat had to observe the condition of the sidewalks. Where snow had been allowed to gather, he would knock on the citizen's door and give warning. When he came round the next time, and saw that nothing had been done, he was supposed to make a note of it. The delinquent would be sent a summons to appear before the Recorder's Court. He could be fined.

This system never worked well. It required the co-operation of too many individuals. Even into the early years of the 20th century the condition of Montreal's sidewalks remained deplorable. "The people of Montreal are not much given to walking," said Rt. Rev. Ashton Oxenden, an Englishman who came out to be the Anglican bishop of Montreal in 1869. He regarded himself as one of the "most persevering pedestrians in the place." But he had to equip himself to confront snow on the sidewalks. "In the majority of streets," said the bishop, "no attempt is made to remove it from the wooden sidewalks... Sometimes the walking is very bad, and almost dangerous, so that elderly gentlemen, like myself, are glad to put on 'creepers,' which are something like the spikes that are attached to cricket shoes, or to the 'crampons,' which are used in Switzerland for crossing the glaciers."

The system of snow removal in Montreal satisfied no one. If the pedestrians were displeased, so were the police. They complained that the courts were far too lenient on those summoned before them. Judges replied that the bylaw about snow removal was so detailed as to be hard to understand, and so unrealistic as to be beyond enforcement with any sort of fairness. They cited an example. How could a citizen, who went to work every day, be expected to return home to shovel the snow from the sidewalk, within an hour "after the ceasing to fall of any snow, whether by snowstorm or from the roofs"?

From time to time the question was raised whether the city should itself remove the snow and tax the citizens for doing it. City Hall repudiated the suggestion as absurd. How could the city be expected to have always on hand tools and labor enough to clear all the sidewalks of Montreal on sudden notice? In 1899, an attempt was made by the city to frighten citizens into doing a better job of clearing the sidewalks. Hitherto, if any pedestrian was injured in a fall on a sidewalk improperly cleared, he sued the city. The city was responsible in law because it had the obligation to see that citizens were doing the required shovelling.

In 1899, the Montreal charter was amended. The city was given "recourse in warranty" against "any person whose fault or negligence had occasioned an accident." Any such person might now have to pay the damages. Not even this menace of legal damages proved enough to solve the problem. In 1905, the city undertook, as an experiment, to remove the snow from the sidewalks in three of the wards. The experiment proved that it could be done. Eventually the city took over the responsibility for snow removal on all sidewalks in town.

Even after this transfer of responsibility had taken place, conditions in the streets remained difficult. Methods and equipment were still comparatively primitive. Sidewalks were now being cleared by small ploughs. Each plough was drawn by a single horse. Only the upper snow was shaved off. Much was left behind.

A true sound of spring in Montreal used to come every year when the city sent out its first gangs of pick and shovel men to dig little ditches alongside the sidewalks, to let the immense accumulation of melting ice and snow run away into the sewers. The swinging picks made a distinctive hollow sound, with a tinkling echo, as they split apart the roadside ice. It was a harbinger of spring, as authentic as the caws of returning crows on the softened air. The murmur of the water in the little ditches, and its gurglings as it streamed into the drains, used to sing like poetry.

Some Unusual Kinds of Streetcars

For ten years (from 1915 to 1925), prisoners of the Bordeaux Jail were sometimes taken for a streetcar ride. It was not exactly the same sort of ride the public used to take. These prisoners rode in special cars, made just for them. These cars (there were two of them) were really prisons on wheels. The sides of the cars were sheathed in metal. Inside, the prisoners sat in a rear compartment, behind a padlocked door. Guards watched them from raised seats. In a forward compartment were seats for travellers who were not prisoners — the court officials and others. Motorman and conductor were both in locked compartments. Entrances and exits to the cars had locks and bars.

These prison cars had been built by the Montreal Tramways Company in an arrangement with the Quebec government. In 1912 the government had built a jail in the country town of Bordeaux. This new jail was more than seven miles from the Montreal courthouse — the old stone-columned building on the north side of Notre Dame Street, backing on the Champ de Mars. Prisoners had to be brought from the jail to the courthouse for trials, as witnesses, or for other reasons. Transporting them in slow-moving, horse-drawn wagons, through fields, was risky. These wagons might be hijacked on the lonely route. Prisoners might be set free.

Special fortified cars, built to be mobile prisons, seemed an answer to the problem. It was a unique solution. This means of transporting prisoners had been adopted nowhere else in Canada. It worked. No prisoner ever escaped en route. The service was discontinued in 1925 because it was no longer needed. Roads had been improved. Motor vans, still uncertain in 1915, had since become dependable.

Another special service was provided — a funeral car. Such a car was needed in 1910. The Mount Royal Cemetery Company had opened an additional burying ground at the eastern end of the island — its Hawthorndale Cemetery. For a fee of $15, the tramways company carried a coffin from Montreal to Hawthorndale. A funeral car had been prepared for the purpose. The funeral car even handled emergency demands during the influenza epidemic of 1918. Nine or ten coffins were transported at one time. Between trips, the car was doused with strong disinfectant. The pungent odor, and the reason for it, kept tramway workers away from the car while it stood between trips in the company's barn at Hochelaga.

The cemetery's trustees saw the need for a funeral car of revised design. The first car had carried coffins only. Mourners had to travel to Hawthorndale Cemetery on the cars regularly used on the route, like any other passengers.

The new type of funeral car was described by V.A. Linnell, who joined Montreal Tramways in 1921: "It was divided into sections. Of course there was a space for the motorman and conductor in the front. Immediately next was a space for the undertaker and his assistants, the middle section being devoted to holding the coffin, and floral arrangements, and the back part of the car was arranged a little bit like a parlor car for the immediate family and mourners."

The funeral car service was discontinued in 1927, about the same time as the prison cars. The reason was the same in both cases. The development of roads and motor transportation made these tramcars no longer necessary.

Another special car run by Montreal Tramways was the band car. It was an open-air car, with a series of raised seats, each row higher than the other. It carried a band around the city. The musicians were the company's own people — the employees' band. Not all the bandsmen could be accommodated on this car, but enough to give a rousing performance. They were in uniform, "ostrich feathers and everything else." It was an advertising car. The sound of the thumping, blaring band attracted attention as it moved about town. The car carried big banners or placards, bearing the advertiser's message. The band car ran in the evenings, as well as the afternoons. Its advertisements, after dark, were illuminated by electric lights.

The demand for still another unusual tramways service had emerged. On July 4, 1907, Mayor Ekers said he was "in receipt of petitions every day from business concerns in the city." They wanted the City Council to authorize the street railway to run freight cars on its tracks. In 1910, permission was given the street railway to become a freight carrier. Difficulties seemed to be solved. As the freight would be transported by electricity, there would be no smoky pollution of the city's air. Freight would not interfere with passenger services on the same rails. No freight would be carried during the rush hours of passenger service. Freight cars would move mostly by night.

The new service began. Freight cars of various types were used, each suitable for the kind of freight carried. Spur lines were laid into the grounds on the industries concerned, where cars could be loaded or unloaded. Where no such spur lines existed, the materials could be dumped on the road. It was then up to the industry being served to get the load off the street by wheelbarrow or wagon, and to get it off as promptly as possible. The tramway company would pay the city for cleaning the street afterwards. "It was a very common sight," Linnell recalled, "to see freight cars rolling up St. Denis Street

Special fortified tramway cars were once used to transport prisoners.

during the night hours and the old Tramways Company had a very nice business developed...'' In the 1920s freight transport by tramcars declined. Cartage companies, now equipped with fleets of motor trucks, were taking over.

Montreal Tramways, having seen its special service cars, one after the other, displaced by competition from motor vehicles, in the end gave up even its passenger trolley cars. Since it could not beat the motor age, it decided to join it. The last of its trolley cars ran on August 30, 1959. The long trolley age was ended.

Perhaps the only abiding monument to the trolley car is the waterfront boardwalk along Lasalle Boulevard in Verdun. Much of it rests on an embankment reclaimed from the river. The material that forms this embankment was deposited there by the dump freightcars of Montreal Tramways, running along a line specially laid for the purpose.

The Governor Who Died of Hydrophobia

In late August, 1819, Montrealers were wondering what had happened to the governor general, the Duke of Richmond. He had left Montreal to tour the backwoods settlements on the Ottawa River. He was expected back in Montreal for the levee and ball to be held in the elegant Mansion House on St. Paul Street. But the day for his arrival came and still he had not appeared.

One account is to be found in the memoirs written by an army officer, Frederick Tolfrey, in 1845. He says he was sent out on horseback on the road to Lachine to see if he could learn anything about the governor's whereabouts. About half way to Lachine, he saw a calèche in the distance. In it was an officer in uniform — Col. Cockburn. Tolfrey rode up to the carriage. "How is the duke?" he asked. "Where is he ?" Col. Cockburn, with "a melancholy shake of the head," pointed to a rough coffin, a "shell," on the floor of the calèche, at his feet. It contained the Duke of Richmond's body. A military guard was sent to accompany the governor's body into the city. The body was taken to Government House, the Château Ramezay, the old building still standing on Notre Dame Street.

On his tour of the pioneer settlements in the backwoods of Upper Canada the Duke of Richmond had wished, in particular, to visit the new township of Richmond, named in his honor. This wilderness journey would be rough, much of it on foot, along forest trails. But it had been well organized. Marquees and tents were part of the equipment, and an ample supply of wines and provisions. Several officers would travel with him, and a Swiss servant who had been attending him for years. They set out on their dutiful adventure as a "merry party." The duke was a strong man in his mid-fifties, ready for the exertion and interested in the novelty of backwoods life.

After the first few days be began to feel unwell. When he went to wash his face in a basin of water, he drew back with a shudder. His attending officers were surprised to see him appear in the morning unwashed and unshaven. Even the sight of wine came to revolt him. At dinner he asked Col. Cockburn to take wine with him. He had no sooner raised the glass to his lips when, horrified, he at once set it down on the table. "Now this is excessively ridiculous," he said to Col. Cockburn.

The tour completed, the duke and his party approached the Ottawa River, to journey by canoe to Montreal. The duke shuddered when they had to pass through marshlands. At the riverside he hesitated to enter the canoe. The canoe moved out into the river. At once the governor general became agitated. He seized his little spaniel, Blücher, clung to it and kissed it in a weird, frantic way. His officers looked at him in alarm. He forced a smile, and tried to control himself. Soon he was hysterical. One account says he seized one of the paddlers by the throat and had to be held down.

They turned the canoe towards the shore. The moment it grated on the pebbles, the Duke of Richmond leaped out. He ran into the woods, "about a mile and a half at a furious pace." One of his officers and a canoe man came after him. He made for a barn. When they arrived he was lying on the hay, exhausted. His attendants persuaded him to move to a farmhouse, where he might have shelter and care. Along the way they had to cross several brooks. His staff needed all their strength to force him over them.

In the backwoods farmhouse the rabies entered its final stage. The governor was desperately ill, groaning in torments, though often lucid. From time to time he spoke kindly to those about him. He said he had forgiven all his enemies. Even while dying of hydrophobia in the backwoods, he kept his sense of rank as Charles Lennox, fourth Duke of Richmond. He remained aware of the obligations his rank imposed upon him. After his groans, he would cry out to himself: "Shame, Richmond! Shame, Charles Lennox! Bear your sufferings like a man!" In the early morning of August 28 he died.

An incident that might explain all was recalled. It had happened when they were on their way up the St. Lawrence from Quebec to Montreal. The governor general had gone ashore to visit Sorel (then called William Henry). While walking about the town, the duke saw a captive fox. He "expressed something like a wish that the fox should be purchased." The hint was attended to by a servant. Next day the fox was tied to a tent pitched for the accommodation of the servants. It had become irritated in the scorching sun.

By the time the governor general came out that morning, the fox had been moved into the shade but was still restless. "Is it you, my little fellow?" the duke said, holding out his hand to caress it. He was warned to be careful. "No, no," he said, "the little fellow will not bite me." The fox snapped at his hand, closing its teeth. The duke drew back, saying: "Indeed, my friend, you bite very hard." The wound bled. A surgeon dressed it. By the time the governor general was beginning his journey into the backwoods beyond Montreal, the wound had healed. Nothing more was thought of it. But the fox may have been rabid.

On the evening at the end of August a procession was

formed to accompany the body of the Duke of Richmond from the Château Ramezay to the waterfront. There John Molson's steamboat *Malsham* was waiting to carry it to Quebec for burial. The procession was long and solemn, moving to the sound of muffled fifes and drums. Officers, clergy and principal citizens were followed by "an immense concourse of people." The evening was late, growing dark, by the time the waterfront was reached. Artillerymen, "bending under the weight," bore the heavy coffin aboard the steamboat. They laid it on a bier in an upper cabin. The cabin was lighted. Its windows were open, giving a full view of "the chamber of death."

The huge crowd stood on the shore and looked on; "not a sound was to be heard — all was still, as if the earth were uninhabited." The *Malsham* steamed out into the river, wheeled round in St. Mary's Current, then moved downstream into the night. At Quebec, in the Anglican Cathedral of the Holy Trinity, the Duke of Richmond was buried. The position of his grave is marked by a brass plate on the chancel floor.

The Duke of Richmond's body was taken to Château Ramezay.

What Happened in Montreal's Earthquakes

Not often does a statue wave at anyone. But a Montreal statue waved at a constable about ten o'clock one evening in the 1870s. The constable was on his beat, walking through Victoria Square. He passed by the statue of Queen Victoria — a statue that depicts the queen with a sceptre in her right hand. As he went by, the queen waved her sceptre at him. The startled constable could not at first believe his eyes. The spectre *was* being waved. A moment later he felt the ground quivering under his feet. He then knew it must be an earthquake.

Queen Victoria ''waved'' her sceptre at a policeman.

The roar that accompanies Montreal earthquakes has been described in many ways during the years, but all to the same effect. In 1663 the noise was likened to an angry sea pounding against rocks; a procession of carriages thundering over cobblestones; or the clash of two armies in combat. The quake of 1879 sounded like the rolling of a ball in a bowling alley, only very much more prolonged, or the vibration caused by a passing train. Often the earthquake's roar has sounded like an explosion of bursting boilers, or heavy machinery crashing through the floor of a factory, or the blowing up of the powder magazine that used to be kept in the military buildings on Ile Ste. Hélène. In 1893, people living in and around Metcalfe Street thought that Murphy's department store (the predecessor of Simpson's), then under construction on St. Catherine Street, had suddenly collapsed. In 1982 the sound was described by Andrea Brewer of LaSalle as ''a rumbling noise that sounded like a strong blast of wind or the concussion sound from an explosion.''

While some sounds and sights of Montreal's earthquakes have been almost invariable, others, while occasionally recurring, are not always present. Such is the sound in the trees. In the terrible tremors of 1663, Montrealers who fled from the town into the countryside saw trees striking one another, as if in battle. Indians said the forest was drunk. A related phenomenon, though far less violent, reappeared in 1897. Just before the tremor was felt, leaves trembled and rustled. ''This was distinctly noticed in Dominion Square,'' says a contemporary account. ''There was no wind at the time, and the attention of passers-by was first called to an unusual occurrence by the noise the trees made. Hardly was there time to remark upon it when the heaving sensation came which solved all doubts as to the cause.''

The strange antics of animals have been observed in all Montreal earthquakes. They took place in Montreal's first recorded earthquake — the great quake of 1663. Dogs, cats, horses and other tamed animals mingled their frenzied howls with those of wild animals in nearby forests. In the earthquake of 1877 horses began running frantically about the fields. In many houses, dogs and cats tried to scratch their way through doors and windows. In 1917 horses on St. James Street went wild. They struggled to run away and could hardly be restrained. In the earthquake Montrealers experienced on October 7, 1982, animals behaved strangely. A cockatoo banged at its cage and pulled out 26 long feathers. A cat acted crazily running about a room, jumping all over the furniture.

The ringing of bells has happened in some earthquakes, but not in all. The earthquake of 1663 set bells ringing in Montreal's belfries. They rang again by themselves in the Montreal earthquake of 1763. On November 4, 1877, tremors rang bells in the towers of Notre Dame Church in Place d'Armes. In 1897, bells ringing in many houses had ''a very uncanny sound.''

In most earthquakes, Montrealers, though scared, have not panicked. There were three panic years — 1663, 1893 and 1897. In 1663 (in the most violent earthquake of all) worshippers in Notre Dame Church (at that time at the northeast corner of St. Paul and St. Sulpice) felt the floorboards heaving under their knees as they knelt in prayer. The prayers ceased. Curé and worshippers scurried outdoors. They were joined by patients from the Hôtel Dieu next door. These patients had struggled out of their beds into the February cold and snow.

In 1893 the earthquake interrupted a trial in the old Court House on Notre Dame Street. Pillars in the court room were jiggling. Jurymen, lawyers, officials, reporters, spectators all tried to squeeze through the doors. In the rush heavy oak benches were overturned ''as though they had been made of matchwood.'' Even the prisoner (charged with embezzlement) was abandoned by the police. He was seen on Notre Dame Street ''in a dazed condition.''

In the Montreal Board of Trade on St. Sacrement Street the grain merchants made a dash for the outdoors. A.G. Thompson, an athlete in his day, was suddenly imbued (the old account says) ''with his old-time ambition to break the 100-yard records and beat them all. Nobody had a split second time-piece on hand, but Mr. Thompson's confreres were all agreed that as a sprinter, when occasion requires, he has no equal. He will subsequently be dubbed the champion sprinter of the Corn Exchange.'' Employees were seen streaming out of Windsor Station, and out of the Windsor Hotel. In Place d'Armes, in the New York Life building (still standing on the east side of the square, at the corner of St. James), employees rushed from offices into the corridors. This building, at eight storeys, was one of Montreal's tallest. Height raised terror. ''Frightened, I should think so,'' said one employee. ''I thought the building was falling sure enough — it would be a long way to fall from here.''

The office of the Bell Telephone Co. tried to answer hundreds of anxious calls. People wanted to know what was happening. The operators, then called ''Hello Girls,'' though much frightened, stuck to their posts and ''resisted the feminine inclination to faint.''

Despite all the tensions, scares and panics earthquakes have caused in Montreal through three centuries, little damage has resulted. Sometimes glasses and china, trembling on shelves or sideboards, have slipped to the floor and crashed. Plaster in walls and ceiling has cracked. In 1897 a chimney fell down. Windows sometimes were shattered. Plate glass, however, was remarkably resistant. In the quake of 1893, H. Foster Chaffee, ticket agent of the Richelieu & Ontario Navigation Co., was astounded to see the big plate glass windows of the company's office on St. James Street bending without splitting.

Not only has damage been comparatively slight in Montreal's earthquakes; no one has ever been killed, and hardly anyone was ever seriously injured.

The Gas Street Lamps
Go Out Forever

One day, early in December 1888, something very strange came over Montreal. People were collapsing in the streets. Only "with great difficulty" could they be resuscitated. Actors in front of the footlights found they could not speak. Audiences deserted theatres, though performances were only half through. Stores were closed. In factories, workers became "suddenly insensible." Judges adjourned courts.

Doctors found those afflicted were suffering from symptoms resembling acute bronchitis. The cause was a poisonous gas, with intolerable odor, that had spread over the entire city. The source was traced to the Montreal Gas Company — the company that lighted the city's streets. Two burners in its manufacturing plant had broken down the day before. They could not be repaired until the day following. The company was left with a hard choice. It could close down the service and leave the city in darkness; or it could try using an inferior gas. It had chosen to use the inferior gas, without realizing that it would be poisonous.

Montreal was in an uproar. Meetings of public protest were held. The Board of Trade denounced the company for its want of responsibility. Some commercial firms refused to pay their bills. Gradually indignation died away. The gas company resumed its usual service. The mistake of December 1888 was one of the few it made. In general it served the public satisfactorily.

Certainly street lighting by gas had been a revolutionary improvement over the old oil lamps erected on St. Paul Street in 1815. Oil lamps were feeble. At times, when the lamps had been over-filled, oil would drip on the hats and shoulders of those passing beneath them. The introduction of gas lamps had provided lighting that was bright by comparison. The company claimed that its gas gave a brightness equal to 17.46 candles.

Gas, however, had its limitations. One old Montrealer, Mrs. Florence May Ramsden, recalled the gas light in her childhood home in the 1880s: "Gas was the universal illuminant and was very impure, burning with a blue flame and hissing a great deal and frequently freezing in very cold weather, when it had to be thawed out with menthylated spirits. Many dinner parties were spoiled by the gas failing and candles having to be pressed into service."

Yet there was a picturesqueness to the ritualistic appearance every twilight of the lamplighter. He went from post to post, carrying a ladder and a long rod. Each post had an iron bracket just below the lamp. The ladder could be supported on the bracket. The lamplighter climbed the ladder. His rod was equipped with a turning key at one side; with it he opened the valve. He then touched the escaping gas with the lighted taper at the other side of his rod. The lamp flared alight. To children looking on, the lamplighter seemed a magician. "Every evening," Mrs. Ramsden recalled, "we children used to flatten our noses on the window pane and watch the lamplighter with his magic wand sparking the lamps all up and down the street."

The Montreal Gas Company (previously the New City Gas Company) was prosperous. Some of the principal financiers of Montreal invested in it. Dividends were being paid at 10 per cent. Anxiety, however, crept into the annual meeting of the company in 1880. A shareholder suggested that the coming of electricity might menace the monopoly held by gas as "the universal illuminant." The reply came from one of the directors of the company, John Ostell, a noted Montreal architect. He said such fears were "very fallacious." He added: "The Board did not think they need be afraid of the electric light."

The coming of the electric age was nearer than the board of the gas company realized. The company had only a few more years to enjoy its monopoly of street lighting in Montreal. Impressive demonstrations of electricity were taking place. One evening in 1879 electricity had illuminated the whole Champ de Mars, while regiments of the Montreal militia drilled in the presence of a large crowd. In 1880 the harborfront was lighted by 14 electric lamps. Montreal that night became the first city in the world to unload ships by electric light. In 1881 an electric light was placed at the entrance of the hydraulic building on St. Gabriel Street. A reporter wrote: "Its dazzling rays are now nightly reflected at a considerable distance around."

Promotors of electricity were aggressive, and in imaginative ways. They achieved the utmost in publicity by introducing electric light into Montreal's winter carnivals. Electric lights were installed inside the great ice palaces on Dominion Square. A reporter, sent to Montreal in 1883 by the *New York World,* wrote in his despatch: "The ice palace is lit up by the electric light, the effect of which is heightened by the myriad facets of the ice blocks through which it shines, so that from a distance the building looks like a great heap of jewels dropped upon a sheet of crystal." In another winter carnival, electric light was brought to the toboggan slides. Laughing crowds were seen shooting down the slides "between rows of brilliant electric lamps and gaudy streamers."

The Montreal Gas Company found in the Royal Electric Company a competitor it could not equal. The Royal Electric Company in the end won the contract to light the streets. On August 1, 1889, its final triumph was reported: "The date will be memorable in the annals of Montreal, being the first time the city was wholly lighted by electricity. The Royal Electric Light Company, despite rumors to the contrary, fulfilled the terms of their contract, and 753 arc and 346 incandescent lights blazed away all over the city, from shortly after 8 p.m. until daybreak."

It was a new burst of progress. But the old order of gas lamps did not pass without some sentimental regrets. A Montrealer, Erol Gervase, was looking up Laval Avenue at 10 minutes to seven in the morning of July 31, 1889. He saw one last gas lamp still burning in the rainy mist, casting its light on a neighboring elm. As he looked, the light sank, flickered for some time, leaped up in a momentary glare, then went out. "This, then," he wrote, "was the death of the old familiar light, that, in spite of all our grumblings, has served us fairly well in the past... But now we were going to give it up. Poor ghostly little light, that lingered so long for the last time."

He then likened its light to life itself: "What, after all, was it but a figure of ourselves? Lights of a little night, we too shine out in the dark... for our fleeting time, then, vanishing like this tiny ghost of the gaslight, that other and newer luminaries may take our place."

Replicas of old gas lamps bring nostalgia to Old Montreal.

Mount Stephen's Mansion on Drummond Street

The Victorians used to apply the word "princely" to the mansions of rich men. It is a word that may be applied still to Lord Mount Stephen's old mansion on the west side of Drummond Street, a little above St. Catherine. Now the Mount Stephen Club, his residence remains monumental. Even a great marble bust of Lord Mount Stephen stands on a pedestal in the entrance hall. He is still a presence in his old home.

Work on this house on Drummond Street was commenced in 1880 and some three years were to pass before it was completed. In the meanwhile, Lord Mount Stephen was living in a house just to the back of the new building. This house faced on Mountain Street. The house on Mountain Street, though not comparable to Lord Mount Stephen's new mansion, was a considerable building in its own right. At the time, before building the new house had begun, the garden of Lord Mount Stephen's house on Mountain Street extended back to Drummond Street, covering the land where the later house was built. In that garden Lord Mount Stephen grew Bartlett pears and fameuse apples.

When Lord Mount Stephen built his mansion on Drummond Street he could well say that "he built it all himself." It was not that he ever laid his hand on stone or wood, but the place that he won for himself in the city, the

Lord Mount Stephen's Mansion is now the Mount Stephen Club.

country and the world was all of his own making. With him, beginning life as "a barefoot boy" was not a figure of speech; it was true. He recalled these barefoot days in a conversation with Dame Nellie Melba, an Australian operatic singer: "Running barefoot over the stubble is the first memory I have, and in a way it is one of the sweetest memories of all. I used to earn a shilling from the laird (the old Duke of Richmond) in those days for going twelve miles to carry a letter, and very lucky I thought myself to get it. Those shillings I earned were the best earned money I ever made, because as you know yourself, if you want to get over stubble with bare feet, the only way of doing it is to run. It's when you drop into a walk that you start to feel it."

Like many another very young Scot, he set out on the great road for London. "I decided," he said, "I would set out for London, having come to the conclusion that there was not enough scope for the capital I had saved out of my shilling letter journeys if I remained where I was." He started by walking, then took the "Parliamentary" train — a train slow but cheap. In London he got a job at a wholesale merchant's at £20 a year. As he was lodged and boarded as well, he was able to save his £20 a year and thought himself more than ever a capitalist. "And then I got out to Canada in a sailing ship which took three months to cross over and worked like a young devil in another cloth business with a cousin of mine. Clever? No. There was no cleverness in it. A man would just have to be born asleep if he could not have got on in Canada in those days." In 1850 Lord Mount Stephen joined a relation of his in an importing business. He became a junior partner, and went on buying trips to England. He made useful contacts, and became active in a wide variety of business, notably in woolen and cotton mills. He rose to be elected president of the Bank of Montreal. And he was chosen by Sir John A. Macdonald to head a group charged with the responsibility of building the Canadian Pacific Railway.

It was just about the time he became president of the Canadian Pacific Railway that Lord Mount Stephen began to build the great house on Drummond Street which today is the Mount Stephen Club. He was in no hurry. He was living comfortably enough in his house on Mountain Street, and had only to stroll to the end of his garden to watch the work in progress. That the house took some three years to complete was due to his insistence that it was not to be just another big house. Every room, every hall and stairway was to be specially planned, and the woodwork everywhere, and the fireplaces, and stonework were to be fashioned and carved and placed not merely by ordinary carpenters' or masons' skills, but by superlative workmanship. He was asking for something beyond the power of local constructors to provide. But this did not discourage him. He imported whole colonies of specialized workers from overseas, notably from Scotland and Italy. Here they lived and worked for months, sparing no pains or cost in achieving not merely the fine but the exquisite.

Tastes and styles inevitably change. But the excellence of what was achieved in the Drummond Street house, though far from modern aesthetics, remains, in its own way, tremendously impressive.

Even before Lord Mount Stephen could move into his new house, troubles and anxieties were crowding in upon him. Building the CPR had seemed an exciting project at first. This railway across a continent appealed to the imagination; it was a truly imperial endeavor. But in the hard light of day it began to appear more like a fantasy.

Sir John A. Macdonald's government began to hesitate in the assistance it would give. The Opposition in Parliament attacked the scheme. The cabinet itself was divided. To some it seemed better to let the CPR go down to ruin, rather than to ruin the whole country in an impossible enterprise. In these desperate times Lord Mount Stephen mortgaged all his property in support of the company. It was a grand gesture, implying that the downfall of the company would carry him with it. In later and better times, he would sometimes tell guests at his Drummond Street house how the building and all its contents had been mortgaged — "this sofa on which we are now sitting, this carpet under our feet, those ornaments on the mantelpiece — everything." But further help was forthcoming from the government. The mortgage was never foreclosed.

Lord Mount Stephen, however, did not live long in the great house he built for himself on Drummond Street. In 1888, only three years after the Canadian Pacific Railway had been completed, he retired as president of the company and went to live in England. The house on Drummond Street became the home of his brother-in-law, Robert Meighen. After the death of Robert Meighen in 1911, it remained as part of the Robert Meighen Estate.

Private mansions on this scale did not belong to the postwar world with its troubles and its taxes. In May 1926 came the announcement that "the property belonging to the Estate Robert Meighen, with frontage of about 300 feet on Drummond and Mountain streets, and a depth of 280 feet, had been sold to a syndicate headed by James H. Maher." Maher, Noah Timmins and Dr. J.S. Dohan incorporated the Mount Stephen Club in the same year, and acquired the building as its clubhouse. The rest of the property was broken up and sold as building lots.

Lord Mount Stephen used to say that the secret of success was "steady application." The building on Drummond Street, in its stately proportions and rich finishings, remains an impressive example of what was accomplished by "steady application" by a boy who had run messages barefoot over the Scottish stubble.

The Comfortable Glamour
of Sohmer Park

The spirit of contented gaiety — something destroyed by the First World War — reigned in Montreal's Sohmer Park. It was a Renoir-like place, a garden by a river, in dappled sunshine under venerable trees, with outdoor music from opera to semi–classical selections, amusements in sideshows and its famous promenade, 200 to 300 feet long, with its view over the St. Lawrence and its passing ships. Along this promenade were chairs and little round tables. Waiters with straw hats, black coats and long white aprons, served beer, lemonade, ice cream, or French fried potatoes — the best French fried potatoes (it was said) in all Montreal. Sohmer Park was created and sustained by the spirit of Ernest Lavigne. Joseph Lajoie was also important, as his partner. But while Lajoie may have been the more practical businessman, it was Lavigne who gave the park the glamour of his own personality. Ernest Lavigne was a tall and graceful man, of fine figure. He had magnificent white hair, like a "pack of snow." He always dressed in a grey top hat and in light grey clothes, just like Sir Wilfrid Laurier.

Lavigne was an accomplisiled musician, a clarinetist, who had studied in Italy, France, Germany and England. He was to compose some 25 "romances," or melodies. Before Sohmer Park was opened in 1889 he was the conductor of the City Band. It performed summer evenings before huge crowds in Viger Gardens (as Place Viger was known). A man tense with energy, Lavigne spared no effort in achieving his effects. One evening the music in Viger Gardens included an impression of a bird singing from a distant tree. Just before his band came to this passage, he rushed from the platform and climbed one of the garden's trees. Concealed by branches, he played the bird's distant song.

Ernest Lavigne, with his partner, Joseph Lajoie, ran a shop where they sold musical instruments. They were the Montreal agents for the Sohmer piano company. Lavigne succeeded in persuading the company to invest in an amusement park. This park, while drawing large crowds with a variety of attractions, would feature concerts of classical and semi-classical music, as well as operas. It would be known as Sohmer Park. In this way the name "Sohmer" would become a household word in Montreal. It would be a means of continual popular advertising, such as no other piano company could equal. With the Sohmer money, and with other sources of investment as well, Lavigne and Lajoie bought a superb site. It was south of Notre Dame Street at the corner of Panet. The land stretched down towards the waterfront.

The whole musical life of Montreal was stimulated by Sohmer Park. But Ernest Lavigne realized that to carry out his ambitious musical programs other features were also needed, to swell the attendance and increase the revenues. Balloon ascensions took place at Sohmer Park. Prince Kinikini and his troupe of Japanese equilibrists performed their balancing acts. And, as another feature, Jean-Baptiste Peynaud leaped from a wooden tower, 150 feet high, to a small mattress suspended on a net. In a performance on September 15, 1889, the net gave way and he landed unconscious on the ground. He recovered sufficiently to appear later before the crowd, for a huge ovation. He defied death once too often, and was killed in an accident from his tower in Cuba.

Sohmer Park also had a zoo. The chief feature among the trained animals was the elephants. They sat on gigantic chairs around a table, with napkins under their chins, having their dinner. The children, and the grown-ups with them, would shout with delight to see the elephants eating whole loaves of bread at a time.

Sohmer Park had so many attractions that it never lacked crowds. It was known as "the best 10-cent show in the world." Wednesday night was the gala night, when some of the finest musical programs were performed. At first the musical performances were given from a bandstand. Everything went so well that in 1893-94 Lavigne and Lajoie constructed a large building, called the Pavilion. Its roof rested on high iron pillars. The sides were open, so that the musicians and their audiences could have all the advantages of the summer's breeze from the river. But there were means for closing the sides in rainy weather. And by enclosing the sides the pavilion could be kept open for concerts in winter.

Lavigne went to Belgium to recruit new musicians. He brought to Sohmer Park many who were to have a large part in the musical life of the city long afterwards — such men as Jean Baptiste Dubois, violincellist; Van Der Meerschen, trumpeter; Jacques van Pouch, clarinetist; and the Goulet brothers. He also formed a local company to perform opera, and would bring in operatic stars from foreign lands to play the leading roles. Notable among them was Madame Ciapelli, who sang for many seasons in Montreal and had a large following. Lavigne presented serious operas, such as *Faust, Carmen and Aida,* and such light operas as *Les Cloches de Corneville.*

When word spread in January 1909 of Ernest Lavigne's death at the Hôtel Dieu it came as a calamity to the city. His funeral at the Church of the Gésu on Bleury Street was

Pavilion at Sohmer Park where Lavigne conducted his orchestra.

one of the largest Montreal had ever seen. It was estimated that over 75,000 people crowded the streets. The funeral march was played by a band at the head of the procession — a band of the musicians he had brought to Sohmer Park.

After Lavigne was gone, Sohmer Park became something very different from what it had been in his day. Sports promoters turned it into an arena for wrestling. Some of the greatest wrestlers of the time fought their matches there. Among them was the celebrated Hackenschmidt. Sohmer Park was lost in a fire on March 24, 1919. Plans to reconstruct it were proposed. They came to nothing. The spirit of Ernest Lavigne never could be recaptured. Whatever might have followed his Sohmer Park never could have been his.

Joe Beef Wasn't All Bad

The Montreal *Witness,* a newspaper of emphatic Evangelical attitudes, gave its opinion of Joe Beef and his tavern. It declared that his tavern "was probably the most disgustingly dirty in the country." It was, indeed, the resort of the evil... "The only step further was to be found murdered on the wharf or dragged out of the gutter or the river, as might happen. It was the resort of the most degraded men. It was the bottom of the pit..."

Certainly Joe Beef's Tavern, at the corner of Common (rue de la Commune) Street and Callières, had attracted a weirdly mixed crowd in a waterfront environment. Some were sailors who made the tavern known around the world. Many more were drifters, toughs, tricksters, people who, for one reason or another, would not be wanted or comfortable anywhere else. It was easy for critics to dismiss them as "the dregs of society." Joe Beef taunted the churches and spurned their attacks. He issued handbills with his picture, declaring: "He cares not for Pope, Priest, Parson... for of Churches, Chapels, Ranters, Preachers, Beechers and such stuff Montreal has already got enough...."

Yet there was another side to Joe Beef. In an age when social services were still only rudimentary, Joe's Tavern was a refuge. There outcasts could find warmth, food and shelter. On the counter of his tavern bread was piled high. Some said the pile almost reached the ceiling. Anyone was invited to take and eat. If he had money, he was expected to pay. If he had none, he could have bread for nothing. Joe closed his tavern every night at 11 o'clock sharp. But he never turned out into the night those who had nowhere to go.

Those needing a night's shelter lined up at his counter. Those who could paid 10-cents; those who couldn't just stayed in line and were equally accepted. Joe Beef inspected them; it was as though he were on the parade ground. The dirtiest had to take a bath; the stubble-bearded were shaved. Those who bathed were afterward dusted by Joe with insecticide powder. Blankets were issued. The men marched up to the second floor. There they were sent to iron or wooden bunks. More than 100 could be accommodated for a night. Silence was required and enforced.

In the morning, a sort of reveille awakened all at seven. They were given breakfast. Then came the cleansing of the dormitories. Floors were swept. Disinfectant was sprinkled freely. Windows were flung open to let in breezes from the river. Joe would even send one of his employees out on winter nights to search the streets, alleys and doorways round about. If he saw anyone lying in the snow, he was to bring him in. "I would be the most unhappy of men," said Joe, "if the public learned one day that some poor wretch died of hunger or cold at my door."

This kind of regimental order was natural for Joe (whose real name was Charles McKiernan). He had been an army sergeant in the Crimean War in the 1850s, and later with the British garrison on Ile Ste. Hélène. In his tavern he was a military presence, a disciplinarian. His barroom could be noisy, but Joe tolerated no disorder. If anyone, having been warned, was still troublesome, out he went.

Joe was a loyal supporter of the city's hospitals. On his counter were iron boxes, each with a slit on top. One was for donations to Notre Dame Hospital, the other for the Montreal General. Joe won the gratitude of labor unions. He relieved the hardships of strikers by coming forward with thousands of loaves of bread, hundreds of gallons of soup.

Joe Beef, this powerful man, bullnecked and bullet-headed, did not live to be old. He died suddenly in 1899, when only 54, from what "was thought to be heart disease." The Montreal *Witness* pursued Joe even to his grave, with a last savage editorial, calling him "the wickedest man." Yet Joe had a stupendous funeral. The procession stretched for blocks along the waterfront. It was said to be the greatest funeral Montrealers had seen since they buried the martyred statesman Thomas D'Arcy McGee in 1868.

Businesses in the whole district round about were closed. The dike along the waterfront was lined by women and children eight deep. Delegations from 50 labor organizations were among those following the hearse. But most conspicuous among those walking in the procession were the outcasts — the ragged, the poor, the homeless. "We have lost our best friend," they were saying.

Joe, always resourceful in controversy, had arranged to have the last word. It would be an enduring word, not printed on newsprint, but carved in stone. For the big granite monument that would be erected over his grave in Mount Royal Cemetery he had composed an inscription. It included some of his doggerel verses. The last verse about "the day of reckoning," referred to the men "of wealth and power" who had condemned him:

Full many a man of wealth and power
and died and gone before
Who scorned to give a poor man bread
When he stood at this door.
But Joe took in the great unwashed,
Who shared his humble fare,

He made their life a merry one
Without a thought of care.
Their eyes are dim for loss of him
Their grief is quite sincere,
He housed them from the winter blast

And filled them with good cheer.
And when the day of reckoning comes
As come it does to all,
Such sincere mourners they'll not have
Behind their funeral-pall.

Joe Beef's Tavern on the Montreal waterfront.